Small Boats on Green Waters

Small Boats
on
Green Waters

A TREASURY OF GOOD READING
ON COASTAL AND INLAND CRUISING

Edited by Brian Anderson

BREAKAWAY BOOKS
HALCOTTSVILLE, NEW YORK
2007

Small Boats on Green Waters: A Treasury of Good Reading on Coastal and Inland Cruising

ISBN-13: 978-1-891369-70-9

Library of Congress Control Number: 2007922682

Published by Breakaway Books

P.O. Box 24

Halcottsville, New York 12438

www.breakawaybooks.com

FIRST EDITION

CONTENTS

INTRODUCTION

I have no ambition to cross oceans in a small boat, either to make long passages to windward against North Atlantic gales or to scoot day after day down wind, rolling horribly, before the beneficent trades. For me the sea is seasickness, and weariness, and the readiness to admit 'This is it—I'm through.' The sea is continual wetness and apprehension and often an absolute terror, and the fact that one is experiencing it not to make a living but for "pleasure" adds an element of madness to it. To my mind, there is more to be said for sailing in shallow water, making use of the eddies along beaches and watching the current swirl through sand; or to pole through marsh channels with eel grass stroking the topsides and the smell of mud fairly high.
—*Anthony Bailey,* The $1,000 Yacht

It has often struck me how, when one speaks of nautical literature, it often seems to be first and foremost stories of wooden ships and iron men, perfect storms, exotic ports, and long passages. In the magazines, one reads of "go-anywhere boats" and "real blue-water cruisers," of selling up and setting off into the blue.

As a boat nut steeped, like many of us, in those kinds of stories, it always seemed the natural thing to think of the ocean passage as the Holy Grail, and a trip in a canoe or rowboat or daysailer as a stopgap. I dreamed of someday spending days alone between sea and sky with maybe an albatross or a school of dolphins for company and then stepping from a sturdy little sailboat onto the quay at Marseilles, Istanbul, Tahiti, Shanghai, or a hundred other ports whose names hung in the air, as pungent as the spices, salt cod, ambergris, whale oil, and incense that drove men over the seas in the first place.

So you can imagine my thoughts when I found myself the owner of a 28-foot "real blue-water cruiser." Over three years, with friends and alone, I stepped from the deck of my sturdy little cutter, *Lookfar*, onto a dock or dropped the hook in some legendary places: Louisiana's bayou country, Norfolk, Horta, Lisbon, Cartagena, Barcelona, Marseilles, Pilos, Rhodes. It was the adventure of a lifetime, I don't think I could have turned my back on it, and given the chance to do it again I probably would.

But there were times, weeks, when I found myself thinking more and more of my time on the river in my hometown. Bobbing around in the Gulf of Mexico, waiting for a tropical storm to arrive; twisted up like a pretzel in the engine "room" trying to get a wrench on a stubborn bolt when everything I touched immediately became slick with sweat; days on end of sea and sky and nothing alive between them except me; when the wind started to blow cold out of the north and the seas built and there was still nothing but sea and sky and after a week or so of it I started to forget that there was a time when I was not tired and cold and wet and afraid.

Wrestling with the engine, I dreamed of a paddle. When I had been days without seeing another living thing, I longed for a river, its banks teeming with life and something new to see around every corner. In bad weather, I thought of paddling a few yards to the bank and snugging down in my tent, a book like this one in my hands (or let's be real here: a certain couch, warm and dry that almost never bounced around like a rubber duck in a washing machine filled with cold salt water).

Some people are just never happy, I guess. You can take the boy out of Ohio, but you can't take Ohio out of the boy. In the arms of an exotic beauty, my thoughts always turned to the girl next door. Go figure.

So when a friend asked me to do a book-excerpt column for his online small boats magazine, Duckworksmagazine.com, I decided to concentrate on stories of small boats on green waters, for want of a better way to put it. Good stories of messing about in small boats one does not need a wad of cash the size of Texas to own, or in places that could be a couple of miles down the road. Although I must say I wasn't able to resist the story of Blackbeard's demise and a naval battle or two when I ran across them. Few of us are likely to take a 600-ton frigate into action these days. But at least they took place on our collective doorsteps, even if they do stray a little into the realm of "wooden ships and iron men." There's plenty of adventure out there, if one is looking for it. As it turned out, there was a lot of material, and so I thought it would be a good idea to gather together the best passages I could find and do a book.

Small Boats is certainly not exhaustive, and there were probably as many good writers I left out as put in. Mostly I figured that if one could walk into one of the big stores and find an author's books on the shelves in the boat or adventure sections, there was little point. But maybe down the road there will be a second book. I hope that the excerpts that are from familiar works will give pleasure again, and the ones from new authors doubly so. One of the best things about reading through the books for *Small Boats* was the number of new writers I discovered in them. People who write books on a subject tend to read quite a bit, and so one good book will often recommend two or three others. One could follow the threads in these books for years.

—Brian Anderson

Acknowledgments

I would like to thank Chuck Leinweber at Duckworksmagazine.com for the prod; Andy Ask for the means, Patricia Eve at Seafarer Books for her generous help; Peter Spectre for his advice and contribution; Don Wallis; Craig O'Donnell for his contributions; Garth Battista of Breakaway Books for his advice and patience; and of course my wife, Valerie Maudet-Anderson, for her encouragement, and for keeping our beloved daughters, Rachel and Maia, more or less at bay evenings and weekends while I was sorting this all out.

For Rachel and Maia

FROM *AN INLAND VOYAGE*
1877

Robert Louis Stevenson

Painting by John Singer Sargent

There are few authors with a reputation for adventure writing like the author of Treasure Island, The Strange Case of Dr. Jekyll and Mr. Hyde *and* Kidnapped. *But in his first book,* An Inland Voyage, *Robert Louis Stevenson showed he also had talent for that most mysterious kind of alchemy: turning an account of simple, everyday pleasures like a day in a canoe on a pleasant little river into something very like gold.*

Stevenson, a native of Scotland, never enjoyed robust health, and in his mid-twenties was ordered by his doctor to the south of France in the hopes of clearing up the lung problems (probably tuberculosis) that would plague him all his life. By the time he had arrived in France, he had already made something of a name for himself in Edinburgh as a journalist and essayist. Stevenson spent his time abroad writing, traveling a bit, and hanging out with other artists and intellectuals, and having several portraits painted by the fashionable American painter, John Singer Sergeant. In 1876, he and a friend took a leisurely canoe trip through Belgium and northern France, to the Seine river just west of Paris.

They used a kind of boat that is no longer common, a decked canoe known as a "Rob Roy" after the original boat, made famous by John MacGregor in his

A Thousand Miles in the Rob Roy Canoe.

It was very much a gentlemen's outing. The two mostly spent the night in inns and hotels in the numerous towns along the way, ate well, enjoyed the local wines, and generally took it easy. They were arrested as German spies (this was just after the war and occupation of France by Germany that toppled Napoleon II's Second Empire) and had various other minor adventures. In this bit, though, Stevenson had a brush with death that came the way that kind of thing often does, suddenly, when you are thinking "What a beautiful day."

THE SAMBRE TO THE OISE: THE OISE IN FLOOD

The canoe was like a leaf in the current. It took it up and shook it, and carried it masterfully away, like a Centaur carrying off a nymph. To keep some command on our direction required hard and diligent plying of the paddle. The river was in such a hurry for the sea! Every drop of water ran in a panic, like as many people in a frightened crowd. But what crowd was ever so numerous, or so single-minded? All the objects of sight went by at a dance measure; the eyesight raced with the racing river; the exigencies of every moment kept the pegs screwed so tight, that our being quivered like a well-tuned instrument; and the blood shook off its lethargy, and trotted through all the highways and byways of the veins and arteries, and in and out of the heart, as if circulation were but a holiday journey, and not the daily moil of three-score years and ten. The reeds might nod their heads in warning, and with tremulous gestures tell how the river was as cruel as it was strong and cold, and how death lurked in the eddy underneath the willows. But the reeds had to stand where they were; and those who stand still are always timid advisers. As for us, we could have shouted aloud. If this lively and beautiful river were, indeed, a thing of death's contrivance, the old ashen rogue had famously outwitted himself with us. I was living three to the minute. I was scoring points against him every stroke of my paddle, every turn of the stream. I have rarely had better profit of my life.

For I think we may look upon our little private war with death somewhat in this light. If a man knows he will sooner or later be robbed upon a journey, he will have a bottle of the best in every inn, and look upon all his extravagances as so much gained upon the thieves. And above all, where instead of simply spending, he makes a profitable investment for some of his money, when it will be out of risk of loss. So every bit of brisk living, and above all when it is healthful, is just so much gained upon the whole-sale filcher, death. We shall have the less in our pockets, the more in our stomach, when he cries stand and deliver. A swift stream is a favourite ar-tifice of his, and one that brings him in a comfortable thing per annum; but when he and I come to settle our accounts, I shall whistle in his face for these hours upon the upper Oise.

Towards afternoon we got fairly drunken with the sunshine and the ex-hilaration of the pace. We could no longer contain ourselves and our con-tent. The canoes were too small for us; we must be out and stretch ourselves on shore. And so in a green meadow we bestowed our limbs on the grass, and smoked deifying tobacco and proclaimed the world excellent. It was the last good hour of the day, and I dwell upon it with extreme complacency.

On one side of the valley, high up on the chalky summit of the hill, a ploughman with his team appeared and disappeared at regular intervals. At each revelation he stood still for a few seconds against the sky: for all the world (as the *Cigarette* declared) like a toy Burns who should have just ploughed up the Mountain Daisy. He was the only living thing within view, unless we are to count the river.

On the other side of the valley a group of red roofs and a belfry showed among the foliage. Thence some inspired bell-ringer made the afternoon musical on a chime of bells. There was something very sweet and taking in the air he played; and we thought we had never heard bells speak so intel-ligibly, or sing so melodiously, as these. It must have been to some such measure that the spinners and the young maids sang, "Come away, Death," in the Shakespearian Illyria. There is so often a threatening note, something blatant and metallic, in the voice of bells, that I believe we have fully more pain than pleasure from hearing them; but these, as they sounded abroad, now high, now low, now with a plaintive cadence that caught the ear like the burthen of a popular song, were always moderate and tunable, and seemed to fall in with the spirit of still, rustic places, like the noise of a wa-terfall or the babble of a rookery in spring. I could have asked the bell-ringer for his blessing, good, sedate old man, who swung the rope so gently to the time of his meditations. I could have blessed the priest or the heritors, or whoever may be concerned with such affairs in France, who had left these sweet old bells to gladden the afternoon, and not held meetings, and made collections, and had their names repeatedly printed in the local paper, to rig up a peal of brand-new, brazen, Birmingham-hearted substitutes, who should bombard their sides to the provocation of a brand-new bell-ringer, and fill the echoes of the valley with terror and riot.

At last the bells ceased, and with their note the sun withdrew. The piece was at an end; shadow and silence possessed the valley of the Oise. We took to the paddle with glad hearts, like people who have sat out a noble performance and returned to work. The river was more dangerous here; it ran swifter, the eddies were more sudden and violent. All the way down we had had our fill of difficulties. Sometimes it was a weir which could be shot, sometimes one so shallow and full of stakes that we must withdraw the boats from the water and carry them round. But the chief sort of obstacle was a consequence of the late high winds. Every two or three hundred yards a tree had fallen across the river, and usually involved more than another in its fall.

Often there was free water at the end, and we could steer round the leafy promontory and hear the water sucking and bubbling among the twigs. Often, again, when the tree reached from bank to bank, there was room, by lying close, to shoot through underneath, canoe and all. Sometimes it was necessary to get out upon the trunk itself and pull the boats across; and sometimes, when the stream was too impetuous for this, there was nothing for it but to land and "carry over." This made a fine series of accidents in the day's career, and kept us aware of ourselves.

Shortly after our re-embarkation, while I was leading by a long way, and still full of a noble, exulting spirit in honour of the sun, the swift pace, and the church bells, the river made one of its leonine pounces round a corner, and I was aware of another fallen tree within a stone-cast. I had my backboard down in a trice, and aimed for a place where the trunk seemed high enough above the water, and the branches not too thick to let me slip below. When a man has just vowed eternal brotherhood with the universe, he is not in a temper to take great determinations coolly, and this, which might have been a very important determination for me, had not been taken under a happy star. The tree caught me about the chest, and while I was yet struggling to make less of myself and get through, the river took the matter out of my hands, and bereaved me of my boat. The *Arethusa* swung round broadside on, leaned over, ejected so much of me as still remained on board, and thus disencumbered, whipped under the tree, righted, and went merrily away down stream.

I do not know how long it was before I scrambled on to the tree to which I was left clinging, but it was longer than I cared about. My thoughts were of a grave and almost sombre character, but I still clung to my paddle. The stream ran away with my heels as fast as I could pull up my shoulders, and I seemed, by the weight, to have all the water of the Oise in my trousers-pockets. You can never know, till you try it, what a dead pull a river makes against a man. Death himself had me by the heels, for this was his last ambuscado, and he must now join personally in the fray. And still I held to my paddle. At last I dragged myself on to my stomach on the trunk, and lay there a breathless sop, with a mingled sense of humour and injustice. A poor figure I must have presented to Burns upon the hill-top with his team. But there was the paddle in my hand. On my tomb, if ever I have one, I mean to get these words inscribed: "He clung to his paddle."

The *Cigarette* had gone past a while before; for, as I might have observed, if I had been a little less pleased with the universe at the moment, there was a clear way round the tree-top at the farther side. He had offered his services to haul me out, but as I was then already on my elbows, I had declined, and sent him down stream after the truant *Arethusa*. The stream was too rapid for a man to mount with one canoe, let alone two, upon his hands. So I crawled along the trunk to shore, and proceeded down the meadows by the river-side. I was so cold that my heart was sore. I had now an idea of my own why the reeds so bitterly shivered. I could have given any of them a lesson. The *Cigarette* remarked facetiously that he thought I was "taking exercise" as I drew near, until he made out for certain that I was only twittering with cold. I had a rub down with a towel, and donned a dry suit from the india-rubber bag. But I was not my own man again for the rest of the voyage. I had a queasy sense that I wore my last dry clothes upon my body. The struggle had tired me; and perhaps, whether I knew it or not, I was a little dashed in spirit. The devouring element in the universe had leaped out against me, in this green valley quickened by a running stream. The bells were all very pretty in their way, but I had heard some of the hollow notes of Pan's music. Would the wicked river drag me down by the heels, indeed? and look so beautiful all the time? Nature's good-humour was only skin-deep after all.

There was still a long way to go by the winding course of the stream, and darkness had fallen, and a late bell was ringing in Origny Sainte-Benoite, when we arrived.

FROM *THE SURVIVAL OF THE BARK CANOE*
1975

John McPhee

One of the amazing things about traditional small boats is the beauty and elegance with which form follows function. If one builds a wooden boat that paddles, rows or sails well, it is going to be beautiful. There are few other things about which one can say the same. Thoreau wrote "Art is all of a boat but the wood." Traditional builders speak, and probably always have spoken, of the "wisdom of the wood." It is difficult to go wrong as long as one listens, and the birch-bark canoe is one of the best examples. Its form, shaped by a mix of what one needs to move people and gear over rivers, lakes and even the open ocean, and what it is possible to shape out of bark and wood, has not changed or been improved upon in at least 500 years. The latest kevlar-and-epoxy, or vacuum-molded polyethylene wonder would be instantly recognizable by a pre-Colombian Malecite indian.

By the mid-1970s, the art of building canoes in birch bark had almost been lost. There were a few Native American builders in Ontario, one old white man in Minnesota, and Henry Vaillancourt in New Hampshire. As a teenager, Vaillancourt, through some obscure process became obsessed with canoes. Knowing nobody in the small, working-class mill town he lived in who had one, and having no money to buy one, he decided to build one himself out of materials available for free in the forest, like the Indians had done. His first efforts were of course crude, but then he stumbled across The Bark Canoes and Skin Boats of North America, *by*

Edwin Tappan Adney and Howard Chapelle. The book is one of the earliest, and still one of the best, ethnographic studies of art and technology. With the book and single-minded concentration, Vaillancourt quickly became an artist/craftsman of the first rank, and people waited for years to buy one of his canoes.

John McPhee has built a career out of writing about odd corners of our world and subjects one might say are hidden in plain sight. The Founding Fish *is a book-length portrait of the shad.* Oranges *is about oranges. He wrote a four-book series on the geology of North America that reads like a detective thriller.* The Curve of Binding Energy, *written in the early 70s, is about the nuclear industry and the likelihood of nuclear terrorism. In his latest,* Uncommon Carriers, *he travels with a trucker, a towboat pilot, a sea captain, and follows Henry David Thoreau's path along the Concord and Merrimack Rivers in a canoe. But since his first book, a portrait of basketball great Bill Bradley entitled* A Sense of Where You Are, *the thing that has separated McPhee from the rest is his knack for tracking down and writing portraits of people who bring a little something extra to the table, some quality of thought or ability that separates them from the rest.*

So when McPhee stumbled across word of Vaillancourt in a canoeing newsletter, the fit was perfect. The Survival of the Bark Canoe, *is a portrait of Vaillancourt and the story of a canoe trip through the Maine woods with Vaillancourt and a couple of friends. Almost any random part would have made a good addition to this book, but this bit looks into Vaillancourt's almost obsessive craftsmanship and a little of the history of the bark canoe.*

In the middle of one morning, Vaillancourt left the shop, got into his car, drove two or three miles down the road, and went into woods to cut a birch. The weather was sharp, and he was wearing a heavy red Hudson's Bay coat. His sandy-brown hair, curling out in back, rested on the collar. He carried a sheathed Hudson's Bay axe and a long wooden wedge and a wooden club (he called it a mallet) of the type seen in cartoons about cave societies. His eyes—they were pale blue, around an aquiline nose over a trapper's mustache—searched the woodlot for a proper tree. It need not be a giant. There were no giants around Greenville anyway.

He wanted it for its sapwood, not its bark—for thwarts (also called cross-pieces and crossbars) in a future canoe. After walking several hundred feet in from the road, he found a birch about eight inches in diameter, and with the axe he notched it in the direction of a free fall. He removed his coat and carefully set it aside. Beneath it was a blue oxford-cloth button-down shirt, tucked into his blue-jeans. He chopped the tree, and it fell into a young beech. "Jesus Christ!" he said. "It is so frustrating when Nature has you beat." The birch was hung up in the beech. He heaved at it and hauled it until it at last came free.

What he wanted of the tree was about six feet of its trunk, which he cut away from the rest. Then he sank the axe into one end of the piece, removed the axe, placed the wedge in the cut, and tapped the wedge with the mallet. He tapped twice more, and the entire log fell apart in two even halves. He said, "You get some birch, it's a bastard to split out, I'll tell you. But, Christ, this is nice. That's good and straight grain. Very often you get them twisted." Satisfied, he shouldered the tools and the wood, went back to the road, and drove home.

In the yard, he split the birch again, and he now had four pieces, quarter-round. One of these he cut off to a length of about forty inches. He took that into the shed. He built a fire, and in minutes the room was warm. He sat in his rocking chair and addressed the axe to the quarter-round log—the dark heartwood, the white sapwood. Holding the piece vertically, one end resting on the floor, he cut the heartwood away. He removed the bark and then went rapidly down the sapwood making angled indentations that caused the wood to curve out like petals. He cut them off, and they fell as big chips to the floor. A pile began to grow there as the axe head moved up and down, and what had been by appearance firewood was in a short time converted to lumber—a two-by-three, knotless board that might almost have been sawn in a mill.

He then picked up his crooked knife and held its grip in his upturned right hand, the blade poking out to the left. The blade was bent near its outer end (enabling it to move in grooves and hollows where the straight part could not). Both blade and grip were shaped like nothing I had ever seen. The grip, fashioned for the convenience of a hand closing over it, was bulbous. The blade had no hinge and protruded rigidly—but not straight out. It formed a shallow V with the grip.

Vaillancourt held the piece of birch like a violin, sighting along it from his shoulder, and began to carve, bringing the knife upward, toward his chest. Of all the pieces of a canoe, the center thwart is the most complicated in the carving. Looked at from above, it should be broad at the midway point, then taper gradually as it reaches toward the sides of the canoe. Near its ends, it flares out in shoulders that arc penetrated by holes, for lashings that will help secure it to the gunwales. The long taper, moreover, is interrupted by two grooved protrusions, where a tumpline can be tied before a portage. The whole upper surface should be flat, but the underside of the thwart rises slightly from the middle outward, then drops again at the ends, the result being that the thwart is thickest in the middle, gradually thinning as it extends outward and thickening again at the gunwales. All of this comes, in the end, to an adroit ratio between strength and weight, not to mention the incidental grace of the thing, each of its features being a mirror image of another. The canoe's central structural element, it is among the first parts set in place. Its long dimension establishes the canoe's width, and therefore many of the essentials of the canoe's design. In portage, nearly all of the weight of the canoe bears upon it.

So to me the making of a center thwart seemed a job for a jigsaw, a band saw, a set of chisels, a hammer, a block plane, a grooving plane, calipers, templates, and—most of all—mechanical drawings. One would have thought that anyone assertive enough to try it with a knife alone would at least begin slowly, moving into the wood with caution. Vaillancourt, to the contrary, tore his way in. He brought the knife toward him with such strong, fast, heavy strokes that long splinters flew off the board. "Birch is good stuff to work with," he said. "It's almost as easy to work as cedar. This feels like a hot knife going through butter. I used to use a drawknife. That God-damned thing. You've got to use a vise to hold the work. With the crooked knife, I can work in the woods if I want. I saw an Indian on TV in Canada using one. I got one, and I worked and worked with it to get the knack. Now it almost feels as if it's part of me. If anybody ever comes out with a tool that will rival a crooked knife, I'd like to hear about it." He sighted along the wood, turned it over, and began whipping splinters off the other side. He said that steel tools had come with the white man, of course, and that most people seemed to imagine that Indian workmanship had improved with steel tools. "But I doubt it," he continued. "With bone and stone tools, it just took longer. The early Indians relied more on abrasion. With the exception of the center thwart, there is no fancy carving in a canoe. It's all flatwork. In fact, I'm doing experiments with bone tools." He stopped carving, reached to a shelf, and picked up a bone awl. "Make two holes with a bone awl in a piece of cedar, take out the wood between the holes with a bone chisel, and you have a mortise for a thwart to fit into." He reached for a piece of cedar (wood debris was all over the shop), made two holes, picked up a wooden mallet and a bone chisel, and made a mortise in the cedar. Then he picked up the long, curving incisor of a beaver. "I made a knife last winter out of a beaver's tooth," he said. "The original crooked knife was made out of a beaver's tooth." He sat down and continued to carve. The strokes were lighter now as he studied the wood, carved a bit, studied the wood, and carved some more. The piece was beginning to look roughly like a thwart, and the gentler motions of the knife were yielding thin, curling shavings that settled down on the bed of chips and splinters around his feet.

"Where the crooked knife was, the bark canoe was," he said. "People from Maine recognize the crooked knife. People from New Hampshire do not. All they knew was the drawknife. The God-damned drawknife— what a bummer."

The bark canoe was also where the big white birches were, and that excluded a good part of New Hampshire, including Greenville. Vaillan- court goes north to find his bark. The range of the tree—*Betula papyrifera,* variously called the white birch, the silver birch, the paper birch, the canoe birch—forms a swath more than a thousand miles wide (more or less from New York City to Hudson Bay) and reaches westward and northwestward to the Pacific. Far in from the boundaries of this enor- mous area, though, the trees are unlikely and always have been unlikely to grow large enough for the building of good canoes, and this exclusion includes most of the West, and even the Middle West. The biggest trees and the best of Indian canoes were in what are now New Brunswick,

Nova Scotia, Maine, Quebec, and parts of Ontario. Even within this region, the most accomplished craftsmen were concentrated in the east. Of these, the best were the Malecites. So Henri Vaillancourt builds Malecite canoes. Before all other design factors, he cares most about the artistic appearance of the canoes he builds, and he thinks the best-looking were the canoes of the Malecites. The Malecites lived in New Brunswick and parts of Maine. Vaillancourt builds the Malecite St. John River Canoe and the Malecite St. Lawrence River Canoe. He builds them with modifications, though. Toward the end of the nineteenth century, tribes started copying one another and gave up some of the distinctiveness of their tribal styles, and to varying extents, he said, he has done the same.

His carving became even slower now, and he studied the piece carefully before making his moves, but he measured nothing. "There's really no need for feet and inches," he said. "I know more or less what's strong and what isn't. If I want to find the middle of this crosspiece, I can put a piece of bark across it from end to end, and then fold it in half to find the center." He had measured the length—thirty-five inches—and had cut to it exactly. In the spring, when the time came to make the gunwales, he would measure them as well. But that is all he would measure in the entire canoe. According to the prescript passed on by Adney and Chapelle, the center thwart he was working on should taper

> slightly in thickness each way from its center to within 5 inches of the shoulders, which are 30 inches apart. The thickness at a point 5 inches from the shoulder is 1/4 inch; from there the taper is quick to the shoulder, which is 5/16 inch thick, with a drop to 1/4 inch in the tenon. The width, 3 inches at the center, decreases in a graceful curve to within 5 inches of the shoulder, where it is 2 inches, then increases to about 3 inches at the shoulder. The width of the tenon is, of course, 2 inches, to fit the mortise hole in the gunwale.

Yet the only instruments Vaillancourt was using to meet these specifications were his eyes.

He finished off the tumpline grooves. The thwart appeared to be perfect, but he picked up a piece of broken glass and scraped it gently all over. Fine excelsior came away, and the surface became shiningly smooth. It was noon. He had cut the birch in the woods at half past nine. Now he held the thwart in his hand, turning it this way and that. It was a lovely thing in itself, I thought, for it had so many blendings of symmetry. He said he could have done it in an hour if he had not been talking so much. And he was glad the tree in the woods had turned into this thwart instead of "all the chintzy two-bit things they make out of birch—clothespins, dowels, toothpicks, Popsicle sticks." As he worked, he had from time to time scooped up handfuls of chips and shavings and fed them into the stove. Even so, the pile was still high around him, and he appeared to be sitting in a cone of snow.

He soon added more to the pile. From the rafters he took down a piece of cedar and, with the knife, sent great strips of it flying to the floor. He was now making a stempiece, the canoe part that establishes the profile of the bow or the stem.

"Sometimes, when there are, you know, contortions in the grain, you can get into a real rat's nest," he said. "Around a knot, there will be waves in the grain. You cut to the knot from one side, then the other, to get a straight edge. At times like that, I'm tempted just to throw the thing out."

The wood he was working now, though, was dear and without complications, and after a short while, in which most of it went to the floor, he had made something that looked very much like a yardstick—albeit a heavy one—a half inch thick. Its comers were all sharp, and it seemed to have been machine-planed. Then he pressed the blade of the crooked knife into one end of the stick and kept pressing just hard enough to split the stick down fifty per cent of its length. He pressed the knife into the end again, near the first cut, and made another split, also stopping halfway. Again and again he split the wood, going far beyond the moment when I, watching him, thought that further splitting would be impossible, would ruin the whole. He split the board thirty-one times—into laminations each a half inch wide and a sixteenth of an inch thick. And all the laminations stopped in the middle, still attached there; from there on, the wood remained solid. "You split cedar parallel to the bark," he commented. "Hickory you can split both ways. There are very few woods you can do that with."

He plunged the laminated end of the piece into a bucket of water and left it there for a while, and then he built up the fire with scraps from the floor. In a coffee can he brought water to a boil. He poured it slowly over the laminations, bathing them, bathing them again. Then he lifted the steaming cedar in two hands and bent it. The laminations slid upon one another and formed a curve. He pondered the curve. It was not enough of a curve, he decided. So he bent the piece a little more. "There's an awful lot of it that's just whim," he said. "You vary the stempiece by whim." He liked what he saw now, so he reached for a strip of basswood bark, tightly wound it around the curve in the cedar, and tied it off. The basswood bark was not temporary. It would stay there, and go into the canoe. Bow or stem, the straight and solid part of the stempiece would run downward from the tip, then the laminated curve would sweep inward, establishing the character of the end—and thus, in large part, of the canoe itself.

The canoe-end profile was the principal feature that distinguished the styles of the tribes. The Ojibway Long-Nose Canoe, for example, had in its bow (and stern) an outreaching curve of considerable tumblehome (an arc-like a parenthesis that turns more than ninety degrees and begins to come back on itself). The end profiles of the Algonquin Hunter's Canoe were straight and almost vertical, with a small-radius ninety-degree curve at the waterline. The departure from the vertical was inward, toward the paddler. The end profiles of certain Malecite canoes were similar, but the departure from vertical was outward. Other Malecite canoes had long-radius, "compass sweep" bows and sterns.

I mentioned to Vaillancourt that, before and during college years, I had spent a lot of time around a place in Vermont that still specializes in sending out canoe trips, and a birch-bark canoe hangs in the dining hall there.

"Near Salisbury," he said. "Lake Dunmore—am I right?" He took down a worn, filled notebook and began to whip the pages. "Let's see. Yeah. Here. Keewaydin. Is that it?"

That was it. He had not been there, but he would stop by someday.

He hoped to see every bark canoe in existence. There were, for example, sixteen bark canoes in Haliburton, Ontario; one in Upper Canada Village, near Morrisburg, Ontario; a couple at Old Jesuit House, in Sillery, Quebec. In his notebook he had the names and addresses of museums, historical societies, and individuals from Maine to Minnesota, Nova Scotia to Alberta, and as far south as Virginia. Peter Paul, a Malecite in Woodstock, New Brunswick, had one. Vaillancourt had been to see him. The most skillfully built birch-bark canoe he had ever seen was made in Old Town, Maine, and was signed "Louis P. Sock." "I've seen only two or three canoes that were near perfect," he said. "But I've never seen a bark canoe that wasn't graceful. I've never seen an Eastern Cree canoe or a Montagnais. Most of the canoes I've seen did not have a definite tribal style. There's a bark canoe on Prince Edward Island. A sign says it's a Micmac canoe. It isn't."

I told him I'd long ago been told that the bark canoe at Keewaydin was an Iroquois.

He said he doubted that very much, because the Iroquois, except in early times, had had limited access to good birch, and had made their canoes—when they made canoes at all—out of elm or hickory bark. Various tribes had also used the bark of the spruce, the basswood, the chestnut. But all were crude compared to birch. If they wanted to get across a river, they might—in one day—build an elm-bark canoe, and then forget it, leave it in the woods. "You couldn't, by any stretch of the imagination, compare an elm-bark or a hickory-bark canoe to a birch canoe," he said. "Barks other than birch bark will absorb water the way wood will. Canoes made from them—even well made—got waterlogged and heavy. Most were just, you know, rough shells. Good for nothing, like automobiles. Automobiles last, you know, five or six years. A birchbark canoe lasted the Indians ten."

I asked him how much experience he had had by now in more modern canoes. He said he had been in an aluminum canoe twice and in wood-and-canvas canoes only a few times in his life. Otherwise, he had never paddled anything but a birch-bark canoe. He did not paddle much around home, he said, because when he went canoeing he wanted to go to Maine.

"Where in Maine?"

"Oh, up north of Moosehead Lake. The Penobscot River. Chesuncook Lake. Caucomgomoc Lake. It's not just to get out in the canoe—it's to get out and see wildlife. A moose, you know, thirty feet away. Next time I go, I'm going down the Penobscot and on to the Allagash lakes."

I said, "Next time you go, I'd like to go with you."

He said, "Bring your own food."

I had been yearning to make a trip into that region for what was now most of my life. Keewaydin had run trips there, but one circumstance or another had always prevented me from going. Just the thought of making a journey there in a birchbark canoe was enough to make me sway like a drunk. I thought of little else through the winter and the spring.

FROM A THOUSAND MILES IN THE ROB ROY CANOE ON RIVERS AND LAKES OF EUROPE

1866

John MacGregor

This was the book that launched a million canoes. John MacGregor, a Scottish barrister, first stepped into a canoe during an extended trip to the United States and Canada. A few years after his return to England he designed what would become known as a Rob Roy canoe: a one-man decked lapstrake boat that also carried a small gaff sail. The design took features from traditional birch bark canoes, but it mostly seems to have been modeled after the Inuit kayaks MacGregor saw while traveling along the Bering Sea. One used a double paddle, sitting on the bottom of the craft; a spray skirt was attached to the cockpit to keep water out of the boat in rough seas or rapids. At around 15 feet, the Rob Roys were a little shorter than the Inuit boats normally were.

After a long trip around Europe in the Rob Roy, mostly in France, Germany and Switzerland, his first book, A Thousand Miles in the Rob Roy Canoe, *became a best seller and launched canoeing as a sport on both sides of the Atlantic. Dozens of boatbuilders were pressed into service building the new craft, most notably J. Henry Rushton, and sportsmen were soon to be found paddling down almost every water-way in the US and Europe in a fad that lasted for several decades. MacGregor went on to write several other books, including* The Rob Roy in the Baltic, The Rob Roy on the Jordan, Nile, Red Sea and Gennesareth, *etc., and* The Voyage Alone in the Yawl Rob Roy.

This excerpt tells the story of MacGregor's first experiences canoeing in Europe through France and Germany. It includes part of an appendix from the book describing the canoe and how she was rigged for sail and equipped for the voyage.

ON THE MEUSE—BARRIERS AND SHALLOWS— HUY—GUN-BARRELS—EARL OF ABERDEEN—A DROWNING BOY—SWIMMERS—A NIGHT CLIMB— THE PREMIER'S SON—NOTHING TO PAY—A DAY'S SAIL—DOWN-HILL—CANOES AND CANNONS—THE PRINCE OF WALES—ALONE AGAIN.

Glancing water, brilliant sun, a pretty canoe, and a light heart, all your baggage on board, and on a fast current,—who would exchange this for any diligence or railway, or steamboat, or horse?

A pleasant stream was enough to satisfy at this early period of the voyage, for the charm of rocks and rapids had not yet been known. It is good policy, too, that a quiet, easy, respectable sort of river like the Meuse should be taken in the earlier stage of a water tour, when there is novelty enough in being on a river at all. The river-banks one would call tame if seen from shore are altogether new when you open up the vista from the middle of the stream. The picture that is rolled sideways to the common traveller now pours out upon you from the front, ever enlarging from a centre, and in the gentle sway of the current the landscape seems to swell on this side and on that with new things ever advancing to meet you in succession.

How careful I was at the first shallow! getting out and wading as I lowered the boat. A month afterwards we would dash over these with a shove here and a stroke there in answer to a hoarse croak of the stones at the bottom grinding against my keel. And the first barrier—how anxious it made me, to think by what means shall we get over. A man appeared just in time

(N.B.—They *always* do), and twopence made him happy for his share of carrying the boat round by land, so I jumped in again as before.

Sailing was easy, too, in a fine wide river, strong and deep, and with a favouring breeze, and when the little steamer passed I drew along side and got my penny roll and penny glass of beer through the porthole, while the wondering passengers smiled, chattered, and then looked grave—for was it not indecorous to laugh at an Englishman evidently mad, poor fellow?

The voyage was chequered by innumerable little events, all perfectly different from those one meets on shore, and when we came to the forts at Huy and knew the first day's work was done, the persuasion was complete that quite a new order of sensations had begun.

Next morning the boat was found safe in the coach-house and the sails still drying on the harness-pegs, where we had left them, but the ostler and all his folks were nowhere to be seen. Everybody had gone to join the long funeral procession of a great musician, who lived fifty years at Huy, though we never heard of him before, or of Huy either; yet you see it is in the map at the end of our log.

The pleasure of meandering with a new river is very peculiar and fascinating. Each few yards brings a novelty, or starts an excitement. A crane jumps up here, a duck flutters there, splash leaps a gleaming trout by your side, the rushing sound of rocks warns you round that corner, or anon you come suddenly upon a millrace. All these, in addition to the scenery and the people and the weather, and the determination that you *must* get on, over, through, or under every difficulty, and cannot leave your boat in a desolate wold, and ought to arrive at a house before dark, and that your luncheon bag is long since empty; all these, I say, keep the mind awake, which would doze away and snore for 100 miles in a carriage.

It is, as in the voyage of life, that each care and hardship is a very Mentor of living. Our minds would only vegetate if all life were like a straight canal, and we in a boat being towed along it. The afflictions that agitate the soul are as its shallows, rocks, and whirlpools, and the bark that has not been tossed on billows knows not half the sweetness of the harbour of rest.

The river soon got fast and lively, and hour after hour of vigorous work prepared me well for breakfast. Trees seemed to spring up in front and grow tall, but it was only because I came rapidly towards them. Pleasant villages floated as it were to meet me, gently moving. All life got to be a smooth and

gliding thing, of dreamy pictures and far-off sounds, without fuss and without dust or anything sudden or loud, till at length the bustle and hammers
of Liege came near the Rob Roy—for it was always the objects and not myself that seemed to move. Here I saw a fast steamer, the Seraing, propelled
by water forced from its sides, and as my boat hopped and bobbed in the
steamer's waves we entered a dock together, and the canoe was soon hoisted
into a garden for the night.

Gun-barrels are the rage in Liege. Everybody there makes or carries or
sells gun-barrels. Even women walk about with twenty stocked rifles on
their backs, and each rifle, remember, weighs 10 lbs. They sell plenty of
fruit in the market, and there are churches well worth a visit here. But gun-
barrels, after all, are the prevailing idea of the place.

However, it is not my purpose to describe the towns seen on this tour. I
had seen Liege well, years before, and indeed almost every town mentioned
in these pages. The charm therefore of this voyage was not in going to
strange lands, but in seeing old places in a way so new.

Here at length the Earl of Aberdeen met me, according to our plans
arranged long before. He had got a canoe built for the trip, but a foot longer
and two inches narrower than the Rob Roy, and, moreover, made of fir instead of strong oak. It was sent from London to Liege, and the "combing"
round the edge of the deck was broken in the journey, so we spent some
hours at a cabinet-maker's where it was neatly mended.

Launching our boats unobserved on the river, we soon left Liege in the
distance and braved the hot sun.

The pleasant companionship of two travellers, each quite free in his own
boat, was very enjoyable. Sometimes we sailed, then paddled a mile or two,
or joined to help the boats over a weir, or towed them along as we walked
on the bank for a change.

Each of us took whichever side of the river pleased him best, and we talked
across long acres of water between, to the evident surprise of sedate folks on
the banks, who often could see only one of the strange elocutionists, the
other being hidden by bushes or tall sedge. When talking thus aloud had am-
plified into somewhat uproarious singing, the chorus was far more energetic
than harmonious, but then the Briton is at once the most timid and shy of
travellers, and the most *outré* and singular when he chooses to be free.

The mid-day beams on a river in August are sure to conquer your fresh energies at last, and so we had to pull up at a village for bread and wine.

The moment I got into my boat again a shrill whining cry in the river attracted my attention, and it came from a poor little boy, who had some how fallen into the water, and was now making his last faint efforts to cling to a great barge in the stream. Naturally I rushed over to save him and my boat went so fast and so straight that its sharp prow caught the hapless urchin in the rear; and with such appointed reminder too that he screamed and struggled, and so got safely on a barge.

On most of the Belgian, German, and French rivers there are excellent floating baths, an obvious convenience which is sadly wanted in Britain, though we have quite as many bathers as there are abroad.

The floating bath consists of a wooden framework, say 100 feet long, moored in the stream, which runs freely through a set of strong bars and chains and iron network, forming a false bottom, shallow at one end and deeper at the other; so that the bather cannot be carried away. Round the sides there are bathing boxes and steps, ladders, and spring boards for the various degrees of proficiency. Now we have one in London.

The youths and even the little boys on the Rhine are very good swimmers, and many of them dive well. Sometimes there is a ladies' bath of similar construction, from which a good deal of very lively noise may be heard when the fair bathers are in a talkative mood.

The soldiers at military stations near the rivers are marched down regularly to bathe, and one day we found a large number of young recruits assembled for their general dip.

While some were in the water others were firing at the targets for ball practice. There were three targets, each made of cardboard sheets, fastened upon wooden uprights. A marker safely protected in a ball-proof *mantelet* was placed so close to these targets that he could see all three at once. One man of the firing party opposite each target having fired, his bullet passed through the pasteboard and left a clear round hole in it, while the ball itself was buried in the earth behind, and so could be recovered again, instead of being dashed into fragments as on our iron targets, and then spattered about on all sides, to the great danger of the marker and everybody else.

When three men had thus fired, signals were made by drum, flag, and bugle, and the firing ceased. The marker then came out and pointed to the bullet-mark on each target, and having patched up the holes he returned within his mantelet, and the firing was resumed. This safe method of ball practice is much better than that always until lately used in our own military shooting, and the French could tell us how terribly effective it was as an instruction in cool aim.

As we rounded a point there was a large herd of cattle swimming across the stream in close column, and the Rob Roy went right into the middle of them to observe how they would welcome a stranger. When in my canoe on the Nile I have seen the black oxen swim over the stream night and morning, reminding one of Pharaoh's dream about the "kine" coming up out of the river, a notion that used to puzzle in boyhood days, but which is by no means incongruous when thus explained. The Bible is a book that bears the fullest blaze of light upon it, for truth looks more true when most clearly seen.

The evening fell sombre long ere we came near the town of Maastricht, in Holland, one of the most strongly fortified places in Europe; that is, of the old fashion, with straight high walls quite impervious to the Armstrong and Whitworth guns—of a century gone by.

But all we knew as we came near it at night was, that the stream was deep and strong, and that no lights appeared. Emerging from trees, the current took us right into the middle of the town, but where were the houses? Had they no windows, no lamps, not even a candle?—no, not a spark!

Two great high walls bounded the river, but not a gate or port could we find, though one of us carefully scanned the right and the other cautiously scraped along the left of this very strange place.

The cause of this was that the commerce and boats all turn into a canal above the old tumbledown fortress, and so the blank brick sides bounded us thus inhospitably. At last we came to a bridge, looming overhead in the blackness, and our arrival there was greeted by some Dutch lads upon it with a shower of stones pattering pitilessly upon the delicate cedar of our canoes.

At last we found a place where we could cling to the wall, which here sloped a little with debris, and now there was nothing for it but to haul the boats up bodily over the impregnable fortification, and thus carry them into the sleepy town. No wonder the *octroi* guard stared as his lamplight fell on two gaunt men in grey, carrying what seemed to him a pair of long coffins, but he was a sensible though surprised individual, and he guided us well, stamping through the dark deserted streets to an hotel.

Though the canoes in a cart made a decided impression at the railway-station next day, and our arguments logically proved that the boats must go as baggage, the porters were dense to conviction, and obdurate to persuasion, until all at once a sudden change took place; they rushed at us, caught up the two neglected "bateaux," ran with them to the luggage-van, pushed them in, banged the door, piped the whistle, and as the train went off.— "Do you know why they have yielded so suddenly?" said a Dutchman, who could speak English. "Not at all," said we. "Because I told them one of you was the son of the Prime Minister, and the other Lord Russell's son."

But a change of railway had to be made at Aix-la-Chapelle, and after a hard struggle we had nearly surrendered the boats to the "merchandise train," to limp along the line at night and to arrive "perhaps to-morrow." The superintendent seemed to clutch the boats as his prize, but as he gloried a little too loudly, his rival in dignity, the "Chef" of the passengers' baggage, came, listened, and with calm mien ordered for us a special covered truck, and on arriving at Cologne there was "nothing to pay."

To be quiet we went to the Belle Vue, at Deutz, which is opposite Cologne, but a great Singing Society had its gala there, and sang and drank prodigiously. Next day (Sunday too) this same quiet Deutz had a "Schutzen Fest," where the man who had hit the target best was dragged about in an open carriage with his wife, both wearing brass crowns, and bowing royally to a screaming crowd, while blue lights glared and rockets shot up in the darkness.

At Cologne, while Lord A. went to take our tickets at the steamer, the boats were put in a handcart, which I shoved from behind as a man pulled it in front. In our way to the river I was assailed by a poor vagrant sort of fellow, who insisted on being employed as a porter, and being enraged at a refusal he actually took up a large stone and ran after the cart in a threatening passion. I could not take my hands from the boats, though in fear that his missile would smash them if he threw it, but I kicked up my legs behind as we trotted along. One of the sentries saw the man's conduct, and soon a policeman brought him to me as a prisoner, but as he trembled now with fear more than before with anger, I declined to give him in charge, though the police pressed this course, saying, "Travellers are sacred here." This incident is mentioned because it was the sole occasion when any discourtesy happened to me during any cruise.

We took the canoes by steamer to a wide part of the Rhine at Bingen. Here the scenery is good, and we spent an active day on the river, sailing in a splendid breeze, landing on islands, scudding about in steamers' waves, and, in fact, enjoying a combination of yacht voyage, picnic, and boat race.

This was a fine long day of pleasure, though in one of the sudden squalls my canoe happened to ground on a bank just at the most critical time, and the bamboo mast broke short. The uncouth and ridiculous appearance of a sail falling overboard is like that of an umbrella turned inside out in a gust of wind. Nobody gets the slightest sympathy for this, or for having the gout or the mumps. I got another stronger mast from a gardener—one of the long, green-painted sticks used as a standard for hollyhocks! This lasted all the voyage, and the broken mast was made into a boom.

Lord Aberdeen went by train to inspect the river Nahe, but reported unfavourably; and I paddled up from its mouth, but the water was very low.

Few arguments were needed to stop me from going against stream anywhere; I have a profound respect for the universal principle of gravitation, and quite allow that in boating it is well to have the earth's strong attraction with you by always going down stream, and so the good rule was to make steam, horse, or man take the canoe against the current, and to let gravity help the canoe to carry me down.

Time pressed for my fellow-paddler to return to England, so we went on to Mayence, and thence by rail to Aschaffenburg on the Main. The canoes again travelled in grand fashion, having a truck to themselves; but instead of the stately philosopher superintendent of Aix-la-Chapelle, who managed this gratuitously, we had a fussy little person to deal with, and to pay accordingly—the only case of good, honest cheating I can recollect during the voyage.

A fellow-passenger in the railway was deeply interested about our tour; and we had spoken of its various details for some time to him before we found that he supposed we were travelling with "two small cannons," mistaking the French word "canots" for "canons." He had even asked about their length and weight, and had heard with perfect placidity that our "canons" were fifteen feet long, and weighed eighty pounds, and that we took them only for "plaisir," not to sell. Had we carried two pet camelopards, he would have been just as little astonished.

The guests at the German inn of this long-named town amused us much by their respectful curiosity. Our dress in perfect unison, both alike in grey flannel, puzzled them exceedingly; but this sort of perplexity about costume and whence why and whither is an everyday occurrence for the paddler abroad.

The Main is an easy river, but the scenery is only so so. In a fine breeze upon it we lost much time by forcing the canoes to do yachts' work. Sailing on rivers is rather a mistake unless with a favourable wind. A storm of rain at length made it lunch-time, so we sheltered ourselves in a bleak sort of arbour attached to an inn, where they could give us only sour black bread and raw bacon. Eating this poor cheer in a wet, rustling breeze and pattering rain, half chilled in our macintoshes, was the only time I fared badly, so little of "roughing it," was there in this luxurious tour.

Fine weather came soon again and pleasure,—nay, positive sporting; for there were wild ducks quite impudent in their familiarity, and herons wading about with that look of injured innocence they put on when you dare to disturb them. So my friend capped his revolver pistol, and I acted as a pointer dog, stealing along the other side of the river, and "pointing" the game with my paddle.

Vast trouble was taken. Lord A. went ashore, and crawled on the bank a long way to a wily bird, but, though the sportsman had shown himself at Wimbledon to be one of the best shots in the world, it was evidently not easy to shoot a heron with a revolver.

As the darker shades fell, even this rather stupid river became beautiful; and our evening bath was in a quiet pool, with pure yellow sand to rest on if you tired in swimming. At Hanau we stopped for the night.

The wanderings and turnings of the Main next day have really left no impression on my memory, except that we had a pleasant time, and at last came to a large Schloss, where we observed on the river a boat evidently English. While we examined this craft, a man told us it belonged to the Prince of Wales, "and he is looking at you now from the balcony." For this was the Duchess of Cambridge's Schloss at Rumpenheim, and presently a four-in-hand crossed the ferry, and the Prince and Princess of Wales drove in it by the river-side, while we plied a vigorous paddle against the powerful west wind until we reached Frankfort, and dried our wet jackets at the *Russie,* one of the best hotels in Europe.

The Frankfort boatmen were amazed next day to see the two English canoes flitting about so lightly on their river; sometimes skimming the surface with the wind, and despising the contrary stream; then wheeling about, and paddling hither and thither, in shallows where it was "only moist." For fun we both got into my canoe, which bore the weight perfectly well. However, there was not room for both of us to use our paddles comfortable in the same canoe.

On Sunday, the Royal personages came to the English church at Frankfort, and, with that quiet good taste which wins more admiration than any pageantry, they walked from the place of worship like the rest of the hearers. There is a true grandeur in simplicity when the occasion is one of solemn things.

Next day my active and pleasant companion had to leave me on his return to England. Not satisfied with a fortnight's rifle practice at Wimbledon, where the best prize of the year was won by his skill, he must return to the moors and coverts for more deadly sport; and the calls of more important business besides required his presence at home. He paddled down the Rhine to Cologne, and on the way several times performed the difficult feat of hooking on his canoe to a steamer going at full speed.

Meantime, my boat went along with me by railway to Freyburg, from whence a voyage really new was ready to begin, for as yet the Rob Roy had not paddled in parts unknown.

For Canoeists

Although the Rob Roy and its luggage were not prepared until after much cogitation, it is well that intending canoeists should have the benefit of what experience has since proved as to the faults and virtues of the arrangements devised for a first trip, after these have been thoroughly tasted in so pleasant a tour.

The best dimensions for the canoe appear to be—length, 13 feet; beam, 2 feet 2 inches; depth outside, from keel to deck, 9 inches; camber, 2 inches; keel, 1 inch, with a strip of iron, half an inch broad, carefully secured all the way below, and a copper strip up the stern and stern posts, and round the top of each of them. The opening in the deck should be 4 feet long (at most) and 20 inches wide, with a strong combing all round, but not more than 1 inch high. This opening should be semicircular at the ends, both for appearance sake and strength and convenience, so as to avoid corners. The macintosh sheet to cover this must be strong, to resist constant wear, light coloured, for the sun's heat, and so attached as to be readily loosened and made fast again, say 20 times a day. A water-tight compartment in the hull is a mistake. Its partition prevents access to breakages within, and arrests the circulation of air, and it cannot be kept long perfectly staunch. There should be extra timbers near the seat. The canoe must be so constructed as to endure without injury, (1) to be lifted by any part whatever; (2) to be rested on any part; (3) to be sat upon while aground, on any part of the deck, the combing, and the interior.

Wheels for transport have been often suggested, but they would be useless. On plain ground or grass you can readily do without them. On rocks and rough ground, or over ditches and through hedges, wheels could not be employed, or would be in the way. Bilge pieces are not required. Strength must be had without them, and their projection seriously complicates the difficulties of pushing the boat over a pointed rock, both when afloat and when ashore.

The paddle should be 7 feet long (not more), strong, with both ends rounded, thick, and banded with copper. There should be conical cups to catch the dribbling water, and, if possible, some plan (not yet devised) for preventing or arresting the drops from the paddle ends, which fall on the deck when you paddle slowly, and when there is not enough centrifugal force to throw this water away from the boat. Painter of best flexible rope, not tarred, well able to bear 200 lb. weight; more than 20 feet is a constant encumbrance. Ends secured through a hole in stem post and another in stern post (so that either or both can be readily cast off), the slack coiled on deck behind you.

There should be a back support of two wooden slips, each 15 inches by 3 inches, placed like the side strokes of the letter H, and an inch apart, but laced together with cord. Rest them against the edge of the combing, and so as to be free to yield to the motion of the back at each stroke, without hurting the spine. If made fast so as always to project, they are much in the way of the painter in critical times. They may be hinged below so as to fold down as you get out.

The mast should be 5 feet long, strong enough to stand gales without stays, stepped just forward of the stretcher, and so as to be struck without your rising when in a squall, or when nearing trees, or a bridge, barrier, ferry-rope, bank, or waterfall, or going aground.

The sail, if a lug, should have a fore leach of 4 feet, a head of 3 feet 6 inches, and a foot of 4 feet 6 inches; yard and boom of bamboo.

The boat can well stand more sail than this at sea, or in lakes and broad channels, but the foregoing size for a lug is quite large enough to manage in stiff breezes and in narrow rocky tortuous rivers.

A spritsail, on the whole, would be better as enabling more canvas to be carried, while it can be reduced at once to a leg of mutton sail by dropping the sprit in a gale.

The material of the sail should be strong cotton, in one piece, without any eyelet or hole whatever, but with a broad hem, enclosing well-stretched cord all round. A jib is of little use as a sail. It is apt to get aback in sudden turns. Besides, you must land to set it or to take in its outhaul, so as to be quite snug. But the job does well to tie on the shoulders when they are turned to a fierce sun. The sails (with the booms or yards) should he rolled up round the mast compactly, to be stowed away forward, so that the end of the mast resting on the stretcher will keep the roll of sails out of the wet. The flag and its staff when not fast at the mast-head should fit into the mast-step, and should be light, so as not to sink if it falls overboard, as one of mine did.

The floor-boards should be strong, and easily detachable, so that one of them can be at once used as a paddle if that falls overboard.

The stretcher should have only one length, and let this be carefully determined after trial before starting. The two sides of its foot-board should be high and broad, while the middle may be cut down to let the hand get to the mast. The stretcher should, of course, be moveable, in order that you may lie down with the legs at full length for repose.

One brass cleat for belaying the halyard should be on deck, about the middle, and on the right-hand side. A stud on the other side, and this cleat will do to make one turn of the sheet round on either tack.

List of Stores on Board the Rob Roy

1. *Useful Stores.*—Paddle, painter (31 feet at first, but cut down to 20 feet), sponge, waterproof cover, 5 feet by 2 feet 3 inches, silk blue union jack, 10 inches by 8 inches, on a staff 2 feet long. Mast, boom, and yard. Lug sail, jib, and spare jib (used as a sun shawl). Stretcher, two back boards, floor boards, basket to sit on (12 inches by 6 inches, by 1 inch deep), and holding a macintosh coat. For repairs—iron and brass screws, sheet copper and

copper nails, putty and white lead, a gimlet, cord, string, and thread, a spare button, needle, and pins, canvas wading shoes (wooden clogs would be better); all the above should be left with the boat. Black bag for luggage, closed by three buttons, and with shoulder-strap, size, 12 inches by 12 inches, by 5 inches deep (just right). Flannel Norfolk jacket (flaps not too long, else they dip in the water, or the pockets are inverted in getting out and in); wide flannel trousers, with broad back buckle, second trousers with belt (braces are better on shore). Flannel shirt on, and another for shore. Thin alpaca black Sunday coat, thick waistcoat, black leather light-soled spring-sided shoes (should be stronger for rocks and village pavements), straw hat, cloth cap (only used as a bag), 2 collars, 3 pocket handkerchiefs, ribbon tie, 2 pair of cotton socks (easily get off for sudden wading, and drying quickly when put on deck in the sun). Brush, comb, and tooth-brush. Testament, passport (scarcely needed after this winter), leather purse, circular notes, small change in silver and copper for frequent use, blue spectacles in strong case, book for journal and sketches, black, blue, end red chalk, and steel pen. Maps, cutting off a six inch square at a time for rocket reference. Pipe, tobacco-case, and light-box (metal, to resist moisture from without and within), guide books and pleasant evening reading book, you should cut off covers and all useless pages of these, and every page as read. No needless weight should be carried hundreds of miles; even a fly settling on the boat must be refused a free passage. Illustrated papers, tracts, and anecdotes in French and German for Sunday reading and daily distribution (far too few had been taken, they were always well received). Box of "Gregory's Mixture," sticking plaster, small knife, and pencil.

2. *Useless Articles.*—Boathook, undervest, water-proof helmet ventilated cap, foreign conversation books, glass seltzer bottle and patent cork (for a drinking flask), tweezers for thorns.

3. *Lost or Stolen Articles.*—Bag for back cushion, waterproof bag for sitting cushion, long knife, necktie, woven waistcoat, box of quinine, steel-hafted knife. These, except the last of them, were not missed.

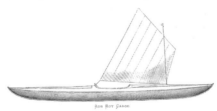

ROB ROY CANOE.

FROM *THE UNLIKELY VOYAGE OF JACK DE CROW:* *A MIRROR ODYSSEY FROM NORTH WALES TO THE BLACK SEA*

2002

A. J. Mackinnon

illustration by A.J. Mackinnon

In September 1998, A. J. (Sandy) Mackinnon found himself floating down the Danube through Serbia in an 11-foot sailing dinghy.

His voyage had started a year before in northern Wales. He was in the process of easing out of his job teaching at a small public school there when he noticed a derelict little plywood boat, half covered in weeds, near the school's boathouse. It struck Mackinnon that the dinghy might be a nice way to go. Pop it in the nearby Llangollen Canal, then down the River Severn, perhaps as far as Gloucester, near the sea. A little adventure, some sightseeing, then back to Australia for another position.

One might suspect that he had a longer trip lurking in the back of his mind, and wisely kept mum about it in case it didn't work out—the thirty-year-old boat came to pieces, he was waylaid by a mermaid, or simply that a trip, by oar and sail, in an 11-foot boat through an English winter might be expected to turn any man into a gibbering wreck well within a couple of hundred miles.

In any case he was probably as surprised as anybody, and his delight infuses every word in the book, to find himself something like 3,000 miles along on his journey a year later. The one tiny cloud on the horizon was that in Kosovo that summer, Serbia's President Slobodan Milosevic had been up to no good again, and NATO, meaning mostly the USA and Britain, was threatening to start bombing if he didn't back down.

So there was Mackinnon, rowing merrily along into what could easily become a war zone, two little Union Jacks fluttering from the rigging, and probably about as far, mentally and spiritually, as one can get from ethnic cleansing, computer-guided bombs, and the insane calculus of that sort of international politics. For those who know the road, there is nothing quite as precious as kindness from a stranger. Mackinnon's experience, though, given the circumstances, was something else again.

LIFE DURING WARTIME

So precious are the memories of my time in Serbia and of the overwhelming kindness and simplicity of the Serbian people that I am tempted to relate in detail each new encounter, each new bend of the river, each new friend met on the way. I feel that if nothing else it would be a tribute to these people who have suffered much of late, not least being maligned by the world press. But as ever, the deeds of the few in power, the politicians and generals, are not representative of the common folk, and from purely personal experience, I found them to be the warmest and most spontaneously hospitable of people.

However, I shall limit myself to the briefest of sketches of that golden time. For golden it was. The sun shone warm and bright with September gold, flaming in the poplars and willows that lined the banks, and silvering the threads of gossamer that drifted in airy swathes across the river to festoon my rigging with fairy pennants. The low, level light made the river always a molten shimmer of silver haze, and at times it felt as though I was rowing into Paradise, or the album cover for a Handel Oratorio. Still the endless trees marched on either side, at times thick and tangled where I was delighted to see wild pigs rooting at the river's edge, unaware of my gliding presence yards away. A species of eagle with a distinct white tail could often be seen sailing across the river and emitting squeaky yelps more suited to a plastic baby's toy than a keen-eyed monarch of the skies. At times the air would turn even hazier and yellower than the autumn sun could account for, and stink of sulphur—a distant factory chimney above the trees would provide the unromantic explanation.

In one particularly lambent wood, I remember, there came a sweet chiming from somewhere high in the goldy-green treetops, a plangent jingling of bells as though elfin wind chimes were sounding. It was remote and musical and faint, unearthly above the clunk-splash of the mortal oars, and I wondered for a moment if I was dreaming. I have no idea what it was, so far from anywhere, and still wonder if perhaps in some odd geographical sideslip, I had passed by Lorien all unknowing.

Another night's stop was somewhat less poetic. South of Novi Sad, I had stopped in another fishermen's camp, but far busier than the previous one. Here I met three university students, Ivan David and Sonja; they were keen to practise their already excellent English, and we talked for a long while abut the present troubles in the country. Once, they said, just a few years ago, Yugoslavian students had had the run of Europe and Asia Minor for their holidays. In fact, so unrestricted were the Yugoslavians in where they could go in the world that a Yugoslavian passport had been the highest priced of all stolen passports on the Black Market. Now, they were restricted only to Hungary and Romania. The rest of the world was closed to them, and these young people were finding the cultural claustrophobia unbearable. They condemned their president's actions in Kosovo, but were angrier still at the stance of the United States and Britain. They were not children, they said.

Our talk was interrupted by a high, ear-splitting squeal from just behind me, and as I jumped in my seat I exclaimed the old cliché, "Goodness me, it sounds like a pig having its throat cut!" When I turned I saw that that was exactly what it was. Just yards away, a fisherman had a little pink pig propped between his booted knees and had just flashed a great knife across the poor creature's face; it was not so much agonised as faintly hurt and bewildered, a gently confused expression one would associate more with Pooh Bear wondering where his last pot of honey had got to than with an animal being slaughtered. "Why is the light dimming so fast, Mother?" it seemed to stay, "and why am I feeling all so floppy and listless all of a sudden?" Poor piggy. Poor me. It was all rather too ethnic for us sensitive English-Drama teaching types.

The last day before I reached Belgrade, where I hoped to replenish my vanishing money supplies, is a beauty. The forest has ended, and now sandy cliffs rear high on the southern bank, the home of thousands of sand martins and swifts. Near lunchtime I am hailed by two fishermen on the bank in a grassy meadow at the foot of the cliffs: Jan and Estovich. Jan is fifty-ish, Estovich is a hundred and two. They ply me with beer and peanuts, and though their English is as non-existent as my Yugoslavian, we seem to communicate with ease. Later they light a little fire and make a pot of coffee, the same river silt which I find hard to like, but drink gamely. Then when I show them a magic trick as a thanks, Jan is so overcome with excitement he does three somersaults in the long meadow grass like a child. I am tickled pink. When I finally indicate I must sail on they solemnly present me with a large glass bottle of something that they call 'Paradijo.' It is most gorgeous, rich orange-red, opaque, and full of little golden-yellow seeds suspended in it, and I think it is made from tomatoes and paprika. Over the next four days, I treasure it, savouring each mouthful; the taste is a little like tomato juice, but there is a rich burning afterglow that goes right to the belly. I could not work out if it was alcoholic or not—I think on balance not—but it had the same warming effect, as did my memory of the middle-aged Jan tumbling for glee in the green grass whenever I swigged that precious stuff.

That night I came to a tiny scattering of huts beneath a cliff, a squalid assortment of boat sheds and dank hovels, and sat on my dinghy preparing the last bit of bread and some salami that I had discovered in the bows. This was left over from Linz and still going strong . . . stronger by the day in fact. I was just about to retire, when a huge man came out of one of the nearby huts and called me over. What I had thought was a private home was in fact a rough sort of taverna; a concrete floor, an open kitchen, but full of guests sitting at the cheap little tables with plastic red and white cloths and bowls of bread. Silently he pointed to a table in the corner, and his daughter brought a bowl of bread.

"Nema dinar . . ." I explained. (No money.)

"Nema problema," he replied.

Before I had finished the bread, the girl had reappeared with a bowl of crumbled eggplant.

"Um . . . thank you, but nema dinar . . ."

"Nema problema," she chirped, and tripped away.

These were people who did not know who I was or where I had come from. I had not yet had a chance to explain my story, not to do anything as impressive as the magic-hanky-into-toy-rabbit trick nor play a haunting air on my tin whistle. And yet throughout the rest of the night as they bustled around, serving their legitimate guests, each time they passed a new dish was set down before me—spiced meats, a dish of paprika in oil, grilled chops, a sweet thing made of poppy seeds, and three beers. It was all done so wordlessly that I couldn't help thinking that there must be a catch somewhere. My worst fears were confirmed when after the fifth apologetic rendition of "Look, I'm terribly sorry, there must be some mistake, I don't have any money and I appear to have eaten a four course dinner," my massive host put an arm around my shoulders and guided me into the kitchen area. There he showed me a framed photo of himself as a younger man dressed in a white kimono, grinning and holding up a trophy.

"Me, Europe karate champion, 1956. Chop, chop! Hyaaii!"

Then he led me gently back to my seat. I translated that as meaning, "Mess with me, laddie, or try that old not-got-any-cash-on-me routine, and I'll kick your kidneys out your ears before you can say chop-suey, chum!"

But no, at the end of the evening, when the rest of the guests had departed, he came and sat at the table where I was rolling like a porpoise, poured the inevitable schnapps, and sat proudly telling me in incomprehensible Yugoslavian about karate, the 1956 Olympics, his beautiful daughter, and what a pleasure it was to have met me. It was all thoroughly puzzling. All I could do in payment was make a little painted origami book the next morning and leave it for them to find, just the sort of thing that is useful and valuable in a country plunged in economic and political disaster on the brink of bombardment, I always think . . .

I am going to race through Belgrade. It has a huge number of bookshops, but most of the books are on the occult. It has a marina called the

Dorcol, meaning 'four corners'—it is here that they used to quarter people using four horses all going in different directions. The marina is shabby but exceptionally friendly—I keep being given plum brandy by different people on old boats, poured out of coloured glass bottles shaped like St. Nicolai, the patron saint of sailors. The Hyatt Hotel, though hugely luxurious, will not give me cash but will allow me to use my Visa card for services. The clerks at reception are immune to both my logic and my charm. They are just charming back. I sit and have a hugely luxurious afternoon tea in a fit of pique and sit and write letters while Handel's Trio Sonata tinkles away in the background. I make long, expensive calls to England. I have a large, piggy dinner. I stop myself actually staying there that night, and sleep on the dinghy and regret it as a lashing thunderstorm soaks me through. I trudge around every bank in Belgrade, telling them to bloody well take down their Visa signs if they are not going to cough up. I climb the great park-like hill of Kalemegdan and watch the junction of the River Sava and the Dunav glow under a post-thunderstorm sky of orange and rose and purple, and all the trees and grass as unnaturally tinted as a Chesterton landscape. It is the Sava down which the beastly Croats sent the corpses of Serbs with nails knocked through their skulls, according to the Serbs I met later, and they fetched up here in Belgrade. The Serbs call it Beograd, which means "White City" though now it is sooty and grey, and sorry, but I hate it. While I am spending a penny behind a bush near the marina, a large brown snake glides away though my legs , and I am not in a position to do anything about it. The subsequent instinctive clenching does something to my bladder that makes it difficult to pee for several days afterwards. Now that we are back in a country where the language has some tenuous roots connected with Latin and Anglo-Saxon, the alphabet capriciously changes to the Cyrillic one, so I remain as baffled as I was in Hungary. For example, the perfectly guessable-at "Restoran" for restaurant transliterates as "PETOPAN" which sounds like something you boil jam in. I am thoroughly fed up, so let us leave Belgrade.

There that was quick, wasn't it?

Over the next three days, things begin to get a little desperate. I have run out of food, and the supply of people on either hand to dole out provisions when needed is suddenly thin. So am I. The landscape slowly changes from pretty vineyards and orchards on gentle slopes (where I am sorely tempted to steal some grapes and apples) to a harsher, drier landscape as I near the Carpathian Mountains and the Iron Gates. This is where the Dunav carves its way though the last great obstacle before its final run to the sea. It does so in a great gorge, sheer sided and and tortuous, the grim gateway into old Transylvania. But whether I will make it there before starving to death, I am not sure. Being hungry is not nearly as adventurous and romantic when you are actually in mid-fast.

The need to get to Bulgaria and to a bank presses me on, past the leaning fortress towers of Smederevo, past the fortress of Ram, through unfriendly Jugovo where in the dark streets men sit and play dominoes and chess with all the grunting and jeering and raucous noise more associated with wrestling matches; through a smart little riverside resort where a hugely fat man bathing with his family shouts out things in a purple rage at the sight of my two little Union Jacks. It still has not occurred to me that my little dinghy flying the British ensign could possibly enrage or offend the people whom Britain were on the point of bombarding. I suppose I might also have been seen as the very first flagboat of an invading British navy, sent out just to reccy round and report back. The point is driven home when I sleep aboard in the town of Veliko Gradiste and wake the next morning to find that someone in the night has slashed both my Union Jacks to shreds. I am furious, furious at the vandal that has done this. Then a sudden thought sobers me. Sleeping just three feet lower down, I am lucky not to have met a similar fate.

I am more fortunate. A doleful-looking Serb called Branko comes along, introduces himself and invites me back to his mother's house for lunch. His English is good . . . good enough to tactfully inquire if I might like to have a hot bath first. The grubby ring around the bath when I have finished would grow root vegetables. Roast pork, potatoes, paprika (I really am a little tired of the paprika), vodka damson-cake and wine and then a cycle ride out to a local beauty spot. On the way we run over two snakes, and see three more. I tell Branko of my snake experience in Belgrade, and he explains that yes, there appears to be a plague of them this summer. There are two possible explanations, he says. One is that it is a plot by the CIA, an experiment in biological warfare as an entree before the main bombardment. The second and more likely one, he says with a perfectly straight face, is that God is punishing the Serbs for their wickedness. That opens the way for a long talk about Serbia and its problems, which are legion. Chief of these is corruption. Every town, every village has its local Mafia boss. Extortion on even the smallest, most local scale is rife. No one owns a business, not an apple cart, not a newspaper stand, without paying a large cut to the hired thugs of the resident Mr. Big. Those who resist meet with violence and terror tactics. Much of this stems from Milosevic and his ministers; the Kosovo problem is just one very visual symptom of the sickness in the land. The poverty I was seeing everywhere—and I was, often worse than I had seen elsewhere in Africa or Laos—was a recent phenomenon. Yugoslavia had been a rich and prosperous country until ten years ago, when the first blockades were imposed. Oh, it had never been as rich as Germany or Austria, for sure, but its farms had been productive, its orchards tended, its vines fruitful. Now everywhere there was filth and waste, and the people were confused and angry. That was the problem with embargoes and blockades, Branko said. They drew the people's anger outwards to the States and Britain, muddying the issue. It was so easy for the politicians to blame all the country's woes on the evil superpowers, and deny responsibility for their own policies.

"Why do the people not rise up against Milosevic if it is clear that it is his actions bringing about the embargoes?" I asked.

"Because," he said with a sigh, "Serbs watch only Serbian television. You don't think Milosevic allows any truth to creep into the news coverage, do you? NATO is blockading us because they are jealous of us, or because they are afraid of us, or because they want to steal all our fruit. Not because of anything our glorious leader has done—dear me, never! Hence the CIA and the snakes," he added, looking more doleful than ever. "It is all very sad."

When I continued on my way that afternoon, I did so with a huge bag of apples, a clove of garlic, and a great jar of home-made honey, a present from Branko's mother Dora. But I also took with me a new insight, a new thoughtfulness—I understood a little, just a little, about my slashed flags now.

FROM *THE WIND IN THE WILLOWS*
1908

Kenneth Grahame

There is a certain kind of person who cannot look at the sea, a river, or (for the really bitten) even a middling puddle without casting about for a boat to beg, borrow, or build so that they can float away on it. It is not an easy feeling to express and even harder to explain, and for solid, sensible, not to say stolid folks, it is inexplicable, almost unconscionable, and clearly a sign of some grave moral defect or other.

Kenneth Grahame's The Wind in the Willows *shows that he was above all one of the breed. And if Grahame also couldn't quite manage to explain why some find so much pleasure on the water, he did at least provide the passage that probably best captures the compulsion:*

> *'Nice? it's the only thing,' said the Water Rat solemnly, as he leant forward for his stroke. 'Believe me, my young friend, there is nothing— absolutely nothing—half so much worth doing as simply messing about in boats. Simply messing,' he went on dreamily, 'messing—about—in— boats; messing—'*

So, as one would imagine, in searching the book for a good bit to excerpt, I found that I was spoiled for choice. A. J. Mackinnon, represented in the previous piece in this anthology, has clearly spent a lot of time thinking about the subject, and in his book The Unlikely Voyage of Jack De Crow *he said he figured "The Piper at the Gates of Dawn" was the best chapter in the English language. Stiff competition, that. But it is one of a handful of passages that will take anyone who loves the wild, magic places where they want to go.*

THE PIPER AT THE GATES OF DAWN

The Willow-Wren was twittering his thin little song, hidden himself in the dark selvedge of the river bank. Though it was past ten o'clock at night, the sky still clung to and retained some lingering skirts of light from the departed day; and the sullen heats of the torrid afternoon broke up and rolled away at the dispersing touch of the cool fingers of the short midsummer night. Mole lay stretched on the bank, still panting from the stress of the fierce day that had been cloudless from dawn to late sunset, and waited for his friend to return. He had been on the river with some companions, leaving the Water Rat free to keep a engagement of long standing with Otter; and he had come back to find the house dark and deserted, and no sign of Rat, who was doubtless keeping it up late with his old comrade. It was still too hot to think of staying indoors, so he lay on some cool dock-leaves, and thought over the past day and its doings, and how very good they all had been.

The Rat's light footfall was presently heard approaching over the parched grass. 'O, the blessed coolness!' he said, and sat down, gazing thoughtfully into the river, silent and pre-occupied.

'You stayed to supper, of course?' said the Mole presently.

'Simply had to,' said the Rat. 'They wouldn't hear of my going before. You know how kind they always are. And they made things as jolly for me as ever they could, right up to the moment I left. But I felt a brute all the time, as it was clear to me they were very unhappy, though they tried to hide it. Mole, I'm afraid they're in trouble. Little Portly is missing again; and you know what a lot his father thinks of him, though he never says much about it.'

'What, that child?' said the Mole lightly. 'Well, suppose he is; why worry about it? He's always straying off and getting lost, and turning up again;

he's so adventurous. But no harm ever happens to him. Everybody hereabouts knows him and likes him, just as they do old Otter, and you may be sure some animal or other will come across him and bring him back again all right. Why, we've found him ourselves, miles from home, and quite self-possessed and cheerful!'

'Yes; but this time it's more serious,' said the Rat gravely. 'He's been missing for some days now, and the Otters have hunted everywhere, high and low, without finding the slightest trace. And they've asked every animal, too, for miles around, and no one knows anything about him. Otter's evidently more anxious than he'll admit. I got out of him that young Portly hasn't learnt to swim very well yet, and I can see he's thinking of the weir. There's a lot of water coming down still, considering the time of the year, and the place always had a fascination for the child. And then there are— well, traps and things—YOU know. Otter's not the fellow to be nervous about any son of his before it's time. And now he IS nervous. When I left, he came out with me—said he wanted some air, and talked about stretching his legs. But I could see it wasn't that, so I drew him out and pumped him, and got it all from him at last. He was going to spend the night watching by the ford. You know the place where the old ford used to be, in bygone days before they built the bridge?'

'I know it well,' said the Mole. 'But why should Otter choose to watch there?'

'Well, it seems that it was there he gave Portly his first swimming-lesson,' continued the Rat. 'From that shallow, gravelly spit near the bank. And it was there he used to teach him fishing, and there young Portly caught his first fish, of which he was so very proud. The child loved the spot, and Otter thinks that if he came wandering back from wherever he is—if he IS anywhere by this time, poor little chap—he might make for the ford he was so fond of; or if he came across it he'd remember it well, and stop there and play, perhaps. So Otter goes there every night and watches—on the chance, you know, just on the chance!'

They were silent for a time, both thinking of the same thing—the lonely, heart-sore animal, crouched by the ford, watching and waiting, the long night through—on the chance.

'Well, well,' said the Rat presently, 'I suppose we ought to be thinking about turning in.' But he never offered to move.

'Rat,' said the Mole, 'I simply can't go and turn in, and go to sleep, and DO nothing, even though there doesn't seem to be anything to be done. We'll get the boat out, and paddle up stream. The moon will be up in an hour or so, and then we will search as well as we can—anyhow, it will be better than going to bed and doing NOTHING.'

'Just what I was thinking myself,' said the Rat. 'It's not the sort of night for bed anyhow; and daybreak is not so very far off, and then we may pick up some news of him from early risers as we go along.'

They got the boat out, and the Rat took the sculls, paddling with caution. Out in midstream, there was a clear, narrow track that faintly reflected the sky; but wherever shadows fell on the water from bank, bush, or tree, they were as solid to all appearance as the banks themselves, and the Mole had to steer with judgement accordingly. Dark and deserted as it was, the night was full of small noises, song and chatter and rustling, telling of the busy little population who were up and about, plying their trades and vocations through the night till sunshine should fall on them at last and send them off to their well-earned repose. The water's own noises, too, were more apparent than by day, its gurglings and 'cloops' more unexpected and near at hand; and constantly they started at what seemed a sudden clear call from an actual articulate voice.

The line of the horizon was clear and hard against the sky, and in one particular quarter it showed black against a silvery climbing phosphorescence that grew and grew. At last, over the rim of the waiting earth the moon lifted with slow majesty till it swung clear of the horizon and rode off, free of moorings; and once more they began to see surfaces—meadows widespread, and quiet gardens, and the river itself from bank to bank, all softly disclosed, all washed clean of mystery and terror, all radiant again as by day, but with a difference that was tremendous. Their old haunts greeted them again in other raiment, as if they had slipped away and put on this pure new apparel and come quietly back, smiling as they shyly waited to see if they would be recognised again under it.

Fastening their boat to a willow, the friends landed in this silent, silver kingdom, and patiently explored the hedges, the hollow trees, the runnels and their little culverts, the ditches and dry waterways. Embarking again and crossing over, they worked their way up the stream in this manner, while the moon, serene and detached in a cloudless sky, did what she could, though so far off, to help them in their quest; till her hour came and she sank earthwards reluctantly, and left them, and mystery once more held field and river.

Then a change began slowly to declare itself. The horizon became clearer, field and tree came more into sight, and somehow with a different look; the mystery began to drop away from them. A bird piped suddenly, and was still; and a light breeze sprang up and set the reeds and bulrushes rustling. Rat, who was in the stern of the boat, while Mole sculled, sat up suddenly and listened with a passionate intentness. Mole, who with gentle strokes was just keeping the boat moving while he scanned the banks with care, looked at him with curiosity.

'It's gone!' sighed the Rat, sinking back in his seat again. 'So beautiful and strange and new. Since it was to end so soon, I almost wish I had never heard it. For it has roused a longing in me that is pain, and nothing seems worth while but just to hear that sound once more and go on listening to it for ever. No! There it is again!' he cried, alert once more. Entranced, he was silent for a long space, spellbound.

'Now it passes on and I begin to lose it,' he said presently. 'O Mole! the beauty of it! The merry bubble and joy, the thin, clear, happy call of the distant piping! Such music I never dreamed of, and the call in it is stronger even than the music is sweet! Row on, Mole, row! For the music and the call must be for us.'

The Mole, greatly wondering, obeyed. 'I hear nothing myself,' he said, 'but the wind playing in the reeds and rushes and osiers.'

The Rat never answered, if indeed he heard. Rapt, transported, trembling, he was possessed in all his senses by this new divine thing that caught up his helpless soul and swung and dandled it, a powerless but happy infant in a strong sustaining grasp.

In silence Mole rowed steadily, and soon they came to a point where the river divided, a long backwater branching off to one side. With a slight movement of his head Rat, who had long dropped the rudder-lines, directed the rower to take the backwater. The creeping tide of light gained and gained, and now they could see the colour of the flowers that gemmed the water's edge.

'Clearer and nearer still,' cried the Rat joyously. 'Now you must surely hear it! Ah—at last—I see you do!'

Breathless and transfixed the Mole stopped rowing as the liquid run of that glad piping broke on him like a wave, caught him up, and possessed him utterly. He saw the tears on his comrade's cheeks, and bowed his head and understood. For a space they hung there, brushed by the purple loose-strife that fringed the bank; then the clear imperious summons that marched hand-in-hand with the intoxicating melody imposed its will on Mole, and mechanically he bent to his oars again. And the light grew steadily stronger, but no birds sang as they were wont to do at the approach of dawn; and but for the heavenly music all was marvellously still.

On either side of them, as they glided onwards, the rich meadow-grass seemed that morning of a freshness and a greenness unsurpassable. Never had they noticed the roses so vivid, the willow-herb so riotous, the meadow-sweet so odorous and pervading. Then the murmur of the approaching weir began to hold the air, and they felt a consciousness that they were nearing the end, whatever it might be, that surely awaited their expedition.

A wide half-circle of foam and glinting lights and shining shoulders of green water, the great weir closed the backwater from bank to bank, troubled all the quiet surface with twirling eddies and floating foam-streaks, and deadened all other sounds with its solemn and soothing rumble. In midmost of the stream, embraced in the weir's shimmering arm-spread, a small island lay anchored, fringed close with willow and silver birch and alder. Reserved, shy, but full of significance, it hid whatever it might hold behind a veil, keeping it till the hour should come, and, with the hour, those who were called and chosen.

Slowly, but with no doubt or hesitation whatever, and in something of a solemn expectancy, the two animals passed through the broken tumultuous water and moored their boat at the flowery margin of the island. In silence they landed, and pushed through the blossom and scented herbage and undergrowth that led up to the level ground, till they stood on a little lawn of a marvellous green, set round with Nature's own orchard-trees—crab-apple, wild cherry, and sloe.

'This is the place of my song-dream, the place the music played to me,' whispered the Rat, as if in a trance. 'Here, in this holy place, here if anywhere, surely we shall find Him!'

Then suddenly the Mole felt a great Awe fall upon him, an awe that turned his muscles to water, bowed his head, and rooted his feet to the ground. It was no panic terror—indeed he felt wonderfully at peace and happy—but it was an awe that smote and held him and, without seeing, he knew it could only mean that some august Presence was very, very near. With difficulty he turned to look for his friend and saw him at his side cowed, stricken, and trembling violently. And still there was utter silence in the populous bird-haunted branches around them; and still the light grew and grew.

Perhaps he would never have dared to raise his eyes, but that, though the piping was now hushed, the call and the summons seemed still dominant and imperious. He might not refuse, were Death himself waiting to strike him instantly, once he had looked with mortal eye on things rightly kept hidden. Trembling he obeyed, and raised his humble head; and then, in that utter clearness of the imminent dawn, while Nature, flushed with fullness of incredible colour, seemed to hold her breath for the event, he looked in the very eyes of the Friend and Helper; saw the backward sweep of the curved horns, gleaming in the growing daylight; saw the stern, hooked nose between the kindly eyes that were looking down on them humorously, while the bearded mouth broke into a half-smile at the corners; saw the rippling muscles on the arm that lay across the broad chest, the long supple hand still holding the pan-pipes only just fallen away from the parted lips; saw the splendid curves of the shaggy limbs disposed in majestic ease on the sward; saw, last of all, nestling between his very hooves, sleeping soundly in entire peace and contentment, the little, round, podgy, childish form of the baby otter. All this he saw, for one moment breathless and intense, vivid on the morning sky; and still, as he looked, he lived; and still, as he lived, he wondered.

'Rat!' he found breath to whisper, shaking. 'Are you afraid?'

'Afraid?' murmured the Rat, his eyes shining with unutterable love. 'Afraid! Of HIM? O, never, never! And yet—and yet—O, Mole, I am afraid!'

Then the two animals, crouching to the earth, bowed their heads and did worship.

Sudden and magnificent, the sun's broad golden disc showed itself over the horizon facing them; and the first rays, shooting across the level water-meadows, took the animals full in the eyes and dazzled them. When they were able to look once more, the Vision had vanished, and the air was full of the carol of birds that hailed the dawn.

As they stared blankly in dumb misery deepening as they slowly realised all they had seen and all they had lost, a capricious little breeze, dancing up from the surface of the water, tossed the aspens, shook the dewy roses and blew lightly and caressingly in their faces; and with its soft touch came instant oblivion. For this is the last best gift that the kindly demi-god is careful to bestow on those to whom he has revealed himself in their helping: the gift of forgetfulness. Lest the awful remembrance should remain and grow, and overshadow mirth and pleasure, and the great haunting memory should spoil all the after-lives of little animals helped out of difficulties, in order that they should be happy and light-hearted as before.

Mole rubbed his eyes and stared at Rat, who was looking about him in a puzzled sort of way. 'I beg your pardon; what did you say, Rat?' he asked.

'I think I was only remarking,' said Rat slowly, 'that this was the right sort of place, and that here, if anywhere, we should find him. And look! Why, there he is, the little fellow!' And with a cry of delight he ran towards the slumbering Portly.

But Mole stood still a moment, held in thought. As one wakened suddenly from a beautiful dream, who struggles to recall it, and can re-capture nothing but a dim sense of the beauty of it, the beauty! Till that, too, fades away in its turn, and the dreamer bitterly accepts the hard, cold waking and all its penalties; so Mole, after struggling with his memory for a brief space, shook his head sadly and followed the Rat.

Portly woke up with a joyous squeak, and wriggled with pleasure at the sight of his father's friends, who had played with him so often in past days. In a moment, however, his face grew blank, and he fell to hunting round in a circle with pleading whine. As a child that has fallen happily asleep in its nurse's arms, and wakes to find itself alone and laid in a strange place, and searches corners and cupboards, and runs from room to room, despair growing silently in its heart, even so Portly searched the island and searched, dogged and unwearying, till at last the black moment came for giving it up, and sitting down and crying bitterly.

The Mole ran quickly to comfort the little animal; but Rat, lingering, looked long and doubtfully at certain hoof-marks deep in the sward.

'Some—great—animal—has been here,' he murmured slowly and thoughtfully; and stood musing, musing; his mind strangely stirred.

'Come along, Rat!' called the Mole. 'Think of poor Otter, waiting up there by the ford!'

Portly had soon been comforted by the promise of a treat—a jaunt on the river in Mr. Rat's real boat; and the two animals conducted him to the water's side, placed him securely between them in the bottom of the boat, and paddled off down the backwater. The sun was fully up by now, and hot on them, birds sang lustily and without restraint, and flowers smiled and nodded from either bank, but somehow—so thought the animals—with less of richness and blaze of colour than they seemed to remember seeing quite recently somewhere—they wondered where.

The main river reached again, they turned the boat's head upstream, towards the point where they knew their friend was keeping his lonely vigil. As they drew near the familiar ford, the Mole took the boat in to the bank, and they lifted Portly out and set him on his legs on the tow-path, gave him his marching orders and a friendly farewell pat on the back, and shoved out into mid-stream. They watched the little animal as he waddled along the path contentedly and with importance; watched him till they saw his muzzle suddenly lift and his waddle break into a clumsy amble as he quickened his pace with shrill whines and wriggles of recognition. Looking up the river, they could see Otter start up, tense and rigid, from out of the shallows where he crouched in dumb patience, and could hear his amazed and joyous bark as he bounded up through the osiers on to the path. Then the Mole, with a strong pull on one oar, swung the boat round and let the full stream bear them down again whither it would, their quest now happily ended.

'I feel strangely tired, Rat,' said the Mole, leaning wearily over his oars as the boat drifted. 'It's being up all night, you'll say, perhaps; but that's nothing. We do as much half the nights of the week, at this time of the year. No; I feel as if I had been through something very exciting and rather terrible, and it was just over; and yet nothing particular has happened.'

'Or something very surprising and splendid and beautiful,' murmured the Rat, leaning back and closing his eyes. 'I feel just as you do, Mole; simply dead tired, though not body tired. It's lucky we've got the stream with us, to take us home. Isn't it jolly to feel the sun again, soaking into one's bones! And hark to the wind playing in the reeds!'

'It's like music—far away music,' said the Mole nodding drowsily.

'So I was thinking,' murmured the Rat, dreamful and languid. 'Dance-music—the lilting sort that runs on without a stop—but with words in it, too—it passes into words and out of them again—I catch them at intervals—then it is dance-music once more, and then nothing but the reeds' soft thin whispering.'

'You hear better than I,' said the Mole sadly. 'I cannot catch the words.'

'Let me try and give you them,' said the Rat softly, his eyes still closed. 'Now it is turning into words again—faint but clear—*Lest the awe should dwell—And turn your frolic to fret—You shall look on my power at the helping hour—But then you shall forget!* Now the reeds take it up—*forget, forget,* they sigh, and it dies away in a rustle and a whisper. Then the voice returns— *Lest limbs be reddened and rent—I spring the trap that is set—As I loose the snare you may glimpse me there—For surely you shall forget!* Row nearer, Mole, nearer to the reeds! It is hard to catch, and grows each minute fainter. *Helper and healer, I cheer—Small waifs in the woodland wet—Strays I find in it, wounds I bind in it—Bidding them all forget!* Nearer, Mole, nearer! No, it is no good; the song has died away into reed-talk.'

'But what do the words mean?' asked the wondering Mole.

'That I do not know,' said the Rat simply. 'I passed them on to you as they reached me. Ah! now they return again, and this time full and clear! This time, at last, it is the real, the unmistakable thing, simple—passionate— perfect—'

'Well, let's have it, then,' said the Mole, after he had waited patiently for a few minutes, half-dozing in the hot sun.

But no answer came. He looked, and understood the silence. With a smile of much happiness on his face, and something of a listening look still lingering there, the weary Rat was fast asleep.

FROM *A WEEK ON THE CONCORD AND MERRIMACK RIVERS*
1849

Henry David Thoreau

Henry David Thoreau is one of the people responsible for instilling in us the idea that one ought to be able to find, without going too far, a place with clean water, trees, and meadow; a bird or a deer to watch; and maybe even a fish or two to catch. So it is no surprise that he understood the appeal of building and messing about in boats.

ART IS ALL OF A SHIP BUT THE WOOD

At length, on Saturday, the last day of August, 1839, we two, brothers, and natives of Concord, weighed anchor in this river port; for Concord, too, lies under the sun, a port of entry and departure for the bodies as well as the souls of men; one shore at least exempted from all duties but such as an honest man will gladly discharge. A warm drizzling rain had obscured the morning, and threatened to delay our voyage, but at length the leaves and grass were dried, and it came out a mild afternoon, as serene and fresh as if Nature were maturing some greater scheme of her own.

After this long dripping and oozing from every pore, she began to respire again more healthily than ever. So with a vigorous shove we launched our boat from the bank, while the flags and bulrushes courtesied a God-speed, and dropped silently down the stream.

Our boat, which had cost us a week's labor in the spring, was in form like a fisherman's dory, fifteen feet long by three and a half in breadth at the widest part, painted green below, with a border of blue, with reference to the two elements in which it was to spend its existence. It had been loaded the evening before at our door, half a mile from the river, with potatoes and melons from a patch which we had cultivated, and a few utensils, and was provided with wheels in order to be rolled around falls, as well as with two sets of oars, and several slender poles for shoving in shallow places, and also two masts, one of which served for a tent-pole at night; for a buffalo-skin was to be our bed, and a tent of cotton cloth our roof. It was strongly built, but heavy, and hardly of better model than usual. If rightly made, a boat would be a sort of amphibious animal, a creature of two elements, related by one half its structure to some swift and shapely fish, and by the other to some strong-winged and graceful bird. The fish shows where there should be the greatest breadth of beam and depth in the hold; its fins direct where to set the oars, and the tail gives some hint for the form and position of the rudder. The bird shows how to rig and trim the sails, and what form to give to the prow that it may balance the boat, and divide the air and water best. These hints we had but partially obeyed. But the eyes, though they are no sailors, will never be satisfied with any model, however fashionable, which does not answer all the requisitions of art. However, as art is all of a ship but the wood, and yet the wood alone will rudely serve the purpose of a ship, so our boat, being of wood, gladly availed itself of the old law that the heavier shall float the lighter, and though a dull water-fowl, proved a sufficient buoy for our purpose.

Some village friends stood upon a promontory lower down the stream to wave us a last farewell; but we, having already performed these shore rites, with excusable reserve, as befits those who are embarked on unusual enterprises, who behold but speak not, silently glided past the firm lands of Concord, both peopled cape and lonely summer meadow, with steady sweeps. And yet we did unbend so far as to let our guns speak for us, when at length we had swept out of sight, and thus left the woods to ring again with their echoes; and it may be many russet-clad children, lurking in those broad meadows, with the bittern and the woodcock and the rail, though wholly concealed by brakes and hardhack and meadow-sweet, heard our salute that afternoon.

(A little later in the voyage, he came upon some boatbuilders.—ed.)

Some carpenters were at work here mending a scow on the green and sloping bank. The strokes of their mallets echoed from shore to shore, and up and down the river, and their tools gleamed in the sun a quarter of a mile from us, and we realized that boat-building was as ancient and honorable an art as agriculture, and that there might be a naval as well as a pastoral life. The whole history of commerce was made manifest in that scow turned bottom upward on the shore. Thus did men begin to go down upon the sea in ships; "and keels which had long stood on high mountains careered insultingly over unknown waves." (Ovid, Metamorphosis I.133.) We thought that it would be well for the traveller to build his boat on the bank of a stream, instead of finding a ferry or a bridge. In the Adventures of Henry the fur-trader, it is pleasant to read that when with his Indians he reached the shore of Ontario, they consumed two days in making two canoes of the bark of the elm-tree, in which to transport themselves to Fort Niagara. It is a worthy incident in a journey, a delay as good as much rapid travelling. A good share of our interest in Xenophon's story of his retreat is in the manoeuvres to get the army safely over the rivers, whether on rafts of logs or fagots, or sheep-skins blown up. And where could they better afford to tarry meanwhile than on the banks of a river?

FROM *THREE MEN IN A BOAT*
1889

Jerome K. Jerome

The "Three Men" and their wives: Olga Hentschel, Jerome, Carl Hentschel ("Harris"), unknown woman, George Wingrove, and Effie Jerome.

This was one of the books that I really wished, reading through it for a good bit, I could just run it through some kind of compress-text program and fit it all into Small Boats. *It is complete nonsense from start to finish. I have never seen any other writer make so much of so little. I started laughing about halfway through the first paragraph, and kept it up pretty much all the way through the book. But of course that is the kiss of death for funny books. You laugh and laugh and feel like you must share it. You think of just the person, who later hands it back to with a quizzical look and tries to be polite. But* Three Men *was of several books that were mentioned time and time again in other books I have read and by people suggesting their favorite books for this one and it has been continuously in print since 1889. So at least this time, I guess I'm not alone.*

WE AGREE THAT WE ARE OVERWORKED, AND NEED REST—A WEEK ON THE ROLLING DEEP?—GEORGE SUGGESTS THE RIVER—MONTMORENCY LODGES AN OBJECTION—ORIGINAL MOTION CARRIED BY MAJORITY OF THREE TO ONE.

At this point, Mrs. Poppets knocked at the door to know if we were ready for supper. We smiled sadly at one another, and said we supposed we had better try to swallow a bit. Harris said a little something in one's stomach often kept the disease in check; and Mrs. Poppets brought the tray in, and we drew up to the table, and toyed with a little steak and onions, and some rhubarb tart.

I must have been very weak at the time; because I know, after the first half-hour or so, I seemed to take no interest whatever in my food—an unusual thing for me—and I didn't want any cheese.

This duty done, we refilled our glasses, lit our pipes, and resumed the discussion upon our state of health. What it was that was actually the matter with us, we none of us could be sure of; but the unanimous opinion was that it—whatever it was—had been brought on by overwork.

"What we want is rest," said Harris.

"Rest and a complete change," said George. "The overstrain upon our brains has produced a general depression throughout the system. Change of scene, and absence of the necessity for thought, will restore the mental equilibrium."

George has a cousin, who is usually described in the charge-sheet as a medical student, so that he naturally has a somewhat family-physicianary way of putting things.

I agreed with George, and suggested that we should seek out some retired and old-world spot, far from the madding crowd, and dream away a sunny week among its drowsy lanes—some half-forgotten nook, hidden away by the fairies, out of reach of the noisy world—some quaint-perched eyrie on the cliffs of Time, from whence the surging waves of the nineteenth century would sound far-off and faint.

Harris said he thought it would be humpy. He said he knew the sort of place I meant; where everybody went to bed at eight o'clock, and you couldn't get a REFEREE for love or money, and had to walk ten miles to get your baccy.

"No," said Harris, "if you want rest and change, you can't beat a sea trip."

I objected to the sea trip strongly. A sea trip does you good when you are going to have a couple of months of it, but, for a week, it is wicked.

You start on Monday with the idea implanted in your bosom that you are going to enjoy yourself. You wave an airy adieu to the boys on shore, light your biggest pipe, and swagger about the deck as if you were Captain Cook, Sir Francis Drake, and Christopher Columbus all rolled into one. On Tuesday, you wish you hadn't come. On Wednesday, Thursday, and Friday, you wish you were dead. On Saturday, you are able to swallow a little beef tea, and to sit up on deck, and answer with a wan, sweet smile when kind-hearted people ask you how you feel now. On Sunday, you begin to walk about again, and take solid food. And on Monday morning, as, with your bag and umbrella in your hand, you stand by the gunwale, waiting to step ashore, you begin to thoroughly like it.

I remember my brother-in-law going for a short sea trip once, for the benefit of his health. He took a return berth from London to Liverpool; and when he got to Liverpool, the only thing he was anxious about was to sell that return ticket.

It was offered round the town at a tremendous reduction, so I am told; and was eventually sold for eighteenpence to a bilious-looking youth who had just been advised by his medical men to go to the sea-side, and take exercise.

"Sea-side!" said my brother-in-law, pressing the ticket affectionately into his hand; "why, you'll have enough to last you a lifetime; and as for exercise! why, you'll get more exercise, sitting down on that ship, than you would turning somersaults on dry land."

He himself—my brother-in-law—came back by train. He said the North-Western Railway was healthy enough for him.

Another fellow I knew went for a week's voyage round the coast, and, before they started, the steward came to him to ask whether he would pay for each meal as he had it, or arrange beforehand for the whole series.

The steward recommended the latter course, as it would come so much cheaper. He said they would do him for the whole week at two pounds five. He said for breakfast there would be fish, followed by a grill. Lunch was at one, and consisted of four courses. Dinner at six—soup, fish, entree, joint, poultry, salad, sweets, cheese, and dessert. And a light meat supper at ten.

My friend thought he would close on the two-pound-five job (he is a hearty eater), and did so.

Lunch came just as they were off Sheerness. He didn't feel so hungry as he thought he should, and so contented himself with a bit of boiled beef, and some strawberries and cream. He pondered a good deal during the afternoon, and at one time it seemed to him that he had been eating nothing but boiled beef for weeks, and at other times it seemed that he must have been living on strawberries and cream for years.

Neither the beef nor the strawberries and cream seemed happy, either— seemed discontented like.

At six, they came and told him dinner was ready. The announcement aroused no enthusiasm within him, but he felt that there was some of that two-pound-five to be worked off, and he held on to ropes and things and went down. A pleasant odour of onions and hot ham, mingled with fried fish and greens, greeted him at the bottom of the ladder; and then the steward came up with an oily smile, and said:

"What can I get you, sir?"

"Get me out of this," was the feeble reply.

And they ran him up quick, and propped him up, over to leeward, and left him. For the next four days he lived a simple and blameless life on thin captain's biscuits (I mean that the biscuits were thin, not the captain) and soda-water; but, towards Saturday, he got uppish, and went in for weak tea and dry toast, and on Monday he was gorging himself on chicken broth. He left the ship on Tuesday, and as it steamed away from the landing-stage he gazed after it regretfully.

"There she goes," he said, "there she goes, with two pounds' worth of food on board that belongs to me, and that I haven't had."

He said that if they had given him another day he thought he could have put it straight.

So I set my face against the sea trip. Not, as I explained, upon my own account. I was never queer. But I was afraid for George. George said he should be all right, and would rather like it, but he would advise Harris and me not to think of it, as he felt sure we should both be ill. Harris said that, to himself, it was always a mystery how people managed to get sick at sea—said he thought people must do it on purpose, from affectation—

said he had often wished to be, but had never been able.

Then he told us anecdotes of how he had gone across the Channel when it was so rough that the passengers had to be tied into their berths, and he and the captain were the only two living souls on board who were not ill. Sometimes it was he and the second mate who were not ill; but it was generally he and one other man. If not he and another man, then it was he by himself.

It is a curious fact, but nobody ever is sea-sick—on land. At sea, you come across plenty of people very bad indeed, whole boat-loads of them; but I never met a man yet, on land, who had ever known at all what it was to be sea-sick. Where the thousands upon thousands of bad sailors that swarm in every ship hide themselves when they are on land is a mystery.

If most men were like a fellow I saw on the Yarmouth boat one day, I could account for the seeming enigma easily enough. It was just off Southend Pier, I recollect, and he was leaning out through one of the port-holes in a very dangerous position. I went up to him to try and save him.

"Hi! Come further in," I said, shaking him by the shoulder. "You'll be overboard."

"Oh my! I wish I was," was the only answer I could get; and there I had to leave him.

Three weeks afterwards, I met him in the coffee-room of a Bath hotel, talking about his voyages, and explaining, with enthusiasm, how he loved the sea.

"Good sailor!" he replied in answer to a mild young man's envious query; "well, I did feel a little queer ONCE, I confess. It was off Cape Horn. The vessel was wrecked the next morning."

I said: "Weren't you a little shaky by Southend Pier one day, and wanted to be thrown overboard?"

"Southend Pier!" he replied, with a puzzled expression.

"Yes; going down to Yarmouth, last Friday three weeks."

"Oh, ah—yes," he answered, brightening up; "I remember now. I did have a headache that afternoon. It was the pickles, you know. They were the most disgraceful pickles I ever tasted in a respectable boat. Did you have any?"

For myself, I have discovered an excellent preventive against sea-sickness, in balancing myself. You stand in the centre of the deck, and, as the ship heaves and pitches, you move your body about, so as to keep it always straight. When the front of the ship rises, you lean forward, till the deck almost touches your nose; and when its back end gets up, you lean backwards. This is all very well for an hour or two; but you can't balance yourself for a week.

George said: "Let's go up the river."

He said we should have fresh air, exercise and quiet; the constant change of scene would occupy our minds (including what there was of Harris's); and the hard work would give us a good appetite, and make us sleep well. Harris said he didn't think George ought to do anything that would have a tendency to make him sleepier than he always was, as it might be dangerous.

He said he didn't very well understand how George was going to sleep any more than he did now, seeing that there were only twenty-four hours in each day, summer and winter alike; but thought that if he DID sleep any more, he might just as well be dead, and so save his board and lodging.

Harris said, however, that the river would suit him to a "T." I don't know what a "T" is (except a sixpenny one, which includes bread-and-butter and cake AD LIB., and is cheap at the price, if you haven't had any dinner). It seems to suit everybody, however, which is greatly to its credit.

It suited me to a "T" too, and Harris and I both said it was a good idea of George's; and we said it in a tone that seemed to somehow imply that we were surprised that George should have come out so sensible. The only one who was not struck with the suggestion was Montmorency. He never did care for the river, did Montmorency.

"It's all very well for you fellows," he says; "you like it, but I don't. There's nothing for me to do. Scenery is not in my line, and I don't smoke. If I see a rat, you won't stop; and if I go to sleep, you get fooling about with the boat, and slop me overboard. If you ask me, I call the whole thing bally foolishness."

We were three to one, however, and the motion was carried.

GEORGE IS INTRODUCED TO WORK—HEATHENISH INSTINCTS OF TOW-LINES—UNGRATEFUL CONDUCT OF A DOUBLE-SCULLING SKIFF.—TOWERS AND TOWED—A USE DISCOVERED FOR LOVERS—STRANGE DISAPPEARANCE OF AN ELDERLY LADY—MUCH HASTE, LESS SPEED—BEING TOWED BY GIRLS: EXCITING SENSATION—THE MISSING LOCK OR THE HAUNTED RIVER—MUSIC—SAVED!

We made George work, now we had got him. He did not want to work, of course; that goes without saying. He had had a hard time in the City, so he explained. Harris, who is callous in his nature, and not prone to pity, said:

"Ah! and now you are going to have a hard time on the river for a change; change is good for everyone. Out you get!"

He could not in conscience—not even George's conscience—object, though he did suggest that, perhaps, it would be better for him to stop in the boat, and get tea ready, while Harris and I towed, because getting tea was such a worrying work, and Harris and I looked tired. The only reply we made to this, however, was to pass him over the tow-line, and he took it, and stepped out.

There is something very strange and unaccountable about a tow-line. You roll it up with as much patience and care as you would take to fold up a new pair of trousers, and five minutes afterwards, when you pick it up, it is one ghastly, soul-revolting tangle.

I do not wish to be insulting, but I firmly believe that if you took an average tow-line, and stretched it out straight across the middle of a field, and then turned your back on it for thirty seconds, that, when you looked round again, you would find that it had got itself altogether in a heap in the middle of the field, and had twisted itself up, and tied itself into knots, and lost its two ends, and become all loops; and it would take you a good half-hour, sitting down there on the grass and swearing all the while, to disentangle it again.

That is my opinion of tow-lines in general. Of course, there may be honourable exceptions; I do not say that there are not. There may be tow-lines that are a credit to their profession—conscientious, respectable tow-lines—tow-lines that do not imagine they are crochet-work, and try to knit themselves up into antimacassars the instant they are left to themselves. I say there MAY be such tow-lines; I sincerely hope there are. But I have not met with them.

This tow-line I had taken in myself just before we had got to the lock. I would not let Harris touch it, because he is careless. I had looped it round slowly and cautiously, and tied it up in the middle, and folded it in two, and laid it down gently at the bottom of the boat. Harris had lifted it up scientifically, and had put it into George's hand. George had taken it firmly, and held it away from him, and had begun to unravel it as if he were taking the swaddling clothes off a new-born infant; and, before he had unwound a dozen yards, the thing was more like a badly-made door-mat than anything else.

It is always the same, and the same sort of thing always goes on in connection with it. The man on the bank, who is trying to disentangle it, thinks all the fault lies with the man who rolled it up; and when a man up the river thinks a thing, he says it.

"What have you been trying to do with it, make a fishing-net of it? You've made a nice mess you have; why couldn't you wind it up properly, you silly dummy?" he grunts from time to time as he struggles wildly with it, and lays it out flat on the tow-path, and runs round and round it, trying to find the end.

On the other hand, the man who wound it up thinks the whole cause of the muddle rests with the man who is trying to unwind it.

"It was all right when you took it!" he exclaims indignantly. "Why don't you think what you are doing? You go about things in such a slap-dash style. You'd get a scaffolding pole entangled you would!"

And they feel so angry with one another that they would like to hang each other with the thing.

Ten minutes go by, and the first man gives a yell and goes mad, and dances on the rope, and tries to pull it straight by seizing hold of the first piece that comes to his hand and hauling at it. Of course, this only gets it into a tighter tangle than ever. Then the second man climbs out of the boat and comes to help him, and they get in each other's way, and hinder one another. They both get hold of the same bit of line, and pull at it in opposite directions, and wonder where it is caught. In the end, they do get it clear, and then turn round and find that the boat has drifted off, and is making straight for the weir.

This really happened once to my own knowledge. It was up by Boveney, one rather windy morning. We were pulling down stream, and, as we came round the bend, we noticed a couple of men on the bank. They were looking at each other with as bewildered and helplessly miserable expression as I have ever witnessed on any human countenance before or since, and they held a long tow-line between them. It was clear that something had happened, so we eased up and asked them what was the matter.

"Why, our boat's gone off!" they replied in an indignant tone. "We just got out to disentangle the tow-line, and when we looked round, it was gone!"

And they seemed hurt at what they evidently regarded as a mean and ungrateful act on the part of the boat.

We found the truant for them half a mile further down, held by some rushes, and we brought it back to them. I bet they did not give that boat another chance for a week.

I shall never forget the picture of those two men walking up and down the bank with a tow-line, looking for their boat.

One sees a good many funny incidents up the river in connection with towing. One of the most common is the sight of a couple of towers, walking briskly along, deep in an animated discussion, while the man in the boat, a hundred yards behind them, is vainly shrieking to them to stop, and making frantic signs of distress with a scull. Something has gone wrong; the rudder has come off, or the boat-hook has slipped overboard, or his hat has dropped into the water and is floating rapidly down stream.

He calls to them to stop, quite gently and politely at first.

"Hi! stop a minute, will you?" he shouts cheerily. "I've dropped my hat over-board."

Then: "Hi! Tom—Dick! can't you hear?" not quite so affably this time.

Then: "Hi! Confound YOU, you dunder-headed idiots! Hi! stop! Oh you—!"

After that he springs up, and dances about, and roars himself red in the face, and curses everything he knows. And the small boys on the bank stop and jeer at him, and pitch stones at him as he is pulled along past them, at the rate of four miles an hour, and can't get out.

Much of this sort of trouble would be saved if those who are towing would keep remembering that they are towing, and give a pretty frequent look round to see how their man is getting on. It is best to let one person tow. When two are doing it, they get chattering, and forget, and the boat itself, offering, as it does, but little resistance, is of no real service in reminding them of the fact.

As an example of how utterly oblivious a pair of towers can be to their work, George told us, later on in the evening, when we were discussing the subject after supper, of a very curious instance.

He and three other men, so he said, were sculling a very heavily laden boat up from Maidenhead one evening, and a little above Cookham lock they noticed a fellow and a girl, walking along the towpath, both deep in an apparently interesting and absorbing conversation. They were carrying a boat-hook between them, and, attached to the boat-hook was a tow-line, which trailed behind them, its end in the water. No boat was near, no boat was in sight. There must have been a boat attached to that tow-line at some time or other, that was certain; but what had become of it, what ghastly fate had overtaken it, and those who had been left in it, was buried in mystery. Whatever the accident may have been, however, it had in no way disturbed the young lady and gentleman, who were towing. They had the boat-hook and they had the line, and that seemed to be all that they thought necessary to their work.

George was about to call out and wake them up, but, at that moment, a bright idea flashed across him, and he didn't. He got the hitcher instead, and reached over, and drew in the end of the tow-line; and they made a loop in it, and put it over their mast, and then they tidied up the sculls, and went and sat down in the stern, and lit their pipes.

And that young man and young woman towed those four hulking chaps and a heavy boat up to Marlow.

George said he never saw so much thoughtful sadness concentrated into one glance before, as when, at the lock, that young couple grasped the idea that, for the last two miles, they had been towing the wrong boat. George fancied that, if it had not been for the restraining influence of the sweet woman at his side, the young man might have given way to violent language.

The maiden was the first to recover from her surprise, and, when she did, she clasped her hands, and said, wildly: "Oh, Henry, then WHERE is auntie?"

"Did they ever recover the old lady?" asked Harris.

George replied he did not know.

Another example of the dangerous want of sympathy between tower and towed was witnessed by George and myself once up near Walton. It was where the tow-path shelves gently down into the water, and we were camping on the opposite bank, noticing things in general. By-and-by a small boat came in sight, towed through the water at a tremendous pace by a powerful barge horse, on which sat a very small boy. Scattered about the boat, in dreamy and reposeful attitudes, lay five fellows, the man who was steering having a particularly restful appearance.

"I should like to see him pull the wrong line," murmured George, as they passed. And at that precise moment the man did it, and the boat rushed up the bank with a noise like the ripping up of forty thousand linen sheets. Two men, a hamper, and three oars immediately left the boat on the larboard side, and reclined on the bank, and one and a half moments afterwards, two other men disembarked from the starboard, and sat down among boat-hooks and sails and carpet-bags and bottles. The last man went on twenty yards further, and then got out on his head.

This seemed to sort of lighten the boat, and it went on much easier, the small boy shouting at the top of his voice, and urging his steed into a gallop. The fellows sat up and stared at one another. It was some seconds before they realised what had happened to them, but, when they did, they began to shout lustily for the boy to stop. He, however, was too much occupied with the horse to hear them, and we watched them, flying after him, until the distance hid them from view.

I cannot say I was sorry at their mishap. Indeed, I only wish that all the young fools who have their boats towed in this fashion—and plenty do—could meet with similar misfortunes. Besides the risk they run themselves, they become a danger and an annoyance to every other boat they pass. Going at the pace they do, it is impossible for them to get out of anybody else's way, or for anybody else to get out of theirs.

Their line gets hitched across your mast, and overturns you, or it catches somebody in the boat, and either throws them into the water, or cuts their face open. The best plan is to stand your ground, and be prepared to keep them off with the butt-end of a mast.

ROWBOAT
1996

Peter H. Spectre

There is a way to guarantee a kid becomes a boat nut. The ingredients are simple: a boy of tender years (girls are by no means immune, but seem a little less susceptible); small boats, preferably sleek wooden ones with lots of glowing brightwork, but almost any harbor mix will do; water to the horizon or a bend in the river. The opposite works too. If one wants to save the kid from himself, give him a farm pond, some kind of miniature barge, and some badly balanced oars too short for the boat. Wait an hour and the kid will be cured forever.

For me, it was a trip to the New England coast when I was maybe 12. I remember a procession of little harbors, museums, and wooden boat shops, and a succession of camping sites on the beach or—even more tantalizingly—on the shore of a cove dotted with small islands, and small boats. My parents very reasonably pointed out to me about a hundred times over the two weeks that we didn't live on the sea, and the only body of water near our house in Ohio was a half-acre pond, ringed by NO TRESSPASSING *signs, and owned by an order of nuns utterly unsympathetic even to natural boyhood pursuits like trespassing with intent to fish, creek-stomp, or just idle away an afternoon. A boat on their pond would have been police kind of trouble. I was perfectly happy to take the risk, my folks were not. So there I was, boatless, reading everything I could on the subject, and waiting for the day when I could lay my hands on something that would float. Three or four years later they did buy me a 13-foot sloop. Too late.*

Peter Spectre, who over the years has run WoodenBoat *magazine, International Marine Publishing, and currently is editor of* Maine Boats, Homes, and Harbors, *grew up on Cape Cod, and clearly had it even worse. The boatyard down the road; the scent of sour oak and cedar shavings, linseed oil, and turpentine; the creek full of boats coming and going; lots and lots of rowboats pulled up on shore, supplied by their thoughtful owners with oars and assorted other useful gear; temptation every day for years. Not that it ever crossed young Peter's mind that one might just hop in, ship oars, and take off when nobody was looking . . .*

ROWBOAT

When I was a boy, growing up in Massachusetts on Cape Cod, I lived for a couple of years in Truro, way down the Cape next to Provincetown. It was a tiny town then, no more than a couple hundred people year round, perhaps 500 or so in the summer, and a general store and a post office and a boatyard down at the mouth of the Pamet River where it emptied into Cape Cod Bay.

There wasn't much for a boy to do. To break the boredom I used to hitchhike into Provincetown and hang around the fish pier, or hunt for Indian arrowheads on Corn Hill, or help a friend who lived on a farm shoot rats in the chicken barn, or, when really desperate, lay pennies on the railroad tracks and wait for the single freight of the week to pass by and flatten them out. But my favorite pastime was to go down to the Pamet and poke around the boatyard.

I can't remember much about the place now, but it was a typical old-style boatyard of the time (mid-1950s): a common variety that you'd find down a narrow Cape Cod road that wound through the beach plum and bayberry bushes. The standard yard of that type would be half on land, half sort of falling into a tidal river, and the owner would live in a shack off to the side. There would be a couple of big sheds filled with boats in storage, boats on cradles sitting in the open out in a field, and a bunch of dinghies by the dock, upside down in the muck with tarps to keep off the winter scudge. Some of these craft would be maintained with a certain measure of pride, depending on the state of their owners' pocketbooks, but a significant number would be in varying degrees of decrepitude, either abandoned or carrying signs that said "For Sale—Make an Offer," which more or less amounted to the same thing.

Over in a corner would be a shop filled with all sorts of fascinating objects. A new wooden boat under construction, an old rowboat being reframed, a bandsaw, a thickness planer, and a table saw running on leather belts off the same motor, benches piled with tools, nails, and rusting engine parts, mounds of sawdust, and a black dog scratching fleas by the side door. Several rather graphically illustrated calendars would hang on the walls; none would be there because the owner and his yard crew were interested in the date, if you know what I mean. The dominant smells would be of native cedar, linseed oil, and wood smoke; sour oak on those days when they were sawing out frames.

Down at the dock there would be an old Flying Horse gas pump with an "Out-of-Order" sign taped above another that said "No Credit Except Regular Customers." You got to be a regular customer by storing a boat in the yard or buying gas for about a month and actually paying for it. Besides credit, the regulars were given skiff privileges at the float and the right to hang around in the spring, getting their boats ready for launching. More boating enthusiasts than you would imagine considered spring fitting-out to be the high point of the season; launching the craft was, in more than one sense, going downhill; actually sailing was anticlimactic.

Spring fitting-out in the boatyard was a ritual. Lots of scraping, lots of burning off built-up paint, lots of jacking garboards back into position after the fastenings let go when water froze in the bilges over the winter. Caulking, puttying, painting, varnishing, grunting, sweating, swearing, drinking beer, listening to Florida exhibition baseball on a portable radio with an antenna jury-rigged from a bent coat hanger.

Oh, pine tar! Oh, turpentine! Oh, memory! Oh, lost!

Lost? Are the boatyards gone?

Some are. Some aren't.

A significant number of the old-style boatyards have, indeed, been made obsolete. Modern times and plastics have seen to that. Damn little need for caulkers, sawyers, plankers, scrapers, painters, and other skilled craftsmen when your hull is inorganic and leak proof, and never requires painting. The black dog with fleas was bad for the image. The calendars were an affront to feminist doctrine. The slapping leather drive belts were an offense to the OSHA inspector.

What do we have now? The worst of it is that the same crowd that gave us condominiumized motel rooms has introduced dockominiums. The only way a docko resembles space in a real boatyard is you get to pay for it on credit if you're a regular.

Fiberglass killed the real boatyard. A miracle material made of inert glass strands surrounded by plastic resin, fiberglass is strong, durable, shiny, reasonably maintenance free, and has about as much heart as a steel boot. (L. Francis Herreshoff, one of the great yacht designers of an earlier era, on seeing fiberglass for the first time, opined that it reminded him of frozen snot.)

Fiberglass is the fast food of the boat biz. Scrape off the barnacles at the end of the season, cover the boat with one of those blue plastic tarps for the winter—or shrink-wrap it like a package of chicken breasts down at the IGA—throw on a little bottom paint at the beginning of the season, rub a little synthetic polishing wax into the topsides, shake the mildew out of the seat cushions, and she's ready to go.

The workshop in a modern boatyard usually involves a huge, hanger-like, rattling-steel industrial building. About four-fifths of the space will be given over to a rack system for storing Donzi-type powerblasters. They'll be stacked about three high and twenty-five long. When an owner wants to go powerblasting for the day he'll drive his BMW to the yard and ask for his boat; an adolescent in a T-shirt that says "Born to Be Bad," or "Jesus Loves You, Everyone Else Thinks You're an Asshole," or something like that will fire up a special forklift tractor, get the boat out of the hanger, and deposit it in the water. The procedure will be reversed when the owner comes back, all tanned out and pumped up after a day of pounding his hairy chest on the water. The other one-fifth of the building will be a sterile room with a few cans of polishing wax and patching resin on the shelves and a table saw with a dull blade gathering dust in a corner. If there is any wood in the place, it will have come from the packing crate used to ship in the new chrome-and-glass power desk for the yard accountant's office.

This isn't a boatshop. It's a warehouse with all the ambience of a Sears Automotive Repair Center. Hanging around here is about as exciting as watching a 23-year-old Coke-swilling computer geek write code for the next Windows operating system.

The latest rage is to move the boatyards out on the highway next to the used-car lots. Galvanized trailers made that possible. With those, there's no need for marine railways or even Travelifts. All you need is a launching ramp and space to park your rig.

In the highway boatyard biz, the automobile-trailer-boat combo is known as a rig. With a used-car lot next door, putting together a rig that meets your specifications won't take much more than an hour or two, providing your credit is good. The roads being what they are these days, you can buy a rig in Millinocket, Maine, in the morning and be down in Kennebunkport in the afternoon. By early evening you'll be into the killer mackerel. The next morning you could move the whole rig down to Rockland, and by afternoon you could be yachting with the Cabots and the Watsons and the Pingrees on the Fox Islands Thoroughfare.

That's the good news. The bad news is that real boatyards are an endangered species. Nowadays you might find a rigger or two, an engine man in a three-piece suit to pronounce your present engine dead and arrange a second mortgage on your home for the next one, enough space to prop her up during the winter, room to swing a polishing rag in the spring, sufficient passage for the Travelift, and a parking lot for the BMWs.

But there are, if you look long and hard enough, a few of the genuine old-style yards left. How will you know they're genuine? For starters they'll have specialized tools, and plenty of them, for working on boats. For finishers they'll have craftsmen who know how to use them. Walk through the gate any day of the week and you'll find plankers spiling off replacement strakes, painters mixing up the proper shade of deckhouse buff, machinists truing a propeller shaft, and a yard man thrashing through the clutch pile for a replacement bushing for a 1933 Palmer twin-banger. The clincher, though, is that you'll see piles of wood. Piles and piles of wood.

People who run genuine boatyards are guided by principles passed down from one generation to the next, and they always involve wood:

A supply of wood beyond that immediately required is money in the bank. If you need 5,000 board feet of cedar for a job and your mill man has 8,000 feet on hand, buy the extra 3,000 and store it under cover. Even if you have to take out a loan. You'll be needing that lumber sooner or later, and when you do, your mill man might not have it. Nobody need be concerned about the moisture content of a pile of lumber that has been stored at the yard for a long period awaiting its time. If it was properly stacked and stickered at the start, it will be properly seasoned at the end.

A good, solid oak plank in inventory for, say, future sawn frames doesn't necessarily represent capital not earning its keep. You can always use the plank for staging or a temporary ramp and revive it for its final purpose later.

A skilled boatwright making $25 an hour planking a boat is still making $25 an hour driving his pickup truck to the lumberyard for that one last stick of white pine for the cockpit sole. Try to run a shop while ignoring that simple truth and you'll be insolvent before the end of the year.

Don't ever—in other words, never—throw away a square-edge, knot- and warp-free seasoned edging over 10 feet long. Sooner or later someone will come around looking for a batten. If you're down at the mill, or at the demolition-debris section of the dump, come to think of it, and someone says that piece of wood over there might make a good stem one of these days, muckle right on to it, because it will.

Of course, a cheap-imitation boatshop can always fool the most discerning eye. They can always call in a tag team of interior designers from Boston or New York and ask them to hoke up the yard with a bunch of stage props to make it look authentic. Hang some pot warp from the rafters; buy some old woodworking tools from a flea market and artfully drape them around the shop; stack a few old boards along the side wall.

Old hands at detecting this sort of ploy won't be fooled, but if you have your doubts, try this: Tell the proprietor that you have a split toerail and ask if he can fix it. If he says you're in luck, that he's been saving a piece of teak out in the shed for just such an eventuality and he'll get Joe right on the case—you know Joe, he's the boatwright with nine fingers (the tenth had an unfortunate encounter thirty years ago with a power jointer) and a bevel gauge made from two pieces of hacksaw blade riveted together at the ends—you're dealing with a genuine boatyard. If he asks for the make, model, and year of your boat, and after looking it up on a wholesale list says he can have a replacement part delivered in three weeks, you're dealing with a mail-order catalog.

The Pamet River boatyard, a regular stop on my daily explorations through town, kicking the can, was no catalog operation. Rather, it was the genuine article, and there, one day when skylarking through the yard and coincidentally suffering from a near-terminal case of I-gotta-have-a-boat, I saw a rowing punt by the door of a shed, carrying a for-sale sign.

It was an unremarkable boat: a couple of side planks, a cross-planked bottom, flat transoms at both ends, and lots of peeling paint, but it reminded me of the punt that Walt Kelley's cartoon character Pogo used to row around the Okeefenokee Swamp with his friends. Pogo's punt would start out in the first frame of a comic strip with a simple name like Frenchie with no hailing port, and in the next frame it would become something like Shikuma, and then Henry Shikuma from Hilo, and then Henry and Ellen from Oahu, and then Missie B from Dubuque, and later the S.S. Helen Barrow from Spokane, and so on. Only primordial boat junkies paid any attention to this running gag. Straight folk were too busy trying to figure out whether Pogo was a Republican or a Democrat or a socialist verging on a pinko Commie fellow traveller.

One of the carpenters at the Pamet River boatyard told me that the asking price for the punt was $35, which doesn't sound like much now and probably wasn't much then, but it might as well have been a thousand dollars as far as I was concerned. My family wasn't living on easy street in those days; I wasn't old enough to have a paying job.

Broke or not, I was at once a rowboat nut and a Pogo fan, and I had to have that boat. So I decided to build a copy of it, even though I had never built a boat before, or anything else more complicated than a tree house lashed together from planks and an old door or two. I ran back home and got a ruler and ran back to the boatyard and took off a few rough dimensions, and then when nobody was looking liberated some boards from a deconstructed barn down the road.

I built that punt in a day, caulking the seams with strips of cloth cut from an old flannel shirt, painted it the next day, and launched it the third.

It wasn't fancy and it was the butt of a lot of jokes, but it was good enough for mucking around in the salt marshes and for fishing in a nearby freshwater pond, and it was stable and it didn't leak and it didn't cost $35 and it was mine.

I was then, and am to this day, a certifiable rowboat junkie, and that little punt, my first rowing craft, couldn't have come at a better time. At least my old man probably thought so. A couple of weeks earlier, I had been collared for stealing someone else's rowboat. I protested that I had merely borrowed it, that I was simply testing it out to see how she rowed, but the town constable who ran me in for Grand Theft, Watercraft failed to appreciate the distinction.

I had been mucking around the waterfront, checking out the important things, when I came across a skiff pulled up on the shore with a pair of oars and locks in place. How thoughtful, I thought, for someone to leave this beautiful little craft for me to try out. The intention was to whip around the harbor before the owner came back, but one thing led to another and then another and another. About five hours later I was pinched by the law way up where the main road crossed a tidal river I had been exploring for blue crabs. (The owner of the rowboat had thoughtfully included, with the oars and the locks, a long-handled net and a pail.)

The constable ran me up to his office in the town hall, sat me on a stool, and discussed crime and its punishment for awhile. I remember he talked a lot about reform school and jail and losing all hope of ever getting a good job and other dire consequences ("Do you know what happens to 12-year-old boys in jail?"). Then he said maybe he should take me home to talk to my old man. I told him thanks but no thanks; I'd rather go to jail.

That, as it turned out, was a big mistake. The constable smiled the way the Grinch did when he told the little Who child that he was just cleaning up around the place, that he definitely wasn't stealing Christmas, and said, "Get in the car."

It was mid-afternoon, and my old man was taking a nap. The constable stayed in the car, the one with the blue bubble light on top and the billy club under the front seat, and sent me in after him.

"What is it?" the old man said when I tapped on the bedroom door.

"There's someone outside who wants to talk to you," I said.

"Who is he?" he said.

"I don't know," I said.

"What does he want?" he said.

"I don't know," I said.

Right, and Grant's Tomb is an ice cream parlor.

It was damned uncomfortable standing out there in the yard while the town constable told my old man that his son was a common boat thief. So, too, was listening to the harangue that followed. What happened? Let's just say that I didn't go to jail and didn't spend much time during the rest of that summer beyond the imaginary line that ran between the stakes defining the corners of my old man's investment in the American dream. I got to go to the dentist's office to have my teeth reamed out and that was about it. Definitely not anywhere near the waterfront.

It was the second time that year I had been caught with a rowboat that didn't belong to me. I have lost track of the number of times I "borrowed" a rowboat and didn't get caught. Let's say it was more than 50, less than 100. In my irrational moments, I've often wondered why my old man didn't recognize this overpowering need to get in a rowboat and buy me one. In my rational moments I recognize that (a) he was not nautically inclined, and therefore didn't know a rowboat from a pitchfork, and (b) he was at the time so close to financial ruin that he had more pressing things to attend to than indulging a son who had criminal tendencies. Such as keeping his creditors from repossessing the family car.

I was a guest at a reception for writers and editors and other literateurs at the Portland Museum of Art in Portland, Maine, a few years ago. The editor of a major general-interest magazine asked me what sort of boat I owned. (People like him never know how to make conversation with people like me. They think we know nothing about politics or sex or drugs or balancing the federal budget or anything else having to do with serious contemporary issues, so they ask us what kind of boats we own.)

I told him I had a rowboat down at the town landing.

The expression on his face was lovely to see. Surely a man of my stature must have a boat with more presence than that, he suggested. A Concordia yawl, perhaps, or a Friendship sloop, or, at the very least, a Beetle cat. My rowboat, in short, must be transportation out to my real boat.

No, I said, I just have a rowboat tied up to the public landing.

When you're a guest at the Portland Museum of Art, it's important to get your artistic sensibilities right out on the table. Thoreauvianism, that's what it was. Wasn't it Henry David Thoreau himself who informed the Concord tax assessor at one point that the only piece of real property he owned was a rowboat? Minimalism: all stripped back to the basics, the essences, the unadorned roots.

It was a pleasant little conceit—a pseudo-intellectual puffball to go along with the hors d'oeuvres and the white wine—but it was also a bald-faced lie. Yes, I owned a rowboat, but not because I had any socio-political statement to make. The truth was that I was merely living out my boyhood dream. I had always wanted a rowboat tied up down there at the public landing, right where I could keep track of it, and I did, and that was all there was to it.

Generally after work in the afternoon or after supper in the evening, spring, summer, and fall—even in the winter, weather permitting—I'd go for a row. Sometimes I'd pull out into the bay and juke around in the southwesterly swell, but more often than not I'd circumnavigate the little island at the mouth of our harbor, or sprint out to a point about a half mile away and back. If there were weed on the boat's bottom and no one was at home in the house on the point, I'd haul her onto a beach there, turn her over, and scrub her down.

During that period I had two rowboats—a winter boat and a summer boat. Neither was much in the speed and elegance departments. Rather, they were extremely utilitarian craft that were noteworthy for being unredeemingly common in an era of shining gel coats and dynamic graphic schemes on the fiberglass boats and wineglass transoms, hand-rubbed varnish, and custom bronze fittings on the renaissance wooden craft.

The summer boat, 12 feet long, was a derivative of the old-style flat-bottomed skiff made a bit more seaworthy by a Maine boatbuilder who understood such things. The bow and sides were shaped just right to take the modest seas of summer, and the flat bottom allowed the boat to be easily beached. Two rowing stations allowed me to take a passenger or two for a little cruise without throwing the trim out of whack. Maintained by me for the long haul, it looked the way a summer boat should; it wasn't out of place even when the New York Yacht Club made its biannual visit to my harbor.

The winter boat was my favorite. A funky old 13-foot round-bottom rowboat said to have been built on Deer Isle, Maine, somewhere between 30 and 50 years previously, it spent a good part of its career in Newport, Rhode Island, though when I took possession it was lying in a barn in Brooklin, Maine. Crudely built yet of moderately fine model, it lasted all those years for reasons that were not entirely clear. The frames were pulling away from the planking, the transom had a huge check—thankfully above the waterline—that opened and closed depending on the strength of the relationship between the humidity and the sun, and the keel had a long hook in it that required a certain touch by the oarsman to keep the boat going in a straight line, when a straight line was what was to be achieved. (On the positive side, she turned fast to port.)

I bought the boat for $50, and, because the seams were so wide "you could throw a cat through 'em," the previous owner included in the deal enough tubes of caulking goop to keep her afloat. I spruced her up with a few new frames and some extra fastenings here and there, and painted her off-white on the outside and light gray on the inside. She was fast, seaworthy, and comfortable, and gave me great service for several years, fair weather and foul.

What with the ice and the snow and the howling gales, nobody in his right mind keeps a rowboat in the water during the winter in Maine, but I did. A few other oddballs did, too. I never discussed the matter with them, but I can tell you what motivated me. I needed a rowboat in the water for peace of mind. I needed to know that in the January Thaw or any other day between November and March when the temperature went above freezing I could row out to the island or the ledges and take a look around. And, yes, I needed an excuse to get out of the house in the darkness of winter. "I'm going down to the harbor to bail the rowboat, my dear," was a sentence heard often around my home, and no one begrudged me the privilege.

Early one winter when I was out of town the boat filled with rainwater during a storm, and then the Montreal Express came through dragging below-zero cold and by the time I got back her bilge was a solid block of ice that lasted until the January Thaw, and that was that. She went loose as a goose. I hauled her out, blocked her up in the backyard, and shifted over to another boat.

One day I was visiting with Dynamite Payson, a professional boatbuilder in South Thomaston, Maine. He was telling me about a boy down the road who had decided that he would be a lobsterman. The boy had the where-withal for some used gear but not for a boat, so he was setting and hauling his traps directly from shore by wading out at low tide.

I don't know about you, but I've done a fair amount of wading around the edges of Penobscot Bay, and I'm here to say that it's a cold, nasty business. Any boy who wants to be a lobsterman so badly that he'll do that on a regular basis deserves anyone's help, so I said, okay, he can have my old winter boat.

I trucked the boat down to South Thomaston, and Dynamite went to work. He cleaned her out and tightened her up, and then he and his wife gave her a nice lobsterboat finish and presented her to the boy. Hauling traps from a rowboat may be hard work, but it sure beats wading around at low tide.

That was several years ago. I recently asked Dynamite for the rest of the story. He said that the boy worked the rowboat until he had saved enough for an outboard skiff; eventually he graduated to an inboard lobsterboat and became a full-fledged lobsterman. My old winter rowboat—my favorite—had done its job.

I sit as I write this on a small island at the mouth of a harbor on Penobscot Bay. The season is high autumn. The mountains by the edge of the western shore are green, with patches of red, orange, and yellow where the hardwoods grow. I can see the barest hint of Matinicus Island on the horizon, out there on the edge of the Atlantic Ocean, and the white foam making up around the ledges out in the bay. The central image is of my summer rowboat, swinging to a buoy connected to the island by a simple haul-off rig.

She is cocked into the wind, her bow slightly higher than her stern and the two connected by a sheer line that could make you weep, it is that perfect. Her bottom is a dark red and her topsides are a deep, rich green, and she carries a manila rope guard that was once part of the main halyard on a big schooner and a line of fenders to protect her from docks and other boats coming alongside.

She's the latest of a long line of rowboats I've owned over the years. Per-haps not the best, perhaps not the one that embodies everything I ever wanted in such a craft, she nevertheless is symbolic of something I have only recently come to recognize: I came to my career—I do what I do—

because when I was a boy I wanted a rowboat just like her.

I remember the first time I was in a rowboat as if it were yesterday. I was six years old. Every detail is clear in my mind: The Oyster River in Chatham, at the elbow of Cape Cod, the fast-ebbing tidal current, the barrenness of early spring by the edge of the sea, the boat a little wooden flat-bottomed skiff, the smell of oiled wood and tarred rope and salt air blowing across the sea grass.

My friend was rowing. He knew what he was doing; I knew nothing. I almost jumped out of my skin with fear when we pushed away from the dock and the current grabbed at the boat and pulled us at a ferocious rate down the river and around a bend.

By the time we pulled into Stage Harbor among the gathered fishing boats—the little draggers, the quahog skiffs, the power catboats—I was no longer scared. I had discovered that all I had to do was know how to work the oars, and in the space of an hour, with my friend yelling instructions and howling hysterically with laughter over my awkwardness, I knew. You didn't have to know anything about engines or sails or rigging. You could walk down the road to the harbor or the shore and step into a little boat without any preparation whatsoever, sit down on the thwart, slide the oarlocks into the sockets, cast off the painter, put the oars into the oarlocks, take a long pull, and be underway. I was hooked by the freedom of the rowboat.

For years I've carried around a piece of paper with several lines from the novel *Flying Colours* by C. S. Forester. The passage has to do with the escape of Captain Horatio Hornblower, Royal Navy, from the interior of France in the early nineteenth century. Hornblower and his two companions didn't elude their pursuers by taking off on horseback or by trekking across the countryside like a band of lubbers. They stole a rowboat and pulled down the Loire River to the sea:

> The coach was poised perilously on the brink of the river; Hornblower could see the black water sliding along almost under his nose. Two yards away a small rowing boat, moored to a post, swayed about under the influence of wind and stream. . . . On a night like this it was easy to lose one's way altogether—except in a boat on the river; in a boat one had only to keep shoving off from shore to allow the current to carry one away faster than any

horse could travel in these conditions . . . .

"We're going to escape down the river in that boat, Brown," he said.

We're going to escape in a rowboat . . . . It was simple, it was elegant, and it could be done by anyone—a captain in His Majesty's Royal Navy who wanted to escape his enemies or a boy who was curious about what lay beyond the next headland or a man who needed a little time now and again to himself.

Yes, it was all about escape. And about romance, too.

FROM *THE STORY OF A BAD BOY*
1870

Thomas Bailey Aldrich

Thomas Bailey Aldrich was well known in his day. He was editor of a number of magazines, including the New York Illustrated News *and* The Atlantic, *during his long career, and one of the literary bright lights of New York in the 1860s. His contemporaries often wondered how he managed also to keep up a steady stream of articles, essays, literary fiction, and poetry on the side. Perhaps his most enduring work was* The Story of a Bad Boy, *a semi-autobiographical novel set in a town called "Rivermouth"—clearly Portsmouth, New Hampshire, the city in which he spent much of his childhood. The book is said to be the first realistic account of childhood in American fiction, and a clear precursor to Mark Twain's classics* The Adventures of Tom Sawyer *and* Adventures of Huckleberry Finn.

It seems a bit of a stretch to call The Story of a Bad Boy *realism—the rosy nos-*

talgia for a childhood in a small port on the Atlantic is stronger even than the salt tang that permeates every word. But Aldrich's ear for the combustible mix that small boats and boys can be is unerring, and perhaps the richest chapter of a vibrant book.

THE CRUISE OF THE *DOLPHIN*

Every Rivermouth boy looks upon the sea as being in some way mixed up with his destiny. While he is yet a baby lying in his cradle, he hears the dull, far-off boom of the breakers; when be is older, he wanders by the sandy shore, watching the waves that come plunging up the beach like white-maned seahorses, as Thoreau calls them; his eye follows the lessening sail as it fades into the blue horizon, and he burns for the time when he shall stand on the quarter-deck of his own ship, and go sailing proudly across that mysterious waste of waters.

Then the town itself is full of hints and flavors of the sea. The gables and roofs of the houses facing eastward are covered with red rust, like the flukes of old anchors; a salty smell pervades the air, and dense gray fogs, the very breath of Ocean, periodically creep up into the quiet streets and envelop everything. The terrific storms that lash the coast; the kelp and spars, and sometimes the bodies of drowned men, tossed on shore by the scornful waves; the shipyards, the wharves, and the tawny fleet of fishing-smacks yearly fitted out at Rivermouth—these things, and a hundred other, feed the imagination and fill the brain of every healthy boy with dreams of adventure. He learns to swim almost as soon as he can walk; he draws in with his mother's milk the art of handling an oar: he is born a sailor, whatever he may turn out to be afterwards.

To own the whole or a portion of a row-boat is his earliest ambition. No wonder that I, born to this life, and coming back to it with freshest sympathies, should have caught the prevailing infection. No wonder I longed to buy a part of the trim little sailboat *Dolphin,* which chanced just then to be in the market. This was in the latter part of May.

Three shares, at five or six dollars each, I forget which, had already been taken by Phil Adams, Fred Langdon, and Binny Wallace. The fourth and remaining share hung fire. Unless a purchaser could be found for this, the bargain was to fall through.

I am afraid I required but slight urging to join in the investment. I had four dollars and fifty cents on hand, and the treasurer of the Centipedes advanced me the balance, receiving my silver pencil-case as ample security. It was a proud moment when I stood on the wharf with my partners, inspecting the *Dolphin,* moored at the foot of a very slippery flight of steps. She was painted white with a green stripe outside, and on the stern a yellow dolphin, with its scarlet mouth wide open, stared with a surprised expression at its own reflection in the water. The boat was a great bargain.

I whirled my cap in the air, and ran to the stairs leading down from the wharf, when a hand was laid gently on my shoulder. I turned and faced Captain Nutter. I never saw such an old sharp-eye as he was in those days.

I knew he wouldn't be angry with me for buying a rowboat; but I also knew that the little bowsprit suggesting a jib, and the tapering mast ready for its few square feet of canvas, were trifles not likely to meet his approval. As far as rowing on the river, among the wharves, was concerned, the Captain had long since withdrawn his decided objections, having convinced himself, by going out with me several times, that I could manage a pair of sculls as well as anybody.

I was right in my surmises. He commanded me, in the most emphatic terms, never to go out in the *Dolphin* without leaving the mast in the boathouse. This curtailed my anticipated sport, but the pleasure of having a pull whenever I wanted it remained. I never disobeyed the Captain's orders touching the sail, though I sometimes extended my row beyond the points he had indicated.

The river was dangerous for sailboats. Squalls, without the slightest warning, were of frequent occurrence; scarcely a year passed that six or seven persons were not drowned under the very windows of the town, and these, oddly enough, were generally sea-captains, who either did not understand the river, or lacked the skill to handle a small craft.

A knowledge of such disasters, one of which I witnessed, consoled me somewhat when I saw Phil Adams skimming over the water in a spanking breeze with every stitch of canvas set. There were few better yachtsmen than Phil Adams. He usually went sailing alone, for both Fred Langdon and Binny Wallace were under the same restrictions I was.

Not long after the purchase of the boat, we planned an excursion to Sandpeep Island, the last of the islands in the harbor. We proposed to start early in the morning, and return with the tide in the moonlight. Our only difficulty was to obtain a whole day's exemption from school, the customary half-holiday not being long enough for our picnic. Somehow, we couldn't work it; but fortune arranged it for us. I may say here, that, whatever else I did, I never played truant ("hookey" we called it) in my life.

One afternoon the four owners of the *Dolphin* exchanged significant glances when Mr. Grimshaw announced from the desk that there would be no school the following day, he having just received intelligence of the death of his uncle in Boston. I was sincerely attached to Mr. Grimshaw, but I am afraid that the death of his uncle did not affect me as it ought to have done.

We were up before sunrise the next morning, in order to take advantage of the flood tide, which waits for no man. Our preparations for the cruise were made the previous evening. In the way of eatables and drinkables, we had stored in the stem of the *Dolphin* a generous bag of hard-tack (for the chowder), a piece of pork to fry the cunners in, three gigantic apple-pies (bought at Pettingil's), half a dozen lemons, and a keg of spring-water—the last-named article we slung over the side, to keep it cool, as soon as we got under way. The crockery and the bricks for our camp-stove we placed in the bows, with the groceries, which included sugar, pepper, salt, and a bottle of pickles. Phil Adams contributed to the outfit a small tent of unbleached cotton cloth, under which we intended to take our nooning.

We unshipped the mast, threw in an extra oar, and were ready to embark. I do not believe that Christopher Columbus, when he started on his rather successful voyage of discovery, felt half the responsibility and importance that weighed upon me as I sat on the middle seat of the *Dolphin*, with my oar resting in the row-lock. I wonder if Christopher Columbus quietly slipped out of the house without letting his estimable family know what he was up to?

Charley Marden, whose father had promised to cane him if he ever stepped foot on sail or rowboat, came down to the wharf in a sour-grape humor, to see us off. Nothing would tempt him to go out on the river in such a crazy clam-shell of a boat. He pretended that he did not expect to behold us alive again, and tried to throw a wet blanket over the expedition.

"Guess you'll have a squally time of it," said Charley, casting off the painter. "I'll drop in at old Newbury's" (Newbury was the parish undertaker) "and leave word, as I go along!"

'Bosh!" muttered Phil Adams, sticking the boat-hook into the string-piece of the wharf, and sending the *Dolphin* half a dozen yards towards the current.

How calm and lovely the river was! Not a ripple stirred on the glassy surface, broken only by the sharp cutwater of our tiny craft. The sun, as round and red as an August moon, was by this time peering above the water-line.

The town had drifted behind us, and we were entering among the group of islands. Sometimes we could almost touch with our boat-hook the shelving banks on either side. As we neared the mouth of the harbor a little breeze now and then wrinkled the blue water, shook the spangles from the foliage, and gently lifted the spiral mist-wreaths that still clung along shore. The measured dip of our oars and the drowsy twitterings of the birds seemed to mingle with, rather than break, the enchanted silence that reigned about us.

The scent of the new clover comes back to me now, as I recall that delicious morning when we floated away in a fairy boat down a river like a dream!

The sun was well up when the nose of the *Dolphin* nestled against the snow-white bosom of Sandpeep Island. This island, as I have said before, was the last of the cluster, one side of it being washed by the sea. We landed on the river-side, the sloping sands and quiet water affording us a good place to moor the boat.

It took us an hour or two to transport our stores to the spot selected for the encampment. Having pitched our tent, using the five oars to support the canvas, we got out our lines, and went down the rocks seaward to fish. It was early for cunners, but we were lucky enough to catch as nice a mess as ever you saw. A cod for the chowder was not so easily secured. At last Binny Wallace hauled in a plump little fellow crusted all over with flaky silver.

To skin the fish, build our fireplace, and cook the chowder kept us busy the next two hours. The fresh air and the exercise had given us the appetites of wolves, and we were about famished by the time the savory mixture was ready for our clamshell saucers.

I shall not insult the rising generation on the seaboard by telling them how delectable is a chowder compounded and eaten in this Robinson Crusoe fashion. As for the boys who live inland, and know naught of such marine feasts, my heart is full of pity for them. What wasted lives! Not to know the delights of a clam-bake, not to love chowder, to be ignorant of lob-scouse!

How happy we were, we four, sitting crosslegged in the crisp salt grass, with the invigorating sea-breeze blowing gratefully through our hair! What a joyous thing was life, and how far off seemed death—death, that lurks in all pleasant places, and was so near!

The banquet finished, Phil Adams drew from his pocket a handful of sweet-fern cigars; but as none of the party could indulge without imminent risk of becoming sick, we all, on one pretext or another, declined, and Phil smoked by himself.

The wind had freshened by this, and we found it comfortable to put on the jackets which had been thrown aside in the heat of the day. We strolled along the beach and gathered large quantities of the fairy-woven Iceland moss, which, at certain seasons, is washed to these shores; then we played at ducks and drakes, and then, the sun being sufficiently low, we went in bathing.

Before our bath was ended a slight change had come over the sky and sea; fleecy-white clouds scudded here and there, and a muffled moan from the breakers caught our ears from time to time. While we were dressing, a few hurried drops of rain came lisping down, and we adjourned to the tent to await the passing of the squall.

"We're all right, anyhow," said Phil Adams. "It won't be much of a blow, and we'll be as snug as a bug in a rug, here in the tent, particularly if we have that lemonade which some of you fellows were going to make."

By an oversight, the lemons had been left in the boat. Binny Wallace volunteered to go for them.

"Put an extra stone on the painter, Binny," said Adams, calling after him; "it would be awkward to have the *Dolphin* give us the slip and return to port minus her passengers."

"That it would," answered Binny, scrambling down the rocks.

Sandpeep Island is diamond-shaped—one point running out into the sea, and the other looking towards the town. Our tent was on the river-side. Though the *Dolphin* was also on the same side, it lay out of sight by the beach at the farther extremity of the island.

Binny Wallace had been absent five or six minutes, when we heard him calling our several names in tones that indicated distress or surprise, we could not tell which. Our first thought was, "The boat has broken adrift!"

We sprung to our feet and hastened down to the beach. On turning the bluff which hid the mooring-place from our view, we found the conjecture correct. Not only was the *Dolphin* afloat, but poor little Binny Wallace was standing in the bows with his arms stretched helplessly towards us—drifting out to sea!

"Head the boat in shore!" shouted Phil Adams.

Wallace ran to the tiller; but the slight cockle-shell merely swung round and drifted broadside on. O, if we had but left a single scull in the *Dolphin*!

"Can you swim it?" cried Adams, desperately, using his hand as a speaking-trumpet, for the distance between the boat and the island widened momentarily.

Binny Wallace looked down at the sea, which was covered with white caps, and made a despairing gesture. He knew, and we knew, that the stoutest swimmer could not live forty seconds in those angry waters.

A wild, insane light came into Phil Adams's eyes, as he stood knee-deep in the boiling surf, and for an instant I think he meditated plunging into the ocean after the receding boat.

The sky darkened, and an ugly look stole rapidly over the broken surface of the sea.

Binny Wallace half rose from his seat in the stem, and waved his hand to us in token of farewell. In spite of the distance, increasing every instant, we could see his face plainly. The anxious expression it wore at first had passed. It was pale and meek now, and I love to think there was a kind of halo about it, like that which painters place around the forehead of a saint. So he drifted away.

The sky grew darker and darker. It was only by straining our eyes through the unnatural twilight that we could keep the *Dolphin* in sight. The figure of Binny Wallace was no longer visible, for the boat itself had dwindled to a mere white dot on the black water. Now we lost it, and our hearts stopped throbbing; and now the speck appeared again, for an instant, on the crest of a high wave.

Finally, it went out like a spark, and we saw it no more. Then we gazed at each other, and dared not speak.

Absorbed in following the course of the boat, we had scarcely noticed the huddled inky clouds that sagged down all around us. From these threatening masses, seamed at intervals with pale lightning, there now burst a heavy peal of thunder that shook the ground under our feet. A sudden squall

DRIFTING AWAY.

struck the sea, ploughing deep white furrows into it, and at the same instant
a single piercing shriek rose above the tempest—the frightened cry of a gull
swooping over the island. How it startled us!

It was impossible any longer to keep our footing on the beach. The wind
and the breakers would have swept us into the ocean if we had not clung
to each other with the desperation of drowning men. Taking advantage of
a momentary lull, we crawled up the sands on our hands and knees, and,
pausing in the lee of the granite ledge to gain breath, returned to the camp,
where we found that the gale had snapped all the fastenings of the tent but
one. Held by this, the puffed-out canvas swayed in the wind like a balloon.
It was a task of some difficulty to secure it, which we did by beating down
the canvas with the oars.

After several trials, we succeeded in setting up the tent on the leeward
side of the ledge. Blinded by the vivid flashes of lightning, and drenched by
the rain, which fell in torrents, we crept, half dead with fear and anguish,

under our flimsy shelter. Neither the anguish nor the fear was on our own account, for we were comparatively safe, but for poor little Binny Wallace, driven out to sea in the merciless gale. We shuddered to think of him in that frail shell, drifting on and on to his grave, the sky rent with lightning over his head, and the green abysses yawning beneath him. We fell to crying, the three of us, and cried I know not how long.

Meanwhile the storm raged with augmented fury. We were obliged to hold on to the ropes of the tent to prevent it blowing away. The spray from the river leaped several yards up the rocks and clutched at us malignantly. The very island trembled with the concussions of the sea beating upon it, and at times I fancied that it had broken loose from its foundation, and was floating off with us. The breakers, streaked with angry phosphorus, were fearful to look at.

The wind rose higher and higher, cutting long slits in the tent, through which the rain poured incessantly. To complete the sum of our miseries, the night was at hand. It came down suddenly, at last, like a curtain, shutting in Sandpeep Island from all the world.

It was a dirty night, as the sailors say. The darkness was something that could be felt as well as seen—it pressed down upon one with a cold, clammy touch. Gazing into the hollow blackness, all sorts of imaginable shapes seemed to start forth from vacancy—brilliant colors, stars, prisms, and dancing lights. What boy, lying awake at night, has not amused or terrified himself by peopling the spaces around his bed with these phenomena of his own eyes?

"I say," whispered Fred Langdon, at length, clutching my hand, "don't you see things—out there—in the dark?"

"Yes, yes—Binny Wallace's face!"

I added to my own nervousness by making this avowal; though for the last ten minutes I had seen little besides that star-pale face with its angelic hair and brows. First a slim yellow circle, like the nimbus round the moon, took shape and grew sharp against the darkness; then this faded gradually, and there was the Face, wearing the same sad, sweet look it wore when he waved his hand to us across the awful water. This optical illusion kept repeating itself.

"And I too," said Adams. "I see it every now and then, outside there. What wouldn't I give if it really was poor little Wallace looking in at us! O boys, how shall we dare to go back to the town without him? I've wished a hundred times, since we've been sitting here, that I was in his place, alive or dead!"

We dreaded the approach of morning as much as we longed for it. The morning would tell us all. Was it possible for the *Dolphin* to outride such a storm? There was a light-house on Mackerel Reef, which lay directly in the course the boat bad taken, when it disappeared. If the *Dolphin* had caught on this reef, perhaps Binny Wallace was safe. Perhaps his cries had been heard by the keeper of the light. The man owned a lifeboat, and had rescued several people. Who could tell?

Such were the questions we asked ourselves again and again, as we lay in each other's arms waiting for daybreak. What an endless night it was! I have known months that did not seem so long.

Our position was irksome rather than perilous; for the day was certain to bring us relief from the town, where our prolonged absence, together with the storm, had no doubt excited the liveliest alarm for our safety. But the cold, the darkness, and the suspense were hard to bear.

Our soaked jackets had chilled us to the bone. To keep warm, we lay huddled together so closely that we could bear our hearts beat above the tumult of sea and sky.

After a while we grew very hungry, not having broken our fast since early in the day. The rain had turned the hard-tack into a sort of dough; but it was better than nothing.

We used to laugh at Fred Langdon for always carrying in his pocket a small vial of essence of peppermint or sassafras, a few drops of which, sprinkled on a lump of loaf-sugar, he seemed to consider a great luxury. I don't know what would have become of us at this crisis, if it hadn't been for that omnipresent bottle of hot stuff. We poured the stinging liquid over our sugar, which had kept dry in a sardine-box, and warmed ourselves with frequent doses.

After four or five hours the rain ceased, the wind died away to a moan, and the sea—no longer raging like a maniac—sobbed and sobbed with a piteous human voice all along the coast. And well it might, after that night's work. Twelve sail of the Gloucester fishing fleet had gone down with every soul on board, just outside of Whale's-back Light. Think of the wide grief that follows in the wake of one wreck; then think of the despairing women who wrung their hands and wept, the next morning, in the streets of Gloucester, Marblehead, and Newcastle!

Though our strength was nearly spent, we were too cold to sleep. Once I sunk into a troubled doze, when I seemed to hear Charley Marden's parting words, only it was the Sea that said them. After that I threw off the drowsiness whenever it threatened to overcome me.

Fred Langdon was the earliest to discover a filmy, luminous streak in the sky, the first glimmering of sunrise.

"Look, it is nearly daybreak!"

While we were following the direction of his finger, a sound of distant oars fell on our ears.

We listened breathlessly, and as the dip of the blades became more audible, we discerned two foggy lights, like will-o'-the-wisps, floating on the river.

Running down to the water's edge, we hailed the boats with all our might. The call was heard, for the oars rested a moment in the row-locks, and then pulled in towards the island.

It was two boats from the town, in the foremost of which we could now make out the figures of Captain Nutter and Binny Wallace's father. We shrunk back on seeing him.

'Thank God!" cried Mr. Wallace, fervently, as he leaped from the wherry without waiting for the bow to touch the beach.

But when he saw only three boys standing on the sands, his eye wandered restlessly about in quest of the fourth; then a deadly pallor overspread his features.

Our story was soon told. A solemn silence fell upon the crowd of rough boatmen gathered round, interrupted only by a stifled sob from one poor old man, who stood apart from the rest.

The sea was still running too high for any small boat to venture out; so it was arranged that the wherry should take us back to town, leaving the yawl, with a picked crew, to hug the island until daybreak, and then set forth in search of the *Dolphin*.

Though it was barely sunrise when we reached town, there were a great many people assembled at the landing eager for intelligence from missing boats. Two picnic parties had started down river the day before, just previous to the gale, and nothing had been heard of them. It turned out that the pleasure-seekers saw their danger in time, and ran ashore on one of the least exposed islands, where they passed the night. Shortly after our own arrival they appeared off Rivermouth, much to the joy of their friends, in two shattered, dismasted boats.

The excitement over, I was in a forlorn state, physically and mentally. Captain Nutter put me to bed between hot blankets, and sent Kitty Collins for the doctor. I was wandering in my mind, and fancied myself still on Sandpeep Island: now we were building our brick-stove to cook the chowder, and, in my delirium, I laughed aloud and shouted to my comrades; now the sky darkened, and the squall struck the island: now I gave orders to Wallace how to manage the boat, and now I cried because the rain was pouring in on me through the holes in the tent. Towards evening a high fever set in, and it was many days before my grandfather deemed it prudent to tell me that the *Dolphin* had been found, floating keel upwards, four miles southeast of Mackerel Reef.

Poor little Binny Wallace! How strange it seemed, when I went to school again, to see that empty seat in the fifth row! How gloomy the playground was, lacking the sunshine of his gentle, sensitive face! One day a folded sheet slipped from my algebra; it was the last note he ever wrote me. I couldn't read it for the tears.

What a pang shot across my heart the afternoon it was whispered through the town that a body had been washed ashore at Grave Point—the place where we bathed. We bathed there no more! How well I remember the funeral, and what a piteous sight it was afterwards to see his familiar name on a small headstone in the Old South Burying Ground!

Poor little Binny Wallace! Always the same to me. The rest of us have grown up into hard, worldly men, fighting the fight of life; but you are forever young, and gentle, and pure; a part of my own childhood that time cannot wither; always a little boy, always poor little Binny Wallace!

FROM *FOUR MONTHS IN A SNEAK-BOX*

1879

Nathaniel H. Bishop

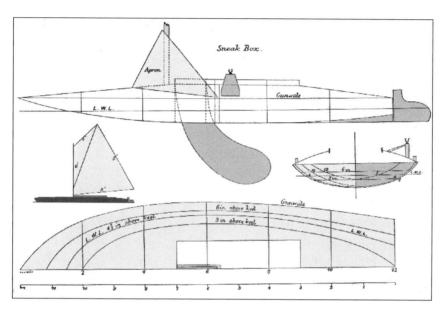

Nathaniel Bishop had the itch. A Yankee, born in Bedford, Massachusetts in 1837, he walked across South America at the age of 17, and later wrote a book on the subject, The Pampas and Andes: A Thousand Miles' Walk Across South America. *In his mid-30s he became a canoeing enthusiast after reading John Mac-Gregor's books about voyaging in Rob Roy canoes. In 1874 he decided to paddle a canoe from Quebec to Florida, 2,500 miles.*

Finishing the trip, he headed north again and had a Barnegat sneakbox built in New Jersey. The sneakbox was developed as a gunning skiff to take into the marshes and shallow bays after waterfowl. They were about 12 feet long with a beam of 4 feet. The ones designed for sport were often sailed with the addition of a daggerboard and a cat mainsail. Modern sailing dinghys like the Sunfish and Lazer owe a lot to the sneakbox.

Starting in Pittsburgh in 1875, Bishop rowed and sailed down the Ohio and Mississippi Rivers to the Gulf of Mexico. After finishing two long open-boat voyages in as many years he wrote up his notes, and The Voyage of the Paper Canoe *and* Four Months in a Sneak-Box *turned out to be popular books. Bishop went on to become something of a cranberry magnate, and also continued to be an active canoeist, helping to found the American Canoe Association in 1880.*

The following excerpt finds Bishop in midwinter near the mouth of the Ohio, and includes an interesting account of passing through flocks of whooping and sandhill cranes in the swamps and backwaters there.

SHANTYBOATS AND CRANES

In the evening, a little creek below Alton (Indiana) was reached, which sheltered me during the night. Soon the rain ceased, and the stars shone kindly upon my lonely camp. I left the creek at half-past four o'clock in the morning. The water had risen two feet and a half in ten hours, and the broad river was in places covered from shore to shore with drift stuff; which made my course a devious one, and the little duck-boat had many a narrow escape in my attempts to avoid the floating mass. The booming of guns along the shore reminded me that it was Christmas, and, in imagination, I pictured to myself the many happy families in the valley enjoying their Christmas cheer. The contrast between their condition and mine was great, for I could not even find enough dry wood to cook my simple camp-fare.

An hour before sunset, while skirting the Indiana shore, I passed a little village called Batesville, and soon after came to the mouth of a crooked creek, out of which, borne on the flood of a freshet, came a long, narrow line of drift stuff. Just within the mouth of the creek, in a deep indenture of the high bank, a shanty-boat was snugly lashed to the trees. A young man stood in the open doorway of the cabin, washing dishes, and as I passed he kindly wished me a "Merry Christmas," inviting me on board. He eagerly inspected the sneak-box, and pronounced it one of the prettiest "tricks" afloat. "How my father and brother would like to see you and your boat!" exclaimed he. "Can't you tie up here, just under yonder p'int on the bank? There's an eddy there, and the drift won't work in enough to trouble you."

The invitation so kindly given was accepted, and with the assistance of my new acquaintance my boat was worked against the strong current into a curve of the bank, and there securely fastened. I set to work about my house-keeping cares, and had my cabin comfortably arranged for the night, when I was hailed from the shanty-boat to "come aboard." Entering the rough cabin, a surprise greeted me, for a table stood in the centre of the room, covered with a clean white cloth, and groaning under the weight of such a variety of appetizing dishes as I had not seen for many a day.

"I thought," said the boy, "that you hadn't had much Christmas to-day, being as you're away from your folks; and we had a royal dinner, and there's lots left fur you—so help yourself." He then explained that his father and brother had gone to a shooting-match on the other side of the river; and when I expressed my astonishment at the excellent fare, which, upon closer acquaintance, proved to be of a dainty nature (game and delicate pastry making a menu rather peculiar for a shanty-boat), he informed me that his brother had been first cook on a big passenger steamer, and had received good wages; but their mother died, and their father married a second time, and— Here the young fellow paused, evidently considering how much of their private life he should show to a stranger. "Well," he continued, "our new mother liked cities better than flatboats, and father's a good quiet man, who likes to live in peace with every one, so he lets mother live in Arkansas, and he stays on the shanty-boat. We boys joined him, fur he's a good old fellow, and we have all that's going. We git plenty of cat-fish, buffalo-fish, yellow perch, and bass, and sell them at the little towns along the river. Then in summer we hire a high flat ashore,—not a flatboat,—I mean a bit

of land along the river, and raise a crop of corn, 'taters, and cabbage. We have plenty of shooting, and don't git much fever 'n ager."

I had rowed fifty-three miles that day, and did ample justice to the Christmas dinner on the flatboat. The father and brother joined us in the evening, and gave me much good advice in regard to river navigation. The rain fell heavily before midnight, and they insisted that I should share one of their beds in the boat; but as small streams of water were trickling through the roof of the shanty, and my little craft was water-tight, I declined the kindly offer, and bade them good-night.

The next day being Sunday, I again visited my new acquaintances upon the shanty-boat, and gathered from their varied experiences much of the river's lore. The rain continued, accompanied with lightning and thunder, during the entire day, so that Monday's sun was indeed welcome; and with kind farewells on all sides I broke camp and descended the current with the now almost continuous raft of drift-wood. For several hours a sewing-machine repair-shop and a photographic gallery floated with me.

The creeks were now so swollen from the heavy rains, and so full of drift-wood, that my usual retreat into some creek seemed cut off; so I ran under the sheltered side of "Three Mile Island," below Newburg, Indiana. The climate was daily improving, and I no longer feared an ice blockade; but a new difficulty arose. The heavy rafts of timber threatened to shut me in my camp. At dusk, all might be open water; but at break of day "a change came o'er the spirit of my dream," and heavy blockades of timber rafts made it no easy matter to escape. There were times when, shut in behind these barriers, I looked out upon the river with envious eyes at the steamboats steadily plodding up stream against the current, keeping free of the rafts by the skill of their pilots; and thoughts of the genius and perseverance of the inventors of these peculiar craft crowded my mind.

In these days of successful application of mechanical inventions, but few persons can realize the amount of distrust and opposition against which a Watts or a Fulton had to contend while forcing upon an illiberal and un-appreciative public the valuable results of their busy brains and fertile genius. It is well for us who now enjoy these blessings,—the utilized ideas of a lifetime of unrequited labors,—to look back upon the epoch of history so full of gloom for the men to whom we owe so much.

At the beginning of the present century the navigation of the Ohio was limited to canoes, bateaux, scows, rafts, arks, and the rudest models of sail-ing-boats. The ever downward course of the strong current must be stemmed in ascending the river. Against this powerful resistance upon tor-tuous streams, wind, as a motor, was found to be only partially successful, and for sure and rapid transit between settlements along the banks of great waterways a most discouraging failure. Down-river journeys were easily made, but the up-river or return trip was a very slow and unsatisfactory af-fair, excepting to those who travelled in light canoes.

The influx of population to the fertile Ohio valley, and the settling up of the rich bottoms of the Mississippi, demanded a more expeditious system of communication. The necessities of the people called loudly for this im-provement, but at the same time their prejudices and ignorance prevented them from aiding or encouraging any such plans. The hour came at length for the delivery of the people of the great West, and with it the man. Ful-ton, aided by Watts, offered to solve the problem by unravelling rather than by cutting the "Gordian knot." It was whispered through the wilderness that a fire-ship, called the "Clermont," built by a crazy speculator named Fulton, had started from New York, and, steaming up the Hudson, had forced itself against the current one hundred and fifty miles to Albany, in thirty-six hours. This was in September, 1807.

The fool and the fool's fire-ship became the butt of all sensible people in Europe as well as in America. Victor Hugo remarks that, "In the year 1807, when the first steamboat of Fulton, commanded by Livingston, furnished with one of Watts's engines sent from England, and manoeuvred, besides her ordinary crew, by two Frenchmen only, Andre Michaux and another, made her first voyage from New York to Albany, it happened that she set sail on the 17th of August. The ministers took up this important fact, and in numberless chapels preachers were heard calling down a malediction on the machine, and declaring that this number seventeen was no other than the total of the ten horns and seven heads of the beasts in the Apocalypse. In America they invoked against the steamboat the beast from the book of Revelation; in Europe, the reptile of the book of Genesis. The SAVANS had rejected steamboats as impossible; the PRIESTS had anathematized them as impious; SCIENCE had condemned, and RELIGION consigned them to perdition."

"In the archipelago of the British Channel islands," this learned author goes on to say, "the first steamboat which made its appearance received the name of the 'Devil Boat.' In the eyes of these worthy fishermen, once Catholics, now Calvinists, but always bigots, it seemed to be a portion of the infernal regions which had been somehow set afloat. A local preacher selected for his discourse the question of, 'Whether man has the right to make fire and water work together when God had divided them.' (Gen. ch. i. v. 4.) No; this beast composed of iron and fire did not resemble leviathan! Was it not an attempt to bring chaos again into the universe?"

So much for young America, and so much for old mother England! Now listen, men and women of to-day, to the wisdom of France—scientific France. "A mad notion, a gross delusion, an absurdity!" Such was the verdict of the Academy of Sciences when consulted by Napoleon on the subject of steamboats early in the present century.

It seems scarcely credible now that all this transpired in the days of our fathers, not so very long ago. Time is a great leveller. Education of the head as well as of the heart has liberalized the pulpit, and the man of theoretical science to-day would not dare to stake his reputation by denying any apparently well-established theory, while the inventors of telephones, perpetual-motion motors, &c., are gladly hailed as leaders in the march of progress so dear to every American heart. The pulpit is now on the side of honest science, and the savant teaches great truths, while the public mind is being educated to receive and utilize the heretofore concealed or undeveloped mysteries of a wise and generous Creator, who has taught his children that they must labor in order to possess.

The Clermont was the pioneer steamer of the Hudson River, and its trial trip was made in 1807. The first steamboat which descended the Ohio and Mississippi rivers was christened the "New Orleans." It was designed and built by Mr. N. J. Roosevelt, and commenced its voyage from Pittsburgh in September, 1811. The bold proprietor of this enterprise, with his wife, Mrs. Lydia M. Roosevelt, accompanied the captain, engineer, pilot, six hands, two female servants, a man waiter, a cook, and a large Newfoundland dog, to the end of the voyage. The friends of this lady—the first woman who descended the great rivers of the West in a steamboat—used every argument they could offer to dissuade her from undertaking what was considered a dangerous experiment, an absolute folly. The good wife, however, clung to her husband, and accepted the risks, preferring to be drowned or blown up, as her friends predicted, rather than to desert her better-half in his hour of trial. A few weeks would decide his success or failure, and she would be at his side to condole or rejoice with him, as the case might be.

The citizens of Pittsburgh gathered upon the banks of the Monongahela to witness the inception of the enterprise which was to change the whole destiny of the West. One can imagine the criticisms flung at the departing steamer as she left her moorings and boldly faced her fate. As the curious craft was borne along the current of the river, the Indians attempted to approach her, bent upon hostile attempts, and once a party of them pursued the boat in hot chase, but their endurance was not equal to that of steam. These children of the forest gazed upon the snorting, fire-breathing monster with undisguised awe, and called it "Penelore"—the fire-canoe. They imagined it to have close relationship with the comet that they believed had produced the earthquakes of that year. The voyage of the "New Orleans" was a romantic reality in two ways. The wonderful experiment was proved a success, and its originator won his laurel wreath; while the bold captain of the fire-ship, falling in love with one of the chambermaids, won a wife.

The river's travel now became somewhat monotonous. I had reached a low country, heavily wooded in places, and was entering the great prairie region of Illinois. Having left my island camp by starlight on Tuesday morning, and having rowed steadily all day until dusk, I passed the wild-looking mouth of the Wabash River, and went into camp behind an island, logging with pleasure my day's run at sixty-seven miles. I was now only one hundred and forty-two miles from the mouth of the Ohio, and with the rising and rapidly increasing current there were only a few hours' travel between me and the Mississippi.

Wednesday morning, December 29th, I discovered that the river had risen two feet during the night, and the stump of the tree to which I had moored my boat was submerged. The river was wide and the banks covered with heavy forests, with clearings here and there, which afforded attractive vistas of prairies in the background. I passed a bold, stratified crag, covered with a little growth of cedars. These adventurous trees, growing out of the crevices of the rock, formed a picturesque covering for its rough surface. A cavern, about thirty feet in width, penetrated a short distance into the rock. This natural curiosity bore the name of "Cave-in-Rock," and was, in 1801, the rendezvous of a band of outlaws, who lived by plundering the boats going up and down the river, oftentimes adding the crime of murder to their other misdeeds. Just below the cliff nestled a little village also called "Cave-in-Rock."

Wild birds flew about me on all sides, and had I cared to linger I might have had a good bag of game. This was not, however, a gunning cruise, and the temptation was set aside as inconsistent with the systematic pulling which alone would take me to my goal. The birds were left for my quondam friends of the shanty-boat, they being the happy possessors of more TIME than they could well handle, and the killing of it the aim of their existence.

The soft shores of alluvium were constantly caving and falling into the river, bringing down tons of earth and tall forest-trees. The latter, after freeing their roots of the soil, would be swept out into the stream as contributions to the great floating raft of drift-wood, a large portion of which was destined to a long voyage, for much of this floating forest is carried into the Gulf of Mexico, and travels over many hundreds of miles of salt water, until it is washed up on to the strands of the isles of the sea or the beaches of the continent.

Having tied up for the night to a low bank, with no thought of danger, it was startling, to say the least, to have an avalanche of earth from the bank above deposit itself upon my boat, so effectually sealing down my hatch-cover that it seemed at first impossible to break from my prison. After repeated trials I succeeded in dislodging the mass, and, thankful to escape premature interment, at once pushed off in search of a better camp.

A creek soon appeared, but its entrance was barred by a large tree which had fallen across its mouth. My heavy hatchet now proved a friend in need, and putting my boat close to the tree, I went systematically to work, and soon cut out a section five feet in length. Entering through this gateway, my labors were rewarded by finding upon the bank some dry fence-rails, with which a rude kitchen was soon constructed to protect me from the wind while preparing my meal. The unusual luxury of a fire brightened the weird scene, and the flames shot upward, cheering the lone voyager and frightening the owls and coons from their accustomed lairs. The strong current had been of great assistance, for that night my log registered sixty-two miles for the day's row.

Leaving the creek the next morning by starlight, I passed large flocks of geese and ducks, while Whooping-cranes (*Grus Americanus*) and Sand-hill cranes (*Grus Canadensis*), in little flocks, dotted the grassy prairies, or flew from one swamp to another, filling the air with their startling cries. Both these species are found associated in flocks upon the cultivated prairie farms, where they pillage the grain and vegetable fields of the farmer. Their habits are somewhat similar, though the Whooping-crane is the most wary of the two. The adult Whooping-cranes are white, the younger birds of a brownish color. This species is larger than the Sand-hill Crane, the latter having a total length of from forty to forty-two inches. The Sand-hill species may be distinguished from the Whooping-crane by its slate-blue color. The cackling, whooping, and screaming voices of an assembled multitude of these birds cannot be described. They can be heard for miles upon the open plains. These birds are found in Florida and along the Gulf coast as well as over large areas of the northern states. They feed upon soft roots, which they excavate from the swamps, and upon bugs and reptiles of all kinds. It requires the most cautious stalking on the part of the hunter to get within gunshot of them, and when so approached the Whooping-crane is usually the first of the two species which takes to the wing. The social customs of these birds are most entertaining to the observer who may lie hidden in the grass and watch them through a glass. Their tall, angular figures, made up of so much wing, leg, neck, and bill, counterpoised by so little body, incline the spectator to look upon them as ornithological caricatures. After balancing himself upon one foot for an hour, with the other drawn up close to his scanty robe of feathers, and his head poised in a most contemplative attitude, one of these queer birds will suddenly turn a somersault, and, returning to his previous posture, continue his cogitations as though nothing had interrupted his reflections. With wings spread, they slowly winnow the air, rising or hopping from the ground a few feet at a time, then whirling in circles upon their toes, as though going through the mazes of a dance. Their most popular diversion seems to be the game of leap-frog, and their long legs being specially adapted to this sport, they achieve a wonderful success. One of the birds quietly assumes a squatting position upon the ground, when his sportive companions hop in turn over his expectant head. They then pirouette, turn somersaults, and go through various exercises with the skill of gymnasts. Their sportive proclivities seem to have no bounds; and being true humorists, they preserve through their gambols a ridiculously sedate appearance. Popular accounts of the nidification of these birds are frequently untrue. We are told that they build their cone-shaped nests of mud, sticks, and grass in shallow water, in colonies, and that their nests, BEING PLACED ON RAFTS of buoyant material, float about in the bayous, and are propelled and guided at the will of the sitting bird by the use of her long legs and feet as oars. The position of the bird upon the nest is also ludicrously depicted. It is described as sitting astride the nest, with the toes touching the ground; and to add still more comicality to the picture, it is asserted that the limbs are often thrust out horizontally behind the bird. The results of close observations prove that these accounts are in keeping with many other related by parlor naturalists. The cranes sit upon their nests like other birds, with their feet drawn up close to the body. The mound-shaped nests are built of sticks, grass, and mud, and usually placed in a shallow pond or partially submerged swamp, while at times a grassy hassock furnishes the foundation of the structure. In the saucer-shaped top of the nest two eggs are deposited, upon which the bird sits most assiduously, having no time at this season for aquatic amusements, such as paddling about with her nest.

The young birds are most hilarious babies, for they inherit the social qualities of their parents, and are ready to play or fight with each other before they are fairly out of the nest. A close observer of their habits writes from the prairies of Indiana: "When the young get a little strength they attack each other with great fury, and can only be made to desist by the parent bird separating them, and taking one under its fostering care, and holding them at a respectable distance until they reach crane-hood, when they seem to make up in joyous hilarity for the quarrelsome proclivities of youth."

Like geese and ducks, cranes winter in one locality so long as the ponds are open, but the first cold snap that freezes their swamp drives them two or three degrees further south. From this migration they soon return to their old haunts, the first thawing of the ice being the signal.

The mouths of the Tennessee and Cumberland rivers were passed, and the Ohio, widening in places until it seemed like a lake, assumed a new grandeur as it approached the Mississippi. Three miles below Wilkinsonville, but on the Kentucky side, I stole into a dark creek and rested until the next morning, Friday, December 31st, which was to be my last day on the Ohio River.

I entered a long reach in the river soon after nine o'clock on Friday morning, and could plainly see the town of Cairo, resting upon the flat prairies in the distance. The now yellow, muddy current of the Ohio rolled along the great railroad dike, which had cost one million dollars to erect, and formed a barrier strong enough to resist the rushing waters of the freshets. Across the southern apex of this prairie city could be seen the "Father of Waters," its wide surface bounded on the west by the wilderness. A few moments more, and my little craft was whirled into its rapid, eddying current; and with the boat's prow now pointed southward, I commenced, as it were, a life of new experiences as I descended the great river, where each day I was to feel the genial influences of a warmer climate.

The thought of entering warm and sunny regions was, indeed, welcome to a man who had forced his way through rafts of ice, under cloudy skies, through a smoky atmosphere, and had partaken of food of the same chilling temperature for so many days. This prospect of a genial clime, with the more comfortable camping and rowing it was sure to bring, gave new vigor to my arms, daily growing stronger with their task, and each long, steady pull TOLD as it swept me down the river.

The faithful sneak-box had carried me more than a thousand miles since I entered her at Pittsburgh. This, of course, includes the various detours made in searching for camping-grounds, frequent crossings of the wide river to avoid drift stuff; &c. The descent of the Ohio had occupied about twenty-nine days, but many hours had been lost by storms keeping me in camp, and other unavoidable delays. As an offset to these stoppages, it must be remembered that the current, increased by freshets, was with me, and to it, as much as to the industrious arms of the rower, must be given the credit for the long route gone over in so short a time, by so small a boat.

FROM **THE JOURNALS OF CONSTANT WATERMAN**

Matthew Goldman
2005

SELDON III

Matthew Goldman is one of those jacks-of-all-trades it is always a pleasure to run into. Toolmaker, playwright, land surveyor, poet, carpenter, he has spent most of his life in coastal Connecticut. These days, he repairs boats in Noank, and once or twice a month writes a column for the magazine Messing About in Boats. Mostly the columns are a look back at some of his youthful adventures and misadventures on the water over the years. They are available in the book The Journals of Constant Waterman.

While trying to choose one for the book, I narrowed things down to two. But after reading them through a couple of times and looking over the other excerpts, there still wasn't an obvious choice. So, considering that they were short and not too sweet, I decided to just include the both of them.

RUDY

It was a squeeze fitting me, Brother John, his wife Marla, and all our gear into my thirteen-foot Grumman canoe. Not to mention Rudy. Rudy was their Doberman and was great in a canoe—except when he wanted to take a walk, which was only every five minutes. We'd put the canoe—and him—in the back of the truck; the three of us climbed up front.

The truck smelled comfortingly of lunch and dog and red oak stove wood and coffee. Brother John—who wasn't my brother—pushed aside his long hair and shifted gears.

"Yep. We're gonna catch us some trout today. I sorta got that feelin'."

We launched the canoe by the ferry slip while Rudy got the kinks out—after our two mile drive—by galloping round and round the parking area. Brother John never bothered to lock his truck. Thirty years back, in a village small as ours, nobody ever locked up. Besides, Brother John's truck didn't have a driver's side window.

"Anyone steals my chain saw's got it comin'," said Brother John.

We paddled down river about ten minutes, cut up the creek and were soon amid the marshes. It's tidal there and the trout don't like it much. We passed the deep hole where all you do is let down some bait to pull up a perch, a bullhead or maybe a bass. It's a good spot to know if you need a few fish for supper.

Another half mile, the water ran clear and fresh—the bottom all sparkly gravel instead of mud. Here you catch nothing but brookies or maybe a perch. Wild brook trout are the Lord's own answer to flavor—there's nothing compares with a fresh one just out of the skillet.

I'd fished the stream out back of our barn as a kid and I'd had to think as a brook trout before I could catch one. There'd been too much brush to consider casting flies. Then it was strictly a boy and a worm and a trout. It wasn't much different, now.

We each baited up while Rudy, employing a tried scientific method, determined that even a dozen worms were more than enough for breakfast. Marla wasn't squeamish at all when she baited her hook. I was in love with Marla—and Brother John knew it. I never exceeded occasional brotherly hugs, so all of us got on well.

I had tried very hard to fall in love with her sister, out in Wisconsin, and taken her paddling all the way down to the dam alongside the cheese works. The creek was slow without many riffles in it and our sole concern had been down in the lower hundred, where two dozen heifers had capered into the shallow ford to greet us.

"It's all right," she'd assured me. "They just want to play a bit."

I'd felt the gravel grating against our bottom and had visions of two dozen Holsteins in my canoe.

"Paddle!" I'd urged, and we'd scooted among them and fled into deeper water. Later, we'd nearly made love on a grassy bank, but thought better of it. Her dad would have chopped me for silage to feed the bull, who needed a high protein diet for *his* line of work. Some time, when the kids aren't around, I'll tell you all about *that* little canoe trip.

Now I watched Marla reel in a lovely trout and explain to Rudy how improved it would be by grilling and how much the hook would disagree with his nose. Rudy was one of those dogs who need convincing. Besides, he felt he was being much ignored.

He decided to take a little walk on the gunwale. A gigantic splash you could hear halfway to Christmas alerted us to the fact that the crew had jumped ship. We stowed our rods with a sigh. Rudy was hanging onto the gunwale and thrashing. Our rail dipped under and the Creek poured in. Marla's trout applauded loudly.

We carefully paddled the few yards to shore, bailed the boat, and stood in the muck to hold the canoe so Rudy could bounce back in. He gratefully shook himself an inch from our faces and spoiled our single trout by treading on it.

But he fell out only once the whole way home.

Originally published in *Messing About in Boats* magazine, September 15, 2005. From *The Journals of Constant Waterman* (Breakaway Books, 2007). Reprinted by permission of the author and Breakaway Books.

Matthew Goldman
2006

Illustration by Matthew Goldman

IN NEED OF A BREEZE

When I was young and quite, quite mad, I took my carvel planked Rhodes 18 from Deep River to South Lyme. Merely fifteen miles. You cruise down the lovely Connecticut River the last few miles to Long Island Sound, go out past the lighthouse at Lynde Neck and follow the channel beside the impressive breakwater down to the second lighthouse—the Jetty Light. Thence you head east, (Did I mention I hadn't a compass?) avoiding Long Sand Shoal, and follow the shore until you round Hatchett Point. A few fierce rocks in a mile wide bay designate this the harbor. You anchor wherever seems likely and take your chances.

Everything went swimmingly from the start. I had the tide behind me as I departed. I hauled up my main and the halyard jammed in the sheave. But the sail had ascended eleven-twelfths of the track, so I made up most of the difference employing the downhaul. Up with the jib, off with the mooring pennant, and away!

Ah, freedom! I was eighteen, invincible, and also perfectly stupid. My first mistake was leaving so late in the day. How long can it take to sail fifteen miles? It wouldn't get dark till nearly eight o'clock. (Did I mention I hadn't a light?) Toward the mouth of the river, the wind turned fluky. My main remained as shapely as a watermelon in a hammock. I headed up and slacked the halyard; yanked on the luff and the main descended a yard. Then I tried to haul it back up.

Wake up, Son—you might just want to undo that downhaul first. This time, it jammed immediately; the halyard had jumped the sheave. Some time, I admonished my clever self, you need to reeve the next size larger line. Now I had more slack than I could possibly take up with just the downhaul. Without a reef point in sight, I decided on the alternative: simply—to climb the mast. I had all the requirements: two hands and two feet. The climbing didn't prove difficult, but the boat heeled over; then heeled over some more and, just as I passed the spreaders, began to welcome the river in over the rail.

So much for that idea. North of the railroad bridge, against the Old Lyme shore, a gas dock juts into the river. Out at the end of it stands a little shack. By this time—half past six—business was done for the day. I moored alongside, climbed the pier and managed to clamber up to the roof of the shack. With me I had brought the recalcitrant halyard.

Now I balanced twenty feet off the water. I pulled on the halyard and the boat rolled toward me until I could grasp the mast. What could be more simple? Then the boat rolled away and nearly twitched me from the ridgepole. Whoopee! Suffice it to say, this little game went on for twenty minutes until I finally managed to clear the sheave.

But the wind had died. (Did I mention I hadn't a motor?) Still, the tide and current would carry me to the Sound. I flopped my way down the channel past both lighthouses; the ebb tide took me eastward toward Hatchett Point. Off I went—no light, no paddle, no motor, no compass, no common sense whatsoever.

A few hours later, drifting at nearly half a knot a couple of miles from shore, I noticed two things: the night, though clear, was also surprisingly dark. Fortunately, the shipping lane lay a mile or two beyond me. Unfortunately, I'd also forgotten to lay in any provisions. My stomach began to complain of cruel neglect.

"Supper!" it cried.

"Shut up," I consoled it. "We've only five miles to go. All we need is a breeze."

Then the tide changed. Very slowly, my little boat drifted back westerly for a second and better view of the Jetty Light. I paid out my fifty feet of rode: it scarcely reached the bottom. Oh, well. Eventually I had to fetch up somewhere. Most of that sleepless, dark, and ravenous night my anchor bounced along the sandy bottom.

By breakfast time (by what time, Mate?!) my hook held fast just off the mouth of the river. Then the tide turned again; the breeze awakened. I rubbed the last bushel of Long Sand Shoal from my blurry eyes, hauled my Danforth and sailed down to South Lyme in only two hours. I anchored out, sloshed the last hundred yards to shore, and squished on up to the village to find some breakfast.

Originally published in *Messing About in Boats* magazine, August 1, 2006. From *The Journals of Constant Waterman* (Breakaway Books, 2007). Reprinted by permission of the author and Breakaway Books.

FROM *ATHLETICS AND MANLY SPORT*
1890

John Boyle O'Reilly

One can see why John Boyle O'Reilly might lean toward the canoe when it came to getting out on the water a bit. He had been most of the way around the world in sailing ships, but the voyages had certainly brought him no pleasure. The first leg of the trip, from Britain to Australia, he made in chains. On the second leg, he was running for his life on a whaling ship headed to the U.S.

He was born in Ireland, and started working as an apprentice for a local newspaper at 13. After a stint in the British army, he returned to Ireland. His family was staunchly Irish nationalist and he joined the Irish Republican Brotherhood, raising a regiment in preparation for an uprising. In 1867 the British authorities became aware of the plans and arrested O'Reilly, among many others. He was sentenced to twenty years of hard labor and transported to Australia.

Most who went there never left. But O'Reilly managed to enlist the help of a

friendly priest, who had him smuggled aboard a whaling ship. After some danger-
ous delays and foul-ups, including a stop in Liverpool, England, he managed to reach
the US in 1869. There he settled in Boston, and again began working for the cause,
becoming involved in a scheme by some fellow Irish expatriates to invade Canada and
snatch it away from the British. It ended in a bloody mess, and O'Reilly swore off
violence. He threw himself into his job as editor of a growing newspaper, The Pilot,
and his writing, which included several books of poetry and a novel. Athletics and
Manly Sport, *which includes several good pieces on canoeing in the U.S., was*
published just before his death in 1890.

DOWN THE SUSQUEHANNA IN A CANOE

This river runs palpably down hill!" said my friend in the other boat,
as our two canoes rounded a sweeping curve, and ran down an unbroken
slope of half a mile.

So it did. Beautiful! That first air-borne sensation of a sheer slide was not
beaten on the next hundred miles of river. The water was not three feet deep;
clear as air—every pebble seen on the bottom, and none larger than your
hand; and the whole wide river slipping and sliding like a great sheet of glass
out of its frame! At the foot of the sloping water was a little rapid, our first
on the Susquehanna, which is even more truly a river of rapids than a river
of bends, though the latter is the meaning of its melodious Indian name.

We had stopped paddling on the "palpable hill," and we let the stream
carry our canoes into the noisy rapid at its foot. Zigzag it crossed the river; and
as I led into a well-defined rushing V, aiming at the angle, I felt the first grumble of a rock along the keel. Next moment we were pitching on sharp little
white-caps below the rush, and scooting down toward the swift, deep water.

We had launched our canoes at Binghamton, J. Smith and I, because
the river above is too low in September. Shame that it should be so! The
beautiful hills above Binghamton, that a few years ago were clothed with
rich foliage for unbroken leagues, are shorn like a stubble-field. The
naked stumps are white and unsightly on the mountains, like the bones
of an old battle-field.

A monster has crept up the valley and devoured the strong young trees.
Every trunk has been swallowed; and the maw of the dragon is belching for
more. On both sides of the river, and through many of the valleys that open

back to the farm-lands, the railroads wind like serpents; and every foot-long joint in their vertebrae is the trunk of a twenty-year-old tree. The hills stand up in the sun, cropped and debased like convicts; their beauty and mystery and shadowed sacredness torn from them; their silence and lone-liness replaced by the selfish chirp of the grasshopper among the dry weeds. Never did the hard utility of civilization appear less disguised and less lovely. An Indian warrior begging on Broadway; a buffalo from the wilds yoked to a market-wagon; any degrading and antagonistic picture of life were more endurable and more hopeful than these majestic ridges stripped and burned into commonplace and repulsive bareness.

But the injured hills, like all old and strong children of nature, curse their destroyer as they die. The railroads have killed the trees, and the death of the trees is as surely killing the river. Year by year its life-blood decreases it grows narrower, shallower, yet more fitfully dangerous. Scores and hundreds of miles it runs, drinking in the volume of the streams; but in all this distance its own volume does not increase.

Marvellous and shocking! The Susquehanna is no deeper at Harrisburg than at Towanda. Its evaporation equals its growth. The shorn hills can hold no moisture. The rain and dew are dried in the morning sun like a breath on a mirror. But when the heavy clouds roll in and rain for weeks, there are no thirsty roots to hold the water, no myriad-leafed miles to be drenched be-fore a rill is formed below. Then the dried veins are suddenly and madly filled, tearing down to the lowlands with unchecked violence. The river, swollen with drunken fury, becomes the brute that civilization is always making—leaping at the bridges, devouring the fields, deluging farm-houses and streets, until its fury is glutted on the blind selfishness that gave it birth.

Pittsburgh riots and Susquehanna devastations are children of the same parents,—Greed and Ignorance. Beautiful trees and beautiful souls, steeped in the coal-pits, scorched by the cinders, thundered over by the roaring wheels that carry treasures to the cultured and luxurious, there is a curse in your defilement and mutilation. Yet our moralists and socialists will not lis-ten and understand.

But who shall be didactic in a canoe on a river that laughs into little rapids every few hundred yards? It was delightful to see Smith take his first rapid. He had only canoed before in still water. A few miles below Bing-hamton we heard the break of the water, and saw the zigzag line ahead.

Not knowing the nature of the thing, whether it was a dam, an "eel-rack," a wood-shoot, or a natural shoal, I paddled ahead, and took a look at it. There was just one place in the line, about three feet wide, where the water rushed down like a sluiceway; and we must go in there. On one side of this passage, a thin spur of black stone rose above the surface, and made a good mark to steer by; but on the other side of the sluice was a great round stone, covered with about six inches of rushing water. I paddled back and asked Smith to observe exactly where my boat entered; and, turning her head, I let her go in "with the swim." It was a delightful little shoot of about fifty yards, and when I had reached the smooth water, I turned to see my friend coming down. He neared the rapids, not letting his boat drift, but paddling with all his force, and moving at tremendous speed down the swift water. He was not heading for the opening, but was coming straight for the big stone at the right side. No use shouting; the din of the water drowned all other sound. I expected to see him strike and swing round, and probably get upset, and rolled over; but instead of that, the bow of his plucky little boat rose at the stone like a steeple-chaser, till I saw half her keel in the air,—and then over she came, without a scratch, and buried her nose in the deep water below the stone, while the canoeist sat straight, laughing with excitement, and dripping with the shower of spray from the plunge.

"How did it feel?" I asked.

"Glorious!" he shouted.

He thought he had come down *secumdum artem*. But before night he knew all about it, for the river was so low that every shallow had an angry brawl. Next day, with a steady hand and cool head, he found the way out for me when I had got into a bad place.

It was in this way: I had gone in first on rather a long and rough descent. There was a bend on the rapid, and in going round I struck heavily and unexpectedly, and swung right athwart the race, amidships fast on a huge brown shelf-rock. The divided water caught bow and stern, and held the canoe against the stone. I got one foot out against the rock and stopped her trembling; and there I was, fast. I could hold her steady, but could do no more. The stone was so shaped that I could not stand on it. The water ran deep and strong, and if I pushed off altogether I should be apt to go down broadside or stern first. So I sat thinking for a second or two; and then I looked back to wave to Smith to keep off. I saw his boat, but not him.

He was swimming, "accoutred as he was," right across the river above, to give me a hand. His judgement had told him that I was badly placed. In a few minutes he had reached the head of the rapid, stepped from stone to stone till he caught hold of my "painter," and next moment my bow came round to the race, and down I shot like a rocket. In a few minutes he followed in the same course.

Just below that rapid we had an unpleasant experience,—the only one on our whole voyage. We fell in with a sordid lout, and up to this day I am sorry we did not thrash him or duck him in the river. We had gone up to a farm-house on the bluff to buy milk and eggs for dinner. Two old women had very kindly served us, and we were coming away when the lout appeared. He was evidently the master of the place: a big, raw-boned, ragged-whiskered, and dirty-skinned brute. He had just caught a snake, about two feet long, and he held it wriggling in his hand, while he laughed a vile chuckle, and opened his filthy mouth in derision as the older woman, his mother, probably, fled, almost screaming with terror. Then he came toward us, and seeing Smith's bare ankles he deliberately put the snake down to bite them, chuckling all the time, and mumbling "You hain't got the sand! He won't bite. *I* ain't afeard. *I've* got the sand. *I* ain't afeard o' snakes," and so on.

We stepped away from him, and at last told him, in a tone he minded, to drop the snake. He did so at once. His mother said to him from the door: "If you did that to me, and I was a man, *I'd kill you!*"

Then the brute insisted on selling us ten cents' worth of honey, which he called "Th' bam'f a thaousand flaours" (balm of a thousand flowers); and, coming to the boat, he begged for a drink, and, at the last moment, wanted us to buy a gallon of "old stock ale, seven year old."

It took us some hours to forget the barbarian. A handsome young trapper, logman, and railroad worker, lower down, who knew him well, told us that the lout was known along the river as a coward, a braggart, and "a man that was no good, anyhow."

The Susquehanna is, in one respect, quite unlike any other river on which I have canoed. There is an endless recurrence of half-mile and mile long deep stretches, and then a brawling rapid. The river rarely makes a bend without shoaling to a foot or two of water; and this is invariably ended by a bar, with a swift descent beyond. These shallow places have been utilized as "eel-racks," by driving stakes or piling stones in a zig-zag line across the river. From Towanda down to Wilkesbarre, with a bold, wooded hill, or "mountain," always on one side, and sometimes on both, the deep stretches become deeper and longer but in a very few places is the "slow water" more than two or three miles in length.

We had brought a small tent with us, and we carried some provisions, prepared coffee, Liebig's extract of beef, a jar of delicious butter (which we broke and lost on the third day), a can of corned beef, some "hard tack," and some bacon. We had tin cups, a little alcohol stove, and a bottle of very old Jamaica (for the malaria).

We had two canoes of the "Shadow" model, Mr. Smith's, a Rushton, decked and hatched; mine without hatches, and built by Partelow, of Riverside, Mass.,—both good boats of their kind, from good builders. But the "Shadow" is not a good kind of canoe for river work. Her keel is too long and too deep. This makes her heavy in turning sharp curves; and, when she runs on a stone,—even a round or flat one,—the keel throws her on one side; and this is really a canoe's unpardonable sin. A canoe should have no keel. The "Shadow" model is really not a canoe at all, but simply a light boat.

The Indian round-bottomed, birch-bark canoe is the best model for American rivers; and it is a pity that our builders do not keep it as their radical study. It should be modified and improved, of course; narrowed for double paddling, and shortened and lightened for portage but its first principle, of a bottom that can run on or over a stone without capsizing, ought never to be forgotten. In my opinion, paper will win against lapstrake in the canoe of the future; all that is needed to insure this is a method of patching the wound on a paper bottom.

Never have I seen river-water so clear and wholesome as the Susquehanna. One of our daily pleasures was to dip our bright tin cups into the river, drink a mouthful, and pour the rest into our mouths without swallowing.

The sun flamed on the water every day of our trip; the records ashore made it the hottest fortnight of the year. So we lovingly hugged the banks when there was any shade; and, unexpectedly, this habit led us into the two greatest pleasures of our voyage.

The first occurred a few miles above the village of Appalaken. We left the main river to run to the left of an island, where the stream was only twenty feet wide. The island was perhaps three-quarters of a mile long, and the trees on both sides reached over, interlaced, and made the stream as dark as late evening. There was a turbulent little rapid at the entrance, as we swung in from the big river and the noonday blaze; and the water all down the narrow stream ran with incredible rapidity. When we felt ourselves carried along in this silent cool shadow, and looked up at the light sifting through the dense foliage, we both exclaimed, "This is too lovely to be repeated!" And the word was true. Such a superlative canoe-ride one could hardly ever expect to enjoy twice. We laid down our paddles, only fearing to come to the end of our marvellous green archway, with its dark gleaming floor; and when, at last, we did sweep out into the broad glare of the river, we sighed and looked back wistfully, as men will. Ten minutes later we were wading over a shallow place and hauling our canoes by the painter.

The other peak of our enjoyment was reached about four miles below the town of Athens. Ah, me! how we did enjoy our evening in that little town! But let the tale bide a little. We had gone down some miles below the bridge at Athens, where the river widened out and grew consumedly slow and commonplace. There was an island, with a narrow opening to the left and a rough little rapid at the entrance,—almost a repetition of the Appalaken archway. After that other experience we did not hesitate, but turned from the big sheet of water, and shot into the narrow turmoil, to the left of the island. Again we dashed into a splendid sweep, but about three times as wide as the Appalaken archway. The water was about four feet deep all the way down, and the bottom was of small pebbles, every one as clearly seen as if laid on a mirror. Once more our paddles were crossed before us, and we sat in profound enjoyment of water, wood, and sky, as we were swept along by the current. Half-way down, we landed on the island, intending to float in the water and be carried down after the canoes, holding on by the "painter."

And here we made a discovery that will redound to the fame of Athens,—a discovery which we present to that town in memory of the genial hospitality of one of its chief citizens, the Rev. Father Costello, who gave us an evening not to be forgotten. Here let me tell how, baked and burned and tired and hungry and thirsty, on the night preceding our discovery, we walked up to the house of the good priest at sunset, and were met at the open door with outstretched hands of welcome; and how, before a word was spoken, we were handed two great goblets filled with iced wine,—rich, fruity, American wine; and how we sat down to a dinner for epicures, even if it were Friday; and how we then were taken into the little moonlit garden, with good cigars, and other comforts, while our amiable and accomplished host charmed us with quaint fancy and strange learning, and played for us on the flute so softly that it could not be heard fifty feet away, but so exquisitely that we knew we were listening to the soul of a poet and a master; and how simply and tenderly he told us that he had discovered a similarity between his little Athens in the Pennsylvania hills and the immortal Athens of the Acropolis.

"Look around," cried Father Costello, pointing to the perfect circle of bold mountains, that were blue even in the moonlight, "those hills are a perfect coronet. This, too, is the City of the Violet Crown!"

Now for our discovery: we give it to Athens with only one condition,— that henceforth the citizen who shall call his town *Aythens* shall be disfranchised or excluded from good society, or both.

Half-way down between the island and the shore we plunged into the swift current, intending to float after the canoes, holding on by the painter,—a most enjoyable and interesting thing to do. When you lie at utter rest in the water and watch the shore go by, it seems too delicious for waking life; but this is not the best. Let your whole body and head sink well under the surface, keeping your eyes open; the river becomes an aquarium,—you see the weeds, the stones, and the fishes as clearly almost as if they were in the air. This is because you have no motion except the motion of the water itself; your eyes are fixed in a crystalline medium, and nothing can express the sense of ease, of utter luxury, which the supporting fluid gives to every limb. You are lolling on or in an air-cushion without surface or friction. The mere swimmer can never feel this, nor even he who is towed after a boat,—though that is an ideal method of taking an invigorating bath. To see the river's inner life, and to enjoy this complete luxury of resting in the water, you must float in and with the stream, without effort or motion, supported by the painter of your boat.

But our discovery waits: half-way down this lovely and lonely island passage we plunged in, as I have many times said; and we had no sooner struck bottom than Smith uttered a strange shout and threw up his hands. I was startled till I looked at his face; and then I was puzzled beyond measure by his motions and expressions. With his hands above his head, he seemed to be dancing on the bottom of the river, and with every step he gave a shout of pleasure. While I looked at him, astonished, I began to feel the infection of his strange conduct. A thrill like soft music ran through me, and seemed to tingle in my ears and under my tongue; and every movement I made brought a repetition of the inexpressible sound, for a sound it was, like a musical echo.

"What is it?" I cried at length. "This is wonderful!"

"It is a musical beach,—a singing beach!" he answered. "And I should say it was the finest in the world!" And then he said, for by strange chance he knew something about such a queer thing, "I believe there are only two or three 'singing beaches' known in the whole world; and this certainly must be the best."

You may be sure we lingered over that mellifluous swim. We pushed the boats ashore, and went in for the weird, sweet music of the stream. It was enough to make one howl with sheer sensuous enjoyment. As we pushed or scraped the pebbly bottom with our feet we felt or heard, I hardly know which, a rich resonance passing through us, clear and sweet as the soft note of distant cow-bells. The slightest displacement of the gravel brought it up, as if it had just escaped from the earth.

When we had tried it a hundred and a thousand times, it occurred to us that neither could hear the note caused by the other,—we only heard the sound of our own feet. Again the tenacious memory of my friend found an explanation. He remembered that divers can only talk under water by placing their heads on the bottom.

Another discovery here: you can't get your head to the bottom of a four-foot stream, unless you catch hold of a stone on the bottom and pull yourself down. You can dive, and get your hands or feet or knees down; but not your chin. We are both good swimmers, and we tried in vain. While under water, on the dive, or crawling along the bottom on hands and knees, the river was a drear and silent sluice. At last we got our chins on the bottom, each on a stone, and we heard it,—oh! we heard such melodious discord, such a mixture of near and remote echo-like sweetness as can only be imagined in dreams. The river became as full of music as it was of water, and the inexpressible fusion of notes played through our senses like intoxication. Smith was twenty or thirty feet from me, and in deeper water; but every sweep he gave the pebbles sounded to me like a thousand cow-bells melted into liquid harmony. Never, until we go to the same spot again, shall we hear such strange, suppressed, elfin music.

FROM

A WOMAN'S WAY THROUGH UNKNOWN LABRADOR

AN ACCOUNT OF THE EXPLORATION OF THE NASCAUPEE AND GEORGE RIVERS

1908

Mrs. Leonidas Hubbard, Junior

Dillon Wallace and George Elson drag their canoe up through some rapids on Susan Brook on July 18, 1903. The photo taken by Mina Hubbard's husband, Leonidas, on his ill-fated expedition.

In July 1903, two explorers from New York, Leonidas Hubbard and Dillon Wallace, arrived in North West River, Labrador. They planned to travel by canoe up the Naskaupi River to Lake Michikamau and then down the George River to witness the Naskaupi tribe's annual caribou hunt. At the time, except for the mouths of the rivers, the area was known only to a few trappers and the Native American tribes that lived there. On maps, it was a large blank space that Hubbard hoped to fill. They hired George Elson, a Scots-Cree trapper, as a guide in North West River. The tiny expedition set off, but an error on the map they used for the first leg of the trip took them up the wrong river. After several months of unremitting toil, endless portages, and plagues of biting insects, they found themselves on the edge of starvation, with winter closing in on the highlands, and very little idea where they were.

Elson made it out of the bush, stumbling across a trapper's cabin after a grueling trek. Help arrived just in time for Wallace, frostbitten and on the edge of death. But it came a week too late for Hubbard. He had spent his last hours writing a letter to his wife, and a final entry in his journal describing the last few days, and his decision to send Elson and Wallace ahead to find help.

Hubbard's wife, Mina, was hit hard by his death. Incredibly, despite having made only a few very casual camping trips with her husband, she decided to go to Labrador and make the trip herself. One might have thought Elson would have had enough of taking greenhorn New Yorkers into terra incognita. But incredibly, he agreed to guide her. In 1905 Mrs. Leonidas Hubbard, Junior, as she called herself, traveled to North West River, and with Elson and three other guides traveled through the heart of Labrador.

EQUIPMENT AND PROVISIONS FOR THE EXPEDITION

There were two canoes, canvas covered and 19 feet long, 13 inches deep, 34 inches wide, and with each of them three paddles and a sponge. The remainder of the outfit consisted of 2 balloon-silk tents, 1 stove, 7 waterproof canvas bags, one dozen 10 lbs. waterproof balloon-silk bags, 3 tarpaulins, 392 lbs. of flour, 4 lbs. baking powder, 15 lbs. rice, 20 cans standard emergency rations, 12 lbs. tea, 12 lbs. chocolate, 60 lbs. sugar, 20 lbs. erbswurst, 1 oz. crystalose, 4 cans condensed milk, 4 cans condensed soup, 5 lbs. hard tack, 200 lbs. bacon, 14 lbs. salt. There were kitchen utensils—3 small axes, 1 crooked knife, and 2 nets. The outfit of firearms consisted of two rifles, a 45-70 with 60 rounds of ammunition, and a 38-55 with 100 rounds. Each of the men had a 22 cal. 10-inch barrel, single-shot pistol for partridges and other small game. Each also carried a hunting knife, a pair of light wool camp blankets, and an extra pair of "shoe-packs."

For myself, I had a revolver, a hunting knife, and some fishing tackle; one three and a quarter by four and a quarter folding pocket kodak, one panorama kodak, a sextant and artificial horizon, a barometer, a thermometer. I wore a short skirt over knickerbockers, a short sweater, and a belt to which were attached my cartridge pouch, revolver, and hunting knife. My hat was a rather narrow brimmed soft felt. I had one pair of heavy leather moccasins reaching almost to my knees, one pair of high seal-skin boots, one pair low ones, which M. Duclos had given me, and three pairs of duffel. Of underwear I had four suits and five pairs of stockings, all wool. I took also a rubber automobile shirt, a long, Swedish dog-skin coat, one pair leather gloves, one pair woollen gloves, and a blouse—for Sundays. For my tent I had an air mattress, crib size, one pair light grey camp blankets, one light wool comfortable, weighing 3 1/2 lbs., one little feather pillow, and a hotwater bottle.

STORM-BOUND ON MICHIKAMATS

We had not reached our haven too soon. Almost immediately the wind rose again, and by noon was blowing so strong that we could have done nothing in any part of Lake Michikamau, not to speak of crossing the upper end in a heavy south wind. Around the point I did not find things look as

I expected. It was only a very shallow bay, and where we looked for the islands a long, narrow point of land stretched out from the west shore to the northeast. Flowing round the eastern end of this point was a rapid, some two hundred yards in length, and at the head of this we found a little lake, between two and three miles in length, lying northeast and southwest. All the eastern portion of it was shallow, and it was with considerable difficulty we succeeded in getting the canoes up to the low shore, where we had lunch. I wondered much if this could possibly be Michikamats, which is mapped in, in dotted lines, as a lake twenty-five miles long lying northwest.

In the afternoon my perplexities were cleared up. A small river, coming down from the northwest, flowed in at the east end of the lake. Three-quarters of a mile of poling, dragging, and lifting brought us up to another lake, and this proved to be Lake Michikamats. For half a mile or more at its lower end the lake is narrow and shoal. Its bed is a mass of jagged rocks, many of which rise so near to the surface that it was a work of art to find a way among them. A low point ran out north on our left, and from this point to the eastern shore stretched a long line of boulders rising at intervals from the water. This line marks the edge of the shallows, and beyond it the lake is deep and broad and stretches away northeast for more than eight miles of its length, when it bends to the northwest.

As we entered it we saw that the low range of wooded hills on our left formed the western boundary of the lake, and over the flat wooded shore on the right we could see the tops of big, barren hills of a range stretching northward. These are a continuation of the round-topped hills which border the east shore of Michikamau south of where the lake narrows. For some miles of our journey up northern Michikamau we could see these hills miles back from the low shoreline. Now we seemed to be turning towards them again. Beyond a point one mile and a quarter north from where we entered the lake a deep bay runs in to the east, and here the hills came into plain view though they were still far back from the shore. Their rounded tops were covered with moss, and low down on the sides dark patches showed where the green woods were.

It was a glorious afternoon, and the canoes scudded at racing pace before a heavy south wind. At a point on the east shore, six miles up the lake, I landed to take bearings. Here we found a peculiar mound of rocks along the edge of the water which proved to be characteristic of the whole shoreline

of the lake. The rocks had been pushed out by the ice and formed a sort of wall, while over the wall moss and willows grew, with here and there a few stunted evergreens, the whole making an effective screen along the water's edge. Back of this were swamps and bogs with low moss-covered mounds running through them, and grown up with scattered tamarack and spruces. On the west shore the hills reached quite to the wall itself.

Behind this wall, at the point, we found a family of ptarmigan. When we appeared the mother bird tried vainly to hurry her flock away to a place of safety. Her mate flew across to an island a short distance north, leaving her alone to her task, but she and her little ones were all taken. Here the first wolf tracks we had seen on the trip were found.

After some time spent at the point it was time to camp. We crossed to the island, north, and as we landed a white-winged ptarmigan flew back to where had just been enacted one of the endless succession of wilderness tragedies. I wondered if he would not wish he had stayed to share the fate of his little family, and what he would do with himself now. It was a beautiful camping place we found. The Indians had found it too, and evidently had appreciated its beauty. There were the remains of many old camps there, well-worn paths leading from one to the other. It was the first place we had come upon which gave evidence of having been an abiding Place of some permanence. There must have been quite a little community there at one time. The prospect south, west, and north was very beautiful.

My tent was pitched in a charming nook among the spruce trees, and had a carpet of boughs all tipped with fresh green. The moss itself was almost too beautiful to cover; but nothing is quite so nice for carpet as the boughs. We were on a tiny ridge sloping to the south shore of the island, and over the screen of willows and evergreens at the water's edge, the wind came in strong enough to drive away the flies and mosquitoes, and leave one free to enjoy the beauty of the outlook. It was an ideal place to spend Sunday, and with a sigh of relief we settled into our island camp. The week had been a wonderfully interesting one; but it had also been an anxious and trying one in a few ways. I was glad to have passed Michikamau so quickly and easily. I wished it might be our good fortune to see some of the Indians.

Through the night the south wind rose to a gale, and showers of rain fell. On Sunday morning I was up at 7 A.M., and after a nice, lazy bath, luxuriously dressed myself in clean clothes. Then came a little reading from a tiny book that had been in Labrador before, and a good deal of thinking. Just after 9 A.M. I lay down to go to sleep again. I had not realised it before, but I was very tired. My eyes had closed but a moment when rat-a-tat-tat on the mixing pan announced breakfast. Joe had prepared it, and the others came straggling out one by one looking sleepy and happy, enjoying the thought of the day's rest, the more that it was the kind of day to make it impossible to travel. Returning to my tent after the meal I lay down to sleep. My head had no sooner touched the pillow than I was asleep, and did not wake till 1.30 P.M.

I could hear Gil outside preparing lunch, and went out to see how he was getting on. It was the first time he had attempted anything in the cooking line, and he looked anxious. We were to have fried cakes and tea, and Gil was cooking the fried cakes. They were not much to look at, for the wind had coated them well with ashes; but they tasted good, and the youngster looked quite relieved at the way they disappeared when we began to eat.

Michikamats was certainly very picturesque in the gale. The wind had six miles of unbroken sweep, and stirred the lake to wild commotion. Out of shelter I could scarcely stand against it. For a long time I watched two gulls trying to fly into the wind. They were very persistent and made a determined fight, but were at last compelled to give up and drop back to land. I spent nearly the whole afternoon watching the storm, running to cover only while the showers passed.

When we gathered for supper in the evening Job was holding a pot over the fire, and did not move to get his plate and cup with the rest. George gave me my plate of soup, and when I had nearly finished it Job set the pot down beside me, saying gently: "I just set this right here." In the pot were three fried cakes, crisp and hot and brown, exactly as I liked them.

There was much speculation as to what we should find at the head of Lake Michikamats, and I wondered how much scouting there would be to do to find the George River waters. If only we could see the Indians. Time was slipping away all too fast; the last week in August was not far distant, and the George River waters might not be easy to find. The days were becoming increasingly anxious for me. Our caribou meat was nearly gone, and a fresh supply of game would have been very welcome. There would be a chance to put out the nets when we reached the head of the lake, and the scouting had to be done. The nets had not yet touched the water.

In the night the wind veered to the north and a steady rain set in, which was still falling when morning came. All were up late for it was too stormy to travel, and rest still seemed very good. While eating breakfast we heard geese calling not far away, and started on a goose hunt. It did not prove very exciting, nor very fruitful of geese. They were at the head of the bay which ran in east of our island. There were a number of small islands in the bay separated by rock-strewn shallows, and having landed Job and Joe on one of the largest of these, George, Gilbert and I paddled round to the south of the group, and came out in the upper part of the bay. There just over the marsh grass at its head we saw five geese, but they saw us too, and before we could get near them were up and away. On the way back four red-throated loons, two old and two young, and a spruce partridge were taken.

It was nearly noon when we reached camp again, and the men were in the midst of preparing dinner when they caught sight of a big caribou stag swimming across to the point south of us. In such circumstances Job was indescribable. He seemed as if suddenly inspired with the energy of a flying bullet, and moved almost as silently. There was a spring for the canoe, and in much less time than it takes to tell it, the canoe was in the water with Job, Gilbert, and George plying their paddles with all their strength.

As had happened before, the splendid creature almost reached the shore when a bullet dropped in front of him, and he turned back. His efforts were now no match for the swift paddle strokes that sent the canoe lightly towards him, and soon a shot from George's rifle ended the struggle. He was towed ashore, bled and gralloched, and brought to camp in the canoe.

Most of the afternoon was spent in cutting up the caribou, and putting it on a stage to dry. While they were busy with their task there came again the sound of the wild goose call. Seizing the rifles, George and Gilbert made off across the island, and soon came back with two young geese, and word that there was another there but too far out in the water for them to get it. Whereupon Job and Joe went off in the canoe, and after a short time came back with a third. This made a pretty good day's hunt. George's record was, one spruce partridge, two young geese, and one caribou.

We had young wild goose for supper that night. I think I never have tasted anything more delicious, and with hot fried cakes it made a supper fit for a king. As we ate the men talked about the calls of the wild birds.

George said: "I do like to hear a wild goose call." Certainly no one who heard him say it would doubt his word. After a little he continued: "There is another bird, too, that the Indians call 'ah-ha-way,' that I used to like so much to listen to when I was a boy. How I used to listen to that bird call. I tell you if you heard that bird call you could just sit and listen and listen. I don't know the English name for it. It is a very small duck, just a very little bird."

Speaking of the loons we had heard calling on Lake Michikamau he said: "You should hear some of the little Indian boys calling the loons. Men's voices are too strong and rough, but some of those little boys, they can do it very well. You will just see the loons come and circle round and round over them when they call."

All day long the rain had fallen steadily. I spent most of it in my tent, but the men had been out the whole day and were soaked. Having done their washing on Sunday they had no dry clothes to put on, and so slept wet that night.

THE MIGRATING CARIBOU

Tuesday morning, August 8th, dawned clear and calm, and Gilbert came forth to light the fire, singing: "Glory, glory, hallelujah! as we go marching along." Yet before the tents were taken down the wind had sprung up from the southwest, and it was with difficulty that the canoes were launched and loaded.

A short distance above our starting-point, we were obliged to run into a sheltered bay, where part of the load was put ashore, and with the canoes thus lightened we crossed to a long, narrow point which reached half-way across from the other side, making an excellent breakwater between the upper and lower parts of the lake. The crossing was accomplished in safety, though it was rough enough to be interesting, and Job and Joe went back for what had been left behind.

The point terminated in a low, pebbly beach, but its banks farther up were ten to twelve feet high, and above it was covered with reindeer moss. Towards the outer end there were thickets of dwarf spruce, and throughout its length scattered trees that had bravely held their heads up in spite of the storms of the dread northern winter. To the south of the point was a beautiful little bay, and at its head a high sand mound which we found to be an Indian burying-place. There were four graves, one large one with three little ones at its foot, each surrounded by a neatly made paling, while a wooden cross, bearing an inscription in Montagnais, was planted at the head of each moss-covered mound. The inscriptions were worn and old except that on one of the little graves. Here the cross was a new one, and the palings freshly made. Some distance out on the point stood a skeleton wigwam carpeted with boughs that were still green, and lying about outside were the fresh cut shavings telling where the Indian had fashioned the new cross and the enclosure about the grave of his little one. Back of this solitary resting-place were the moss-covered hills with their sombre forests, and as we turned from them we looked out over the bay at our feet, the shining waters of the lake, and beyond it to the blue, round-topped hills reaching upward to blend with exquisite harmony into the blue and silver of the great dome that stooped to meet them. Who could doubt that romance and poetry dwell in the heart of the Indian who chose this for the resting-place of his dead.

Walking back along the point we found it cut by caribou trails, and everywhere the moss was torn and trampled in a way that indicated the presence there of many of the animals but a short time since. Yet it did not occur to me that we might possibly be on the outskirts of the march of the migrating caribou. Ptarmigan were there in numbers, and flew up all along our way. We passed a number of old camps, one a large oblong, sixteen feet in length, with two fireplaces in it, each marked by a ring of small rocks, and a doorway at either end. Near where we landed, close in the shelter of a thicket of dwarf spruce, was a deep bed of boughs, still green, where some wandering aboriginal had spent the night without taking time or trouble to erect his wigwam, and who in passing on had set up three poles pointing northward to tell his message to whoever might come after.

The wind continued high, and squalls and heavy showers passed. Nevertheless, when lunch was over we pushed on, keeping close to the west shore of the lake. Little more than a mile further up the men caught sight of deer feeding not far from the water's edge. We landed, and climbing to the top of the rock wall saw a herd of fifteen or more feeding in the swamp. I watched them almost breathless. They were very beautiful, and it was an altogether new and delightful experience to me. Soon they saw us and trotted off into the bush, though without sign of any great alarm. George and Job made off across the swamp to the right to investigate, and not long after returned, their eyes blazing with excitement, to say that there were hundreds of them not far away.

Slipping hurriedly back into the canoes we paddled rapidly and silently to near the edge of the swamp. Beyond it was a barren hill, which from near its foot sloped more gradually to the water. Along the bank, where this lower slope dropped to the swamp, lay a number of stags, with antlers so immense that I wondered how they could possibly carry them. Beyond, the lower slope of the hill seemed to be a solid mass of caribou, while its steeper part was dotted over with many feeding on the luxuriant moss.

Those lying along the bank got up at sight of us, and withdrew towards the great herd in rather leisurely manner, stopping now and then to watch us curiously. When the herd was reached, and the alarm given, the stags lined themselves up in the front rank and stood facing us, with heads high and a rather defiant air. It was a magnificent sight. They were in summer garb of pretty brown, shading to light grey and white on the under parts. The horns were in velvet, and those of the stags seemed as if they must surely weigh down the heads on which they rested. It was a mixed company, for male and female were already herding together. I started towards the herd, kodak in hand, accompanied by George, while the others remained at the shore. The splendid creatures seemed to grow taller as we approached, and when we were within two hundred and fifty yards of them their defiance took definite form, and with determined step they came towards us.

The sight of that advancing army under such leadership, was decidedly impressive, recalling vivid mental pictures made by tales of the stampeding wild cattle in the west. It made one feel like getting back to the canoe, and that is what we did. As we ran towards the other men I noticed a peculiar smile on their faces, which had in it a touch of superiority. I understood in part when I turned, for the caribou had stopped their advance, and were again standing watching us. Now the others started towards the herd. Emboldened by their courage, and thinking that perhaps they held the charm that would make a close approach to the herd possible, I accompanied them. Strange to relate it was but a few minutes till we were all getting back to the canoes, and we did not again attempt to brave their battle front. We and the caribou stood watching each other for some time. Then the caribou began to run from either extreme of the herd, some round the south end of the hill, and the others away to the north, the line of stags still maintaining their position.

After watching them for some time we again entered the canoes. A short paddle carried us round the point beyond which the lake bent to the northwest, and there we saw them swimming across the lake. Three-quarters of a mile out was an island, a barren ridge standing out of the water, and from mainland to island they formed as they swam a broad unbroken bridge; from the farther end of which they poured in steady stream over the hill-top, their flying forms clearly outlined against the sky. How long we watched them I could not say, for I was too excited to take any note of time; but finally the main body had passed.

Yet when we landed above the point from which they had crossed, companies of them, eight, ten, fifteen, twenty in a herd, were to be seen in all directions. When I reached the top of the ridge accompanied by George and Gilbert, Job and Joe were already out on the next hill beyond, and Job was driving one band of a dozen or more toward the water at the foot of the hill, where some had just plunged in to swim across. Eager to secure a photo or two at closer range than any I had yet obtained, I handed George my kodak and started down the hill at a pace which threatened every second to be too fast for my feet, which were not dressed in the most appropriate running wear. However the foot of the hill was reached in safety. There a bog lay across our way. I succeeded in keeping dry for a few steps, then gave it up and splashed through at top speed. We had just hidden ourselves behind a huge boulder to wait for the coming of the herd, when turning round I saw it upon the hill from which we had just come. While exclaiming over my disappointment I was startled by a sound immediately behind me, and turning saw a splendid stag and three does not twenty feet away. They saw us and turned, and I had scarcely caught my breath after the surprise when they were many more than twenty feet away, and there was barely time to snap my shutter on them before they disappeared over the brow of the hill.

The country was literally alive with the beautiful creatures, and they did not seem to be much frightened. The apparently wanted only to keep what seemed to them a safe distance between us, and would stop to watch us curiously within easy rifle shot. Yet I am glad I can record that not a shot was fired at them. Gilbert was wild, for he had in him the hunter's instinct in fullest measure. The trigger of Job's rifle clicked longingly, but they never forgot that starvation broods over Labrador, and that the animal they longed to shoot might some time save the life of one in just such extremity as that reached by Mr. Hubbard and his party two years before.

The enjoyment of the men showed itself in the kindling eyes and faces luminous with pleasure. All his long wilderness experience had never afforded Job anything to compare with that which this day had brought him. He was like a boy in his abandon of delight, and I am sure that if the caribou had worn tails we should have seen Job running over the hills holding fast to one of them.

Before proceeding farther we re-ascended the hill which we first climbed to take a look at the lake. It could be seen almost from end to end. The lower part which we had passed was clear, but above us the lake was a network of islands and water. The hills on either side seemed to taper off to nothing in the north, and I could see where the land appeared to drop away beyond this northern horizon which looked too near to be natural. North of Michikamats were more smaller lakes, and George showed me our probable route to look for "my river". Squalls and showers had been passing all the afternoon, and as it drew towards evening fragments of rainbow could be seen out on the lake or far away on the hills beyond it. Labrador is a land of rainbows and rainbow colours, and nowhere have I ever seen them so brilliant, so frequent and so variedly manifested. Now the most brilliant one of all appeared close to us, its end resting directly on a rock near the foot of the hill. George never knew before that there is a pot of gold at the end of the rainbow. I suspect he does not believe it yet for I could not persuade him to run to get it. Gilbert, more credulous, made a determined attempt to secure the treasure, but before he reached the rock the rainbow had moved off and carried the gold to the middle of the lake.

Camp was made a little farther up. When it was ready for the night Job and Joe were again off to watch the caribou. They were feeding on the hills and swimming back and forth from islands to mainland, now in companies, now a single caribou. Job was so near one as he came out of the water that he could have caught him by the horns. Now and then a distant shout told that Job and the caribou had come to close quarters.

While George and Gilbert prepared supper, I sat writing in my diary with feet stretched to the fire, for I was wet and it was cold that night. Suddenly I was startled to hear George exclaim in tragic tones: "Oh! look there! Isn't that too bad!"

Looking up quickly to see what was the trouble I saw him gazing regretfully at a salt shaker which he had just drawn from his pocket.

"Just see," he exclaimed, "what I've been carrying round in my pocket all the time you were running after those caribou, and never thought about it at all. Well, I am sorry for that. I could just have given you a bit and you would have been all right."

For fifty miles of our journey beyond this point we saw companies of the caribou every day, and sometimes many times a day, though we did not again see them in such numbers. The country was a network of their trails, in the woodlands and bogs cut deep into the soft soil, on the barren hillsides broad, dark bands converging to the crossing place at the river.

FROM *TRAVELS IN ALASKA*

1915

John Muir

Muir spent the last months of his life at work on Travels in Alaska. *Working from entries in his journals compiled over a number of trips to the territory, the book in many ways sums up the major themes of his life's work. It is a study of the geologic effects of glaciers, and a fascinating record of the people and places he traveled. Muir was one of the most popular writers of his time. He had a deft hand for sketching in prose the people and places he encountered, and was also an important early contributor to the study of glaciers and their effect on geology. But perhaps the most enduring portion of his work was his tireless environmental advocacy. He was almost single-handedly responsible for the creation of Yosemite National Park, and worked, with some success, to protect other areas.*

One of the best stories that pops up when reading about Muir is the time he went camping with then-President Theodore Roosevelt.

When I first visited California, it was my good fortune to see the "big trees," the Sequoias, and then to travel down into the Yosemite, with John Muir. Of course of all people in the world he was the one with whom it was best worth while thus to see the Yosemite. . . .

John Muir met me with a couple of packers and two mules to carry our tent, bedding, and food for a three days' trip. The first night was clear, and we lay down in the darkening aisles of the great Sequoia grove. The majestic trunks, beautiful in color and in symmetry, rose round us like the pillars of a mightier cathedral than ever was conceived even by the fervor of the Middle Ages. Hermit thrushes sang beautifully in the evening, and again, with a burst of wonderful music, at dawn. . . . The second night we camped in a snow-storm, on the edge of the cañon walls, under the spreading limbs of a grove of mighty silver fir; and next day we went down into the wonderland of the valley itself. I shall always be glad that I was in the Yosemite with John Muir. . . . —Theodore Roosevelt

Muir and Roosevelt spent a couple of days wandering Yosemite, hiking and camping under the stars, accompanied only by a cook and a packer. Think of that, a sitting U.S. president scrambling up and down cliffs and sleeping rough under the stars in the snow with a couple of locally hired hands and a wild-eyed environmentalist writer, of all people. No Secret Service, no briefcase, no helicopter support. Unbelievable . . .

"Auroras," an account of a hair-raising solo canoe trip and an evening spent watching the aurora borealis, turned out to be the last thing Muir ever wrote for publication.

AURORAS

A few days later I set out with Professor Reid's party to visit some of the other large glaciers that flow into the bay, to observe what changes have taken place in them since October, 1879, when I first visited and sketched them. We found the upper half of the bay closely choked with bergs, through which it was exceedingly difficult to force a way. After slowly struggling a few miles up the east side, we dragged the whale-boat and canoe over rough rocks into a fine garden and comfortably camped for the night.

The next day was spent in cautiously picking a way across to the west side of the bay; and as the strangely scanty stock of provisions was already about done, and the ice-jam to the northward seemed impenetrable, the party decided to return to the main camp by a comparatively open, roundabout way to the southward, while with the canoe and a handful of food-scraps I pushed on northward. After a hard, anxious struggle, I reached the mouth of the Hugh Miller fiord about sundown, and tried to find a camp-spot on its steep, boulder-bound shore. But no landing-place where it seemed possible to drag the canoe above high-tide mark was discovered after examining a mile or more of this dreary, forbidding barrier, and as night was closing down, I decided to try to grope my way across the mouth of the fiord in the starlight to an open sandy spot on which I had camped in October, 1879, a distance of about three or four miles.

With the utmost caution I picked my way through the sparkling bergs, and after an hour or two of this nerve-trying work, when I was perhaps less than halfway across and dreading the loss of the frail canoe which would include the loss of myself, I came to a pack of very large bergs which loomed threateningly, offering no visible thoroughfare. Paddling and pushing to right and left, I at last discovered a sheer-walled opening about four feet wide and perhaps two hundred feet long, formed apparently by the splitting of a huge iceberg. I hesitated to enter this passage, fearing that the slightest change in the tide-current might close it, but ventured nevertheless, judging that the dangers ahead might not be greater than those I had already passed. When I had got about a third of the way in, I suddenly discovered that the smooth-walled ice-lane was growing narrower, and with desperate haste backed out. Just as the bow of the canoe cleared the sheer walls they came together with a growling crunch. Terror-stricken, I turned back, and in an anxious hour or two gladly reached the rock-bound shore that had at first repelled me, determined to stay on guard all night in the canoe or find some place where with the strength that comes in a fight for life I could drag it up the boulder wall beyond ice danger. This at last was happily done about midnight, and with no thought of sleep I went to bed rejoicing.

My bed was two boulders, and as I lay wedged and bent on their up-bulging sides, beguiling the hard, cold time in gazing into the starry sky and across the sparkling bay, magnificent upright bars of light in bright prismatic colors suddenly appeared, marching swiftly in close succession along the northern horizon from west to east as if in diligent haste, an auroral display very different from any I had ever before beheld. Once long ago in Wisconsin I saw the heavens draped in rich purple auroral clouds fringed and folded in most magnificent forms; but in this glory of light, so pure, so bright, so enthusiastic in motion, there was nothing in the least cloud-like. The short color-bars, apparently about two degrees in height, though blending, seemed to be as well defined as those of the solar spectrum.

How long these glad, eager soldiers of light held on their way I cannot tell; for sense of time was charmed out of mind and the blessed night circled away in measureless rejoicing enthusiasm. In the early morning after so inspiring a night I launched my canoe feeling able for anything, crossed the mouth of the Hugh Miller fiord, and forced a way three or four miles along the shore of the bay, hoping to reach the Grand Pacific Glacier in front of Mt. Fairweather. But the farther I went, the ice-pack, instead of showing inviting little open streaks here and there, became so much harder jammed that on some parts of the shore the bergs, drifting south with the tide, were shoving one another out of the water beyond high-tide line. Farther progress to northward was thus rigidly stopped, and now I had to fight for a way back to my cabin, hoping that by good tide luck I might reach it before dark. But at sundown I was less than half-way home, and though very hungry was glad to land on a little rock island with a smooth beach for the canoe and a thicket of alder bushes for fire and bed and a little sleep. But shortly after sundown, while these arrangements were being made, lo and behold another aurora enriching the heavens! and though it proved to be one of the ordinary almost colorless kind, thrusting long, quivering lances toward the zenith from a dark cloudlike base, after last night's wonderful display one's expectations might well be extravagant and I lay wide awake watching. On the third night I reached my cabin and food. Professor Reid and his party came in to talk over the results of our excursions, and just as the last one of the visitors opened the door after bidding good-night, he shouted, "Muir, come look here. Here's something fine."

I ran out in auroral excitement, and sure enough here was another aurora, as novel and wonderful as the marching rainbow-colored columns— a glowing silver bow spanning the Muir Inlet in a magnificent arch right under the zenith, or a little to the south of it, the ends resting on the top of the mountain-walls. And though colorless and steadfast, its intense, solid, white splendor, noble proportions, and fineness of finish excited boundless admiration. In form and proportion it was like a rainbow, a bridge of one span five miles wide; and so brilliant, so fine and solid and homogeneous in every part, I fancy that if all the stars were raked together into one windrow, fused and welded and run through some celestial rolling-mill, all would be required to make this one glowing white colossal bridge.

After my last visitor went to bed, I lay down on the moraine in front of the cabin and gazed and watched. Hour after hour the wonderful arch stood perfectly motionless, sharply defined and substantial-looking as if it were a permanent addition to the furniture of the sky. At length while it yet spanned the inlet in serene unchanging splendor, a band of fluffy, pale gray, quivering ringlets came suddenly all in a row over the eastern mountain-top, glided in nervous haste up and down the under side of the bow and over the western mountain-wall. They were about one and a half times the apparent diameter of the bow in length, maintained a vertical posture all the way across, and slipped swiftly along as if they were suspended like a curtain on rings. Had these lively auroral fairies marched across the fiord on the top of the bow instead of shuffling along the under side of it, one might have fancied they were a happy band of spirit people on a journey making use of the splendid bow for a bridge. There must have been hundreds of miles of them; for the time required for each to cross from one end of the bridge to the other seemed only a minute or less, while nearly an hour elapsed from their first appearance until the last of the rushing throng vanished behind the western mountain, leaving the bridge as bright and solid and steadfast as before they arrived. But later, half an hour or so, it began to fade. Fissures or cracks crossed it diagonally through which a few stars were seen, and gradually it became thin and nebulous until it looked like the Milky Way, and at last vanished, leaving no visible monument of any sort to mark its place.

I now returned to my cabin, replenished the fire, warmed myself, and prepared to go to bed, though too aurorally rich and happy to go to sleep. But just as I was about to retire, I thought I had better take another look at the sky, to make sure that the glorious show was over; and, contrary to all reasonable expectations, I found that the pale foundation for another bow was being laid right overhead like the first. Then losing all thought of sleep, I ran back to my cabin, carried out blankets and lay down on the moraine to keep watch until daybreak, that none of the sky wonders of the glorious night within reach of my eyes might be lost.

I had seen the first bow when it stood complete in full splendor, and its gradual fading decay. Now I was to see the building of a new one from the beginning. Perhaps in less than half an hour the silvery material was gathered, condensed, and welded into a glowing, evenly proportioned arc like the first and in the same part of the sky. Then in due time over the eastern mountain-wall came another throng of restless electric auroral fairies, the infinitely fine pale-gray garments of each lightly touching those of their neighbors as they swept swiftly along the under side of the bridge and down over the western mountain like the merry band that had gone the same way before them, all keeping quivery step and time to music too fine for mortal ears.

While the gay throng was gliding swiftly along, I watched the bridge for any change they might make upon it, but not the slightest could I detect. They left no visible track, and after all had passed the glowing arc stood firm and apparently immutable, but at last faded slowly away like its glorious predecessor.

Excepting only the vast purple aurora mentioned above, said to have been visible over nearly all the continent, these two silver bows in supreme, serene, supernal beauty surpassed everything auroral I ever beheld.

TIME ON THE RIVER
2006

Brian Anderson

So, here are my two bits. It is a version of a story I first wrote for Duckworks
Magazine *in 2006. I hope it won't seem too out of place among the other pieces here.
But it describes a kind of voyage that I didn't run across among the other works I read
through, and anyway, what the heck, I'm the editor.*

TIME ON THE RIVER

My last summer in college, I finished my first boat. It was a boyhood
daydream, a little 13-foot canoe, half inspired by an Inuit skin boat I had
seen in an encyclopedia, and half by Rushton's Wee Lassie. It had a wooden
framework, with white pine stringers, keel, stem and stern posts, supported
by steamed oak ribs, fixed together with epoxy and brass screws. With Inuit
boats, the frame is covered with seal skins. I settled for painted canvas
though. All told, it cost me less than a hundred dollars. It is stronger and
tougher than it sounds, and has given me twenty years of service.

Coincidentally, just as I was putting the last coat of paint on the boat, my
old friend Rodman picked up a kayak from a friend leaving town, and we
began getting together every once in a while to have a paddle. One night
we were sitting at the Cedars Lounge in downtown Youngstown, Ohio, and

over a nip of Wild Turkey or three, we started planning our next trip. We had made a couple of trips on the Mahoning River which ran through town, but upstream, out of the urban area. That night we decided to have a paddle through the center of town, and see what there was to see.

That stretch of the Mahoning was *terra incognita,* at least as far as anyone we knew was concerned. The river flows mostly through abandoned industrial land, and with the exception of a few bridges, it was very difficult to scout for old weirs, locks, or other surprises that might have turned nasty. Friends and family thought we were nuts. Youngstown was a steel town, until the mills closed around 1980, and for more than a hundred years the banks of the Mahoning were lined with mills and factories that pretty much dumped what they wanted to into the river. When I was a kid the Mahoning was basically a bilious cesspool, more or less devoid of life. A local urban legend told of a boy foolish enough to go swimming in it who emerged from the water minus his skin, which had been stripped off like old paint by the river.

Undaunted, we put the boats in the water at the mouth of Mill Creek, where John Young landed in his canoe in 1796, liked what he saw, and founded Youngstown. Almost two hundred years later we found, to our delight, a river full of wildlife with long stretches of natural flow, little islands, and wooded banks. The industrial ruins that dotted its course made it, if anything, more interesting than the wilder and more pristine stretches we knew already. All of this downtown in a city that at its height had boasted 200,000 people.

So when I got back to town to visit family and show off my daughters in the summer of 2006, Rodman met me and my family down at the Cedars for dinner. The talk naturally turned to paddling, and the stretch through Youngstown was really the only choice.

In the event, the day was gray, and threatened rain, but it was good to be on the Mahoning again after a couple of years. We pulled out of Mill Creek into the current, and paddled past an island, just behind the old building in which I had built a loft apartment to live in while I spent a couple of years working at the local newspaper. I would go there to fish in the afternoon, laying back in my canoe, a thwart tied to a root, often half asleep with the line wrapped once around my index finger so that a carp taking the bait would wake me up.

One hazy August afternoon, the river frosted white with the seeds of the cottonwoods, it was not a carp, but four baby raccoons that woke me up. They apparently had swum across the river, and I cracked an eye, lying still in my canoe, to see two masked eyes peering at me over the crest of the island twenty feet away. His fur was rimmed in pink light from the setting sun. I didn't move, and after a few moments, he hopped over the top and followed by three siblings, walked over to a mulberry tree a couple of feet away. The first one headed up the tree and the others followed until I must have made some slight motion or other, and the second one stopped a few feet off the ground to look at me. The third and the fourth ones hadn't spotted me, though, and didn't pause, so there was a double rear-end collision in the tree. The second coon hissed at and cuffed the third and the third hissed and cuffed the fourth, and then they all looked at me for a long moment. When I didn't move, they continued up the tree and were soon easing their way through the highest, thinnest branches, stuffing berries into their mouths as fast as they could.

As I watched, I forgot about fishing, and I must have at some point wrapped the line around my finger more than once, because a carp took the bait and before I knew it I was playing a nice-sized fish with a couple of turns of 8-pound-test monofilament wrapped around my index finger. Things were getting really painful and I was thrashing and flailing around trying to get the string off, keep control of the rod and avoid an unexpected swim. Just as my fingertip was turning a really violent purple, the carp wrapped the line around a snag downstream and broke off. I looked up and saw the last of the raccoons disappearing over the edge of the high riverbank.

At that time I was a crime reporter at the local newspaper: day after day of talking to criminals and cops, and writing about the daily mayhem in the homes and on the streets of my city. It was enormously depressing, and I have often thought that things would have gotten really bad for me, had I not been able to escape, once a week or so, into my canoe with my fishing pole and a pair of binoculars.

It had started to clear up a bit. We cracked beers, and sipped as we passed through a long slow stretch. Next up was a long-ruined dam that had been put in something like two hundred years ago to provide power for a flour mill. With a lot of water in the river, you can sort of scooch over the top of the line of loose rocks that marks the old dam. But normally the only real water to be found is in a chute on the far left. You paddle over around a small point formed by the mouth of a stream, turn in the current, dodge the rock that sits up in the middle of the chute, and then paddle like mad to turn back into midstream before you pile up on a twenty-four-inch steel pipe that angles out into the current about one quarter out of the water, maybe thirty feet downstream before curving down into the streambed. I ran the chute, and Peter and Rodman went over the top in their sturdy plastic boats. Peter and I surfed the eddies below the dam for a few minutes while Rodman took some photos and heckled us, especially Peter when he dipped a gunnel under the current flowing over the top. The abandoned Water Street Bridge spans the river just down from the dam, and the sight of the rusting girders took me back to another evening on the Mahoning.

Very often I would fish for carp through the afternoon, and then at dusk, drift slowly down the river to the pool just above the old milldam. Bread-balls dipped in vanilla and cast into the pool just after dark were almost a sure thing for a channel cat or two, and that night, I was tied up to a small wooded sandbar just below a railroad bridge abutment, waiting for the first bite. It was dark, and a three-quarters moon was just peeking above the tree line, when I saw something surface in the water next to the front of the canoe. It looked like a head, and while one can tell oneself that there is nothing in the river that could possibly be dangerous, it still gave me a start.

As quietly as possible I got out the flashlight. It turned out to be a very large beaver, and not, as I had run across a couple of times in the course of my work, the decomposing corpse of someone with a couple of extra holes in them. So the beaver watched me and I watched the beaver, and neither of us moved. Then a car, playing rap music loud enough to wake the dead, pulled up to the end of the bridge where it was blocked off by a guardrail. The beaver disappeared with a swop of its tail, and I doused the light, not knowing what was going on. I looked up at the bridge, rusted girders, crumbling blacktop at the edges where the sidewalk had fallen though into the river many years ago. Like a vision, a woman half-danced, half-walked, out onto the bridge from the other side. She was dressed in white. White running shoes, white lycra biking shorts, a white jacket, and what seemed like a thousand tiny white beads strung on a hundred braided tresses, and all of it in motion in the moonlight thirty yards away. She yelled something as she disappeared off the end of the bridge toward the car, and the music went low, and after a minute or two she walked back over the bridge, still with a spring in her step.

I fished for a while and caught a nice channel cat, maybe two pounds, with corded muscle under tight, speckled green skin in the net as I eased the hook out with a pair of pliers under the flashlight. It had jumped while I was playing it. The moonlight had glittered off its flanks and the water its fins had flung in the air.

I had just re-baited and cast when another car pulled up, beeped twice, and the woman reappeared and glided across the bridge. She was at the car for just a couple of minutes again. I remember thinking that if she was a prostitute, she must have been extremely good at her work. But she was almost certainly selling cocaine. It was a good setup—the customers pulled up at one end, she took a bag across, but could not be followed in a car if there was a problem with the customer or the police. There was dense brush on either side of the bridge with several paths leading up and down the river, and there was the river itself. With a pebble in the bag, any evidence could be gone in an instant. The police apparently had thought so too, because when I happened by a year or so later, one side of the bridge was blocked off with a wall in concrete, steel, and barbed wire that could have stopped an army.

We finished surfing around under the old bridge, and then passed the floating dock behind the train station where most afternoons I went by a couple of retired guys, Gene and Robert, would be carp fishing. But not today. Just downstream from the dock was a weir. I always made a short portage in my skin boat, but Peter and Rodman decided to run a chute over by the left bank. Peter came through fine, but Rodman hung up on something about halfway down, and a minute after he was through the chute, he was bailing like crazy.

We headed for an island about a hundred yards downstream, and once we had his boat out and turned over we could see that the plastic was cracked a couple of ways and overlapped wrong. Worse, it was under a seat, and we couldn't get at both sides of the hull without a socket set because of the way the nuts that held the seat in were rusted to the bolts and recessed in the plastic. Normally, I carry a roll of duct tape for situations like this in my more fragile skin boat, but that day I didn't have any.

About this point a homeless guy popped his head out of his little tarp-cabin on the bank a few feet away. He was maybe forty, with long blond hair going gray, wearing black jeans and a black leather jacket—kind of an Axl Rose type with a high, penetrating voice. So we asked him if he had any duct tape. He turned his camp inside out, but apparently one of his friends had used the last of his roll putting up another shelter downstream a bit. He did have some beer, though, and lots of questions and advice.

In the meantime, Rodman had another idea. He gathered up a couple of plastic bags and some styrofoam Chinese take-out boxes. With a Leatherman tool Pete carried in his kit, Rodman pried the edges of plastic more or less back into place, and then started a fire with the foam on the bottom of his boat. This was too much for Axl, who was sure that you should hold the burning plastic in your hand and drip it onto the crack. He jumped up and down, put his hands to his head, and shouted advice when he saw what was happening. But Rodman had a plan and pretty soon he had a nice little fire going and was sort of spooning the gooey plastic around over the cracks. It was touch-and-go there for a minute, because the plastic hull kept a lot of heat and was softening and threatening to collapse into a really big hole until we doused it in water to cool off and harden. In the end it worked just fine. Not a leak for the rest of the trip.

It was time for lunch and another beer and we drifted down through the town, the roofs of buildings showing here and there through the trees. All along the river we had been scaring up great blue herons, and now there were about five of them hopscotching, along with a bunch of kingfishers, down the river in front of us. We had also seen cormorants and wood ducks. Overhead, a couple of red-tailed hawks had been circling off and on all day.

Whenever I hear about a polluted site, and someone arguing that it is past saving, too polluted to ever come back, I always think of the Mahoning, and how far it has come in just twenty-five years. I have seen snapping turtles, mink, deer, fox, beaver; I have caught walleyes, channel cats, smallmouth bass, and even once a rainbow trout (certainly stocked in some stream or pond upstream, but still alive anyway). In the winter, when the Mahoning often lies on the southern edge of the frost line, the river is packed with birds of all kinds. A guy from the state fish and game did an electroshock survey near where I fish and found musky, pike, walleye, perch, bluegill, bass, and a half-dozen other species. In other words, while it still would not be a good idea to eat what you catch, the river has in some ways recovered, at least in terms of the range of species of animals, fish, and birds that you find along it. But just a few years back, the joke was that you could use the river water for antifreeze in a pinch. All it took was to stop poisoning it, and let it be for a while.

After lunch we took a detour up Crab Creek for a couple of hundred yards. When I was a child, I lived across the road from the creek, about ten miles upstream from here, where it joins the Mahoning. At that end it is a beautiful little stream, full of turtles, crayfish, minnows, and fish, winding through a wooded ravine where I learned to love the forest, to fish, and to spend long summer days just exploring, wondering what I might see around the next bend. At this end, though, after running through much of the city, it is not so nice. Long ago it was channelized where it ran through the old Republic Steel property. Walls twelve feet high were cut from stone in 1879 (from a date carved into one of the blocks) and the land filled in behind. It makes an interesting trip, though, if one can stomach paddling through the water, which can get pretty ripe, especially in warm weather. A guy from the local EPA office told me once that there were essentially no functioning septic systems attached to houses more than twenty years old in the county, and Crab Creek is the evidence.

But still, paddling up among the old stone walls and under the arched stone bridges is a treat, and I wanted to check out a painting I had seen a ways upstream. It was a nude woman, perhaps eight by twelve feet, painted on the sloping cement wall of the channel. It was essentially a line sketch, drawn in red paint by some budding street artist, and nicely done at that. But what made it really interesting is that looked at standing next to the painting, the proportions were all wrong, the feet too small and the head too big. But if you looked at it from the other side of the creek, sitting on a log near a campfire that had been used over and over again through the years, she was just right. A kind of naive Rubens, with wide hips and heavy, unsiliconed breasts and wearing a big smile. The artist must have sketched her in chalk, wading back and forth across the creek to have a look, before he laid the red paint on the raw concrete. In any case he got it right.

I had always intended to come down with some friends at night, drink some beers and see how she looked in the firelight, but never made it. And on this trip the water was too low and it would have meant a long walk to see if she was even still there after the years of spring floods washing over her.

So we turned around and paddled back out. At the creek mouth, we turned into the current, and passed a reinforced-concrete bridge abutment that had apparently simply been too much trouble to remove when they built an elevated bypass in the 1970s. It is an arch, perhaps fifty feet high, and when you round a bend upstream and see it towering over the scrubby sandbanks and backwaters at the mouth of the creek, it feels like nothing so much as stumbling across some lost bit of Stonehenge or section of Roman aqueduct.

The river here passes through an area of wasteland; the factories, warehouses, and railroad switching yards that covered it are long gone, taken to pieces and sold for scrap. There are some nice little riffles, and an island or two, and this is the stretch where you can see deer and fox, groundhogs, minks, and other wildlife in the evenings. For years there was a nesting pair of barred owls in a big old oak on the bank. They would often start up at my approach and fly heavily off among the trees.

In one part, the water deepens, and through some hydraulic quirk an eddy runs upstream a few feet down. It must have been a day in November sometime when I noticed this. It was overcast, but bright and cold, and for some reason I hadn't been able to get much done at the newspaper. Muttering some excuse to the boss, I slipped out of the office and a half hour later was loose on the river.

The water was running very cold and clear that day. Autumn leaves dotted the surface. As I drifted through over this stretch, I happened to look down into the water, and found I could see straight to the bottom, many feet down. Leaves in a hundred shades between red and yellow glowed against the dark streambed, some drifting with me, others at rest on the bottom, still others moving upstream, with strays tumbling in the eddies between the layers of current. I watched, drifting, so hypnotized that it was a struggle to stay upright in my little canoe and not be drawn down to fly through the frigid, shifting constellations in this unexpected starry night.

A turkey buzzard had replaced the hawks circling overhead now, and as a bonus, there was a new, awkward and dangerous strainer in a chute where the whole river narrowed down to about twenty feet and ran strong and deep.

Rodman and Peter and I managed to dodge the strainer, and passed the island where for several years there was a big plywood cabin cruiser, something like thirty feet long, beached up against the sun and water-bleached tree trunks of a giant towhead. There aren't too many places on the Mahoning where one could cruise for more than a mile in a boat that big, so it was always a mystery where it had come from. The first year I saw it, it was resting on a ledge under a highway bridge about twenty miles upstream. Every spring it would get washed a little farther down the river. One year someone had painted "Youngstown Navy" on the transom, and later some fan of Gilligan and the Skipper had daubed it "USS Minnow." But the floods and the giant tree trunks they dumped on the island's head gradually broke it up, and this time there was nothing left when we passed.

A couple of hundred yards before our pullout, there was one last low weir with an island built up behind it. The river runs between walls here, dug in and built up over the years to protect the railroad yards and tracks. In the early spring, when the river is high, the island and weir are covered with a maelstrom, whirlpools fifteen feet across, big standing waves, hydraulics, the works. I have run the river a couple of times when it is up, but mostly I pull out upstream. One time, though, after writing up a particularly horrible murder-suicide, I just had to get in my canoe and paddle it off. The river that day was running at least eight feet above normal. The various dams and weirs were so far under water that they were little more than bumps in the water and the trip went twice as fast as usual. When I got to the place where I usually pulled out at high water I got out, and then decided to walk down and scout the rapids. I didn't want the trip to end that day, and after a minute, I saw what looked like a workable line through. When I pulled out at the other end of the rapids, I was walking on a cloud, and the feeling lasted through the ride home and a party. Then I checked my messages.

My girlfriend at the time was also a reporter and was working that night, and a couple of hours after I left she heard a report on the police radio of a guy who had gone over a dam in the next town upstream. His boat came out of the hydraulic at the bottom of the dam, but he didn't. The only description of the guy was about thirty with brown hair and a red canoe. There were several messages from her, each one increasingly frantic. I called her to tell her I was okay, and then spent the next day watching the fire department fishing below the dam with grappling hooks for the guy. It turned out he was two days younger than me, but with a wife and a kid, and a new sea kayak he had saved up for several years to buy. The fire chief, when asked by one of the TV reporters what they would do after two days of grappling had turned up nothing, said, "We will just have to wait until the river gives him back." They found him twenty-eight days later, floating in an eddy about fifty yards down from the dam.

One of the best things about the run through the city was that I could do it alone, without needing a car relay. The end of the run was below a railroad bridge on the edge of a switching yard. I would leave the boat in some bushes, and walk out to Center Street. There at the corner with Wilson Avenue sat the Guess Who Lounge. I would buy a shot of Jim Beam and a beer, and use the change to call a taxi to take me home to get my car. A guy named Frank Lentine owned the bar, and there were a couple of things about the Guess Who. One was that the walls were covered in photos of Marilyn Monroe, hundreds of them, and there was a brass pole running from floor to ceiling in a back corner with a dusty mirror ball hanging next to it.

Another thing was a woman named Stella worked there. She wasn't the most talkative woman around, but for a while there I was stopping by once a week or so, and even at the Guess Who, anyone who walked in wearing knee-length rubber boots and carrying an orange dry box got noticed. After a while, Stella started pouring my shots a little long, and one time she told me she had danced for years for Lentine, and his boss, Ernie Biondillo, and Biondillo's boss, Joey Naples. These were well-known men in town.

Lentine had more or less inherited the bar in 1995 when Biondillo was driving to work one morning and a car stalled out in front of him. Two guys with shotguns got out of the car, and when Biondillo went to back up, he found that another car had stopped just behind him too, and two guys with shotguns were already out of that car and walking his way. Biondillo had more or less inherited the Guess Who in 1991 when Joey Naples was checking out how the work was going on his new mansion south of town one evening. He came back to his car, one he had borrowed from a man who had had a small part in the movie *Goodfellas,* and didn't notice somebody hiding in the cornfield across the street with a shotgun. Both men had been connected to the Cleveland mafia. It turned out later that a guy named

Lennie Strollo, who was connected to the Pittsburgh family, was behind it all. Youngstown had traditionally been a more or less open town, but lately it had become poorer and poorer and there just wasn't enough business to go around, apparently.

Stella wouldn't say much about her dancing days. When Lentine, who was about five feet six inches tall and five feet six inches thick, with a nose mashed flat on his face, walked in the room, she wouldn't say anything to anybody at all. Interesting place for a beer.

Rodman and Peter ran a chute through the last weir, and I made a short portage around. Rodman had been working hard on a big computer programming project all summer, and Peter had a new baby who had kept him close to home, and it was a happy bunch that loaded the boats on the car. I wanted to stop for a shot and a beer at the Guess Who, but we were running late. Next time.

FROM *THE RIVER AT GREEN KNOWE*
1959

Lucy M. Boston

illustration by Peter Boston

It is always with trepidation that one returns to the magic books of one's childhood. Too often whatever one found in them as a child is gone, and they are pale and thin. They disappoint and the childhood enchantment itself also fades and is finally erased as one reads.

So I hesitated to open The River at Green Knowe *when I stumbled across it in a pile of old books. Lucy Boston wrote a series of six books in the 1950s and '60s centered on the adventures of children spending their holidays at an ancient house, called "Green Knowe" in the books, where she lived near Cambridge in England. One of them was handed to me by a perceptive librarian during a brutal and endless winter when I was nine or ten. I remember being entranced from the first chapter, and spending what seem now like endless days playing in the snow piled up by the wind in great hills, and then when my toes were numb, coming into the house to change into dry socks and spending another couple of hours with the children in the Norman manor house while my boots dried. Boston was sixty when she started writing, but I remember as I read as a child an almost dreamlike connection with the books—as if Boston had taken her life far enough around the circle for her to know what a child might really think and feel and do, and at the same time how to take me where I had no idea I wanted to go, but did. To my delight, when opening the book again, I found some things do not change.*

"Let's shut our eyes," said Ida, "and say everything we can hear."

FIRST VOYAGE

The first morning was fine and windless. Ida, Oskar and Ping went off after breakfast. At the bottom of the garden there was a wooden boathouse, its four corner posts planted in a marshy piece on the bend of the river. They ran across the unsteady gangway and opened the boathouse door. Inside it was half dark. There was a smell of concentrated river water. The roof and the walls were greened with perpetual damp and wriggly with elastic water patterns. Low down, level with their feet, a canoe lay fretting and tugging gently on its mooring. It was painted blue and brown, and the water that reflected it received it as part of itself. The canoe was lightly built and beautifully balanced, and it would comfortably hold three children. When Ida put the weight of one foot into it, it was like treading on the water itself. It yielded so far that she feared it was sinking under her, but then the water resisted, and she sat down feeling like a water-lily on its leaf. The boys followed her in. Ping sat in front and Oskar in the stern. They parted the willow strands that hung like a net across the opening, and the river was theirs.

The sun had not yet pierced the haze of morning. The water was like a looking-glass with a faint mist of breath drying off it. The children felt it so bewitching that without even a discussion they turned downstream, drifting silently along, willing to become part of the river if they could. Along the edge of the water ran a ribbon of miniature cliff, the top edge undulating like the cliffs of Dover, the vertical sides pierced with holes the size of a golf ball. Sometimes the cliff was high enough to show seams of gravel or strata of different soils. Above it willow-herb or loosestrife or giant dock heavy with seed rose against the sky, and reflected themselves in the water with an effect like 'skeleton' writing. The canoe seemed to hover between two skies. The banks of the river were richly alive. Moorhens hurried from side to side trailing a widening V, fish leapt along the surface, water rats swam underwater, their V trailing from the end of their projecting noses. Or they peeped out from holes, or it might be mice, or martins, or a kingfisher. The rushes ticked like clocks, meadowsweet suddenly bowed down from above almost to the children's noses as a bumble bee landed on it; or a rush waved desperately as something attacked it out of sight at the bottom.

They drifted happily along, a twist of the paddle now and again being enough to keep them on a straight course. Presently the sun came out and beautifully warmed them in the shell of the canoe, and with the sun appeared another host of living things, butterflies, dragonflies, water boatmen, brightly colored beetles and lizards; and high up in the sky a weaving of swallows. The canoe drifted to a standstill.

Ping's eyes were fixed on a small spider that was descending from the branch of a tree, playing out its rope as it came, its many feet all busy. It landed on the point of the prow, made its rope fast and immediately swarmed up again.

"We're tethered," Ping said, smiling indulgently. "Are there no big things in English rivers—no water buffaloes, no tigers in the bamboo, no crocodiles or hippopotamuses?" As he spoke there was a sound of a large body being jerked up out of the mud, and a shadow-flecked bullock on the edge of the bank that had escaped Ping's notice snorted in his ear. He fell over backward into Ida's lap, while the other two laughed and the bullock squared its forelegs and lowered its head. Ping stared up at it from underneath.

"I can see all of us in its eyes," he said, "reflected quite clearly. But you can see it means nothing to him. They are awful stupid eyes. He isn't quite sure that we aren't a dog or a motor-car." Ping stuck one leg straight up in the air. "I don't believe he knows it isn't a stick." The bullock stared a long time and other bullocks came and stared too. Then it lifted its nose and began a tremendous bellow which suddenly tailed off into a foolish query, mild and puzzled. Ping put his leg down again and the bullock sighed deeply in relief.

"Let's shut our eyes," said Ida, "and say everything we can hear."

They all began together so that their voices sounded like a cluster of ducks or any other young things that might be sunning themselves on the river. Ida however said they must take it in turns so that they wouldn't count anything twice.

Water under the canoe's ribs, whirlpool round my paddle, drip off the end of Ping's paddle, bird flying off tree, larks singing, rooks circling, swallows diving, rustling in grass, grasshoppers, honeybees, flies, frogs, bubbles rising, a weir somewhere, tails swishing, cow patting, aeroplanes, a fishing rod playing out; zizz, buzz trill crick, whizz plop, flutter, splash; and all the time everywhere whisper, whisper, lap, chuckle and sigh. If someone moved in the canoe, a moment later on the far side of the river all the rushes nudged each other and whispered about the ripple that had arrived.

"Everything's trying to say something," said Ping. "Fishes poke up round mouths as if they were stammering."

"Do you think," said Ida out of a silence, "that the sound I can hear now might be singing fish?"

They all listened. There was a new sound coming from farther downstream, round the next bend, a musical bubbling, warbling whistle.

With one accord all three paddles went in and the canoe shot off. They were very vigourous after so much time drifting and listening. The whistling grew louder every minute, and then appeared a huge white swan, sailing menacingly, a warship at action stations. Behind him came seven small grey cygnets, whose infant chatter was the noise that had brought the children, and behind them the mother swan guarding the rear. She now hurried forward tossing on the water with the violence of her foot strokes, and both parents bore down on the canoe, slapping their terrible wooden sounding wings, shooting out necks like snakes and hissing in the children's faces. Their open beaks were rough-edged mincers. Fortunately the canoe had enough momentum to be swerved at speed to a safer distance. The mother swan turned back to her brood and the cob contented himself with patrolling up and down between them and the fleeing canoe, keeping his implacable eye sideways to the intruders. As soon as the children felt safe they paused to watch.

"Look there is one tiny cygnet quite left out. It's only half the size of the others."

While the alert had been on there had indeed been seven cygnets in a cluster. The smallest having succeeded in joining them while the parents' attention was elsewhere. Now however, the mother swan had headed it off, and it swam with great agitation alone, uttering heart-rending peeps. Its only and persistent wish was to join the others, but this was not allowed. Whenever it thought it had, by sneaking round behind, achieved its aim, a long white snake would descend, and a beak used like a spoon flip it away.

"Why is she so horrid to it? The littlest ought to be her favourite," said Ida in distress. "She won't let it eat anything." But when the cob saw the poor little thing trying to get round behind him, he hissed, and closing his wicked mincers on its back held it under water.

This was too much for Ida, who leapt to her feet, nearly upsetting the canoe, and hurled her paddle. The attack and the noise—for the two boys shouted at Ida as the canoe rocked—brought the cob back to his duties. He wheeled to rap with his beak on the paddle that was now floating beside him. The poor dazed cygnet came to the surface and paddled away for dear life, straight into Ida's hands. As she had now no paddle she cradled it tenderly in her lap while the boys worked to get out of range of the angry parent. They were not pursued. The six remaining cygnets cuddled up together and whistled contentedly. The mother swan up-ended herself and searched the river bottom for food. After a decent interval to cool his temper, the cob did so too.

"Their feet remind me of umbrellas blown inside out," said Ping,

The little cygnet continued to make the most mournful squeaking.

"Ours must be an orphan," said Oscar. "It's a Displaced Cygnet."

"We'll keep it and bring it up, and have a tame swan swimming beside us wherever we go," said Ida. "I wonder if swans fight? Suppose it's a he-swan and there are fights whenever we go out. A sparrow fight is bad enough. Imagine a swan fight! Think of the noise their wings make taking off! Like a paddle steamer."

"I don't think they fight like dogs," said Ping. "I think they wrestle, each holding the other's right wing in his beak. I would like to see it."

"It won't even be grown up by the end of the holiday," said Oskar. "It will still be a baby. And what are we going to do with it then? And where will it sleep?"

"I'll make it a nest in a box. In the cupboard there is an old eiderdown with a hole in the corner. We'll shake out a lot of feathers and make it feel at home."

But the grief of the cygnet was very hard to bear. It went on and on. The children could hardly talk because of it. It never stopped to take breath. It made the river journey one long execution party. The children got quite miserable.

"It will go on squeaking till it dies," said Ida.

At this point they came to a mill and a dock. The lock keeper happened to be on the bridge, so they paddled straight into the narrow stone passage and the gate was closed behind them. As the water sank, it was like going down in a lift. The walls rose till it was frightening to believe that the river anywhere in its course was as deep as that. The plug gurgling of this giant's bath sucked and tugged. The cygnet's cries, magnified in the enclosing slimy walls, filled Oskar's ears like anguish in a prison. At last the gate was lifted, and after a final push and babble of conflicting waters the new level was established and the canoe could be paddled out into the mill pool. This was as big as a lake and as wild as a marsh. Near the mill it was overhung with trees, but its distant edge was fringed with tall rushes in which were openings where smaller streams flowed into the pool.

Just below the lock two more swans were sailing. They had none of the majesty and organisation of the family upstream. They were restless, nervous and appeared to be looking for something, thrusting their long necks at water level into the rushes, or turning round and round in one spot with their necks stretched up into watchtowers.

When the canoe breasted the pool and carried the squealing cygnet into earshot, the two swans heard at once. They sailed along wing to wing turning their heads sideways to the canoe while they circled round it. As they drew nearer, their bearing stiffened and grew fiercer, while the cygnet now quite hoarse, yelled and fought in Ida's hands. The swans came so close they could have overturned the canoe, their unwinking eyes level with the children's.

"What shall I do now?" Ida cried, shrinking away.

"Let it go," said Oskar, "I think these are its proper parents."

Ida opened her hands, and the cygnet wildly scrambling on its elbowy little black legs and flapping wings hardly stronger than a butterfly's, left the canoe for its mother's back. She fluffed up her wing feathers to hold it there, and both swans paddled off at full speed into the distant rushes.

"Whew! What a relief!" said Ida, but Oscar was following the course of the swans with happy eyes, his jaw thrust out.

"I suppose it got trapped in the lock the last time somebody went through in the other direction. Look Ida, it's off her back now and they are both showing it how to nibble water."

While they were watching, the canoe drifted into a grass bank and Ping put his arm round a post that stood there.

"Here's a good place for mooring. Let's have a bathe." They all scrambled out onto the bank, and soon had dived in like three frogs.

"I'm going to practice up-ending like the swans, and see what I can find on the bottom," said Ida. "Let's see who can find the most interesting thing on the bottom." She vanished leaving only her little feet and ankles on the surface. When she came up for breath she saw Oskar's long shanks waving madly about and Ping's neat gilded legs cool like fish. At the first attempt nobody found anything. The bottom felt unpleasant to the hands. It was deep slime with here and there the rusty edge of a tin, or things that did not feel quite alive and yet moved.

"There must be all kinds of things," Ida persisted, looking with her wet plastered hair and chattering teeth very determined, like a hunting otter. "People always drop things getting in and out of boats. I expect this has been a mooring place ever since boats were invented. We might find Hereward the Wake's dagger."

Up came all their feet again; and again. The third time was lucky. Ida came panting to the surface with a bent piece of iron, and Ping with a live eel held firmly in both hands. When he had showed it to the others he hurled it up into the sky where it shone silver for a moment before entering the water again with no splash at all, like a needle entering silk. Ping seemed supremely satisfied, his almond eyes lifted at the corners making the same kind of smile as his mouth.

"What's this I've got?" said Ida. "It's like a starting handle. It was awfully heavy to swim with. It would be useful if we had a motor boat."

"It's a lock key," said Oscar. "Much more useful. Now we can go anywhere we want quite by ourselves."

"What a lucky find! Because this pool seems the centre point for exploring lots of islands. I can see five or six waterways from here. We shall always be coming and going. What have you found, Oskar?"

"I don't know what it is—some kind of metal bowl. But it is such an odd shape—as if it really was for something special. It might be silver. Do you suppose this is all of it? It wouldn't stand steadily on this knob thing underneath. Perhaps it's the lid of something." He turned it the other way up.

"Its a helmet!" screeched Ida.

"A head lid," said Ping. "An Oskar lid."

Oskar put it on. It fitted him perfectly. As his hands passed over it, the raised part on top that he had thought was the pedestal, became obviously the socket for his plumes.

They picked flowering rushes and tied the stalks into a firm base to fit the socket, and there was Oskar looking like King Arthur himself, at least to Ida's eyes. And because the helmet seemed to demand it of its wearer, Oskar stood up in the canoe all the way home—an art requiring much practice if the canoe was not to be overturned, and leaving all the work to the other two. But it looked magnificent.

illustration by Peter Boston

FROM *A GENERAL HISTORY OF THE ROBBERIES AND MURDERS OF THE MOST NOTORIOUS PYRATES*

1724

Captain Charles Johnson (Daniel Defoe)

Daniel Defoe is probably best known as the author of Robinson Crusoe *and* Moll Flanders. *But he also found time to write political pamphlets for both the Whigs and the Tories in the early 1700s. In 1724 he apparently published yet another classic, on the pirates of the Americas. The book was published under the name Capt.*

Charles Johnson, and there remains some doubt about the author. But considering the subject matter and the need of a well-regarded and politically connected writer like Defoe to steer clear of such a seamy subject, it seems understandable that he might use a pen name for what turned out to be a best seller that probably made him more than his subjects ever dreamed of.

Blackbeard was born Edward Teach (or Thatch) in Bristol, England, around 1685. He turned up in the Caribbean in the early part of the 1700s, and made his name as the right-hand man of another pirate, Captain Benjamin Hornigold, in about 1716. When Hornigold retired and accepted the king's pardon, Blackbeard inherited a French ship, which he renamed the Queen Anne's Revenge. *He fitted her out with 40 guns and took her to sea. He cruised from the Gulf of Honduras to Cape Hatteras, taking prizes, blockading the port of Charleston, and even claimed to have fought a single-ship action with a British navy sloop before taking a pardon from Charles Eden, the royal governor of North Carolina. Defoe writes that along the way Blackbeard greased the palms of a number of Royal Governors, especially Eden, to good effect. "These proceedings show that Governors are but men," Defoe noted delicately.*

In any case, after a short time ashore, either the solid-citizen act paled or he drank all his money, and Blackbeard hoisted his black flag once more. The worthies of the southern seaboard, seeing which way the wind was blowing, decided to petition the governor of Virginia, Alexander Spotswood.

ON THE TURBULENT DEATH
OF BLACKBEARD THE PIRATE

Together with a Short Addendum Concerning his Beard, the Location of his Treasure, and his Nefarious Association with the Devil Himself.

Therefore, with as much secrecy as possible, they sent a deputation to Virginia, to lay the affair before the Governor of that Colony, and to solicit an armed force from the men-of-war lying there to take or destroy this Pirate.

This Governor consulted with the captains of the two men-of-war, viz., the Pearl and the Lime, who had lain in James's River about ten months. It was agreed that the Governor should hire a couple of small sloops, and the men-of-war should man them. This was accordingly done, and the command of them given to Mr. Robert Maynard, first lieutenant of the Pearl, an experienced officer and a gentleman of great bravery and resolution, as will appear by his gallant behaviour in this expedition. The sloops were well manned and furnished with ammunition and small arms, but had no guns mounted.

About the time of their going out, the Governor called an Assembly in which it was resolved to publish a proclamation offering certain rewards to any person or persons, who, within a year after that time, should take or destroy any Pirate. The original proclamation being in our hands is as follows:

By His Majesty's Lieutenant Governor and Commander in Chief of the Colony and Dominion of Virginia,

A PROCLAMATION.

Publishing the Rewards Given for Apprehending or Killing Pirates.

WHEREAS, by an Act of Assembly, made-at a Session of Assembly, begun at the Capital in Williamsburg, the eleventh day of November in the fifth year of His Majesty's Reign, entitled An Act to Encourage the Apprehending and Destroying of Pirates: It is amongst other things enacted, that all and every person or persons, who, from and after the fourteenth day of November, in the Year of Our Lord One Thousand Seven Hundred and Eighteen, and before the fourteenth day of November, which shall be in the Year of our Lord One Thousand Seven Hundred and Nineteen, shall take any Pirate or Pirates, on the sea or land, or in case of resistance, shall kill any such Pirate or Pirates, between the degrees of thirty four and thirty nine Northern latitude, and within one hundred leagues of the Continent of Virginia, or within the Provinces of Virginia, or North Carolina, upon the conviction, or making due proof of the killing of all, and every such Pirate, and Pirates, before the Governor and Council, shall be entitled to have, and receive out of the public money, in the hands of the

Treasurer of this Colony, the several rewards following that is to say, for Edward Teach, commonly called Captain Teach or Black-beard, one hundred pounds; for every other commander of a pirate ship, sloop or vessel, forty pounds; for every lieutenant, master or quartermaster, boatswain or carpenter, twenty pounds; for every other inferior officer, fifteen pounds, and for every private man taken aboard such ship, sloop, or vessel, ten pounds; and that for every Pirate which shall be taken by any ship, sloop or vessel, belonging to this colony, or North Carolina, within the time aforesaid, in any place whatsoever, the like rewards shall be, paid according to the quality and condition of such pirates. Wherefore, for the encouragement of all such persons as shall be willing to serve His Majesty and their Country, in so just and honourable undertaking, as the suppressing a sort of people, who may be truly called enemies to mankind: I have thought fit, with the advice and consent of His Majesty's Council to issue this Proclamation; hereby declaring, the said rewards shall be punctually and justly paid, in current money in Virginia, according to the directions of the said Act. And, I do order and appoint this Proclamation, to be published by the Sheriffs at their respective County houses, and by all Ministers and Readers in the several Churches and Chapels throughout this Colony.

Given at Our Council Chamber at Williamsburg, this 24th day of November, 1718. In the Fifth year of His Majesty's Reign.

GOD SAVE THE KING.

A. Spotswood.
[Governor of Virginia, 1710-1722]

The 17th of November, 1718, the lieutenant sailed from Kicquetan, in James River, in Virginia, and the 21st in the evening came to the mouth of the Ocracoke Inlet where he got sight of the pirate. This expedition was made with all imaginable secrecy, and the officer managed with all the prudence that was necessary, stopping all boats and vessels he met with in the river from going up, and therefore preventing any intelligence from reaching Blackbeard, and receiving at the same time an account from them all of the place where the pirate was lurking. But notwithstanding this caution, Blackbeard had information of the design from His Excellency of the province, whose secretary, Mr. Knight, wrote him a letter particularly concerning it, intimating that he had sent him four of his men, which were all he could meet with in or about town, and so bid him be upon his guard. These men belonged to Blackbeard, and were sent from Bath-Town to Ocracoke Inlet, where the sloop lay, which is about twenty leagues.

Blackbeard had heard several reports which happened not to be true, and so gave the less credit to this, nor was he convinced till he saw the sloops, whereupon he put his vessel in a posture of defence. He had no more

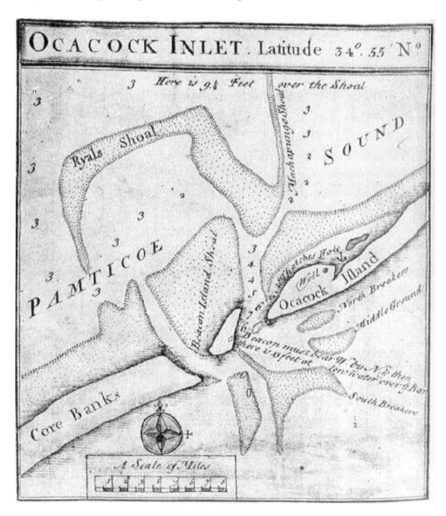

than twenty-five men on board, so he gave out to all the vessels he spoke with that he had forty. When he had prepared for battle, he set down and spent the night in drinking with the master of a trading sloop who, 'twas thought, had more business with Teach than he should have had.

Lieutenant Maynard came to an anchor, for the place being shoal and the channel intricate, there was no getting in where Teach lay that night. But in the morning he weighed and sent his boat ahead of the sloops to sound, and coming within gunshot of the Pirate, received his fire. Whereupon Maynard hoisted the King's colours and stood directly towards him, with the best way that his sails and oars could make. Blackbeard cut his cable, and endeavoured to make a running fight, keeping a continual fire at his enemies with his guns. Mr. Maynard not having any, kept a constant fire with small arms, while some of his men laboured at their oars. In a little time Teach's sloop ran aground, and Mr. Maynard's drawing more water than that of the Pirate, he could not come near him; so he anchored within half a gunshot of the enemy, and in order to lighten his vessel, that he might run him aboard, the lieutenant ordered all his ballast to be thrown overboard, and all the water [i.e., water casks] to be staved, and then weighed and stood for him. Upon which Blackbeard hailed him in this rude manner: *Damn you for villains, who are you? And from whence came you?* The Lieutenant made him answer, *You may see by our colours we are no pirates.* Blackbeard bid him send his boat on board, that he might see who he was: but Mr. Maynard replied thus, *I cannot spare my boat, but I will come aboard of you as soon as I can, with my sloop.* Upon this, Blackbeard took a glass of liquor, and drank to him with these words: *Damnation seize my soul if I give you quarter or take any from you.* In answer to which Mr. Maynard told him *That he expected no quarter from him, nor should he give any.*

By this time Blackbeard's sloop floated, as Mr. Maynard's sloops were rowing towards him, which, being not above a foot high in the waist and consequently the men all exposed, as they came near together (there being hitherto little or no execution done on either side), the Pirate fired a broadside, charged with all manner of small shot—a fatal stroke to them—the sloop the lieutenant was in having twenty men killed and wounded and the other sloop nine. This could not be helped for, there being no wind, they were obliged to keep to their oars, otherwise the Pirate would have got away from him, which, it seems, the lieutenant was resolute to prevent.

After this unlucky blow Blackbeard's sloop fell broadside to the shore. Mr. Maynard's other sloop, which was called the Ranger, fell astern, being, for the present disabled. So the lieutenant finding his own sloop had way and would soon be on board of Teach, he ordered all his men down for fear of another broadside, which must have been their destruction and the loss of the expedition. Mr. Maynard was the only person that kept the deck, except the man at the helm, whom he directed to lie down snug, and the men in the hold were ordered to get their pistols and their swords ready for close fighting, and to come up at his command; in order to which, two ladders were placed in the hatchway for the more expedition. When the lieutenant's sloop boarded the other, Captain Teach's men threw in several new-fashioned sort of grenadoes, viz., case bottles filled with powder and small shot, slugs, and pieces of lead or iron, with a quick match at the end of it, which, being lighted outside, presently runs into the bottle to the powder. As it is instantly thrown on board, it generally does great execution, besides putting all the crew into a confusion; but by good providence, they had not that effect here, the men being in the hold. And Blackbeard, seeing few or no hands aboard, told his men that *They were all knocked on the head except three or four; and therefore, says he, let's jump on board and cut them to pieces.*

Whereupon, under the smoke of one of the bottles just mentioned, Blackbeard enters with fourteen men, over the bows of Maynard's sloop, and were not seen by him until the air cleared. However, he just then gave a signal to his men, who all rose in an instant and attacked the Pirates with as much bravery as ever was done upon such an occasion. Blackbeard and the lieutenant fired the first pistol at each other, by which the Pirate received a wound; and then engaged with swords, till the lieutenant's unluckily broke, and [he] stepping back to cock a pistol, Blackbeard, with his cutlass, was striking at that instant that one of Maynard's men gave him a terrible wound in the neck and throat; by which the lieutenant came off with a small cut over his fingers.

They were so closely and warmly engaged, the lieutenant and twelve men against Blackbeard and fourteen, till the sea was tinctured with blood round the vessel. Blackbeard received a shot in his body from the pistol that Lieutenant Maynard, discharged, yet he stood his ground, and fought with great fury till he received five-and-twenty wounds, and five of them by shot. At length, as he was cocking another pistol, having fired several before, he fell down dead; by which time eight more out of the fourteen dropped, and all the rest, much wounded, jumped overboard and called out for quarter, which was granted; though it was only prolonging their lives for a few days. The sloop *Ranger* came up, and attacked the men that remained in Blackbeard's sloop, with equal bravery, till they likewise cried for quarter.

Here was an end of that courageous brute, who might have passed in the world for a hero had he been employed in a good cause. His destruction, which was of such consequence to the plantations, was entirely owing to the conduct and bravery of Lieutenant Maynard and his men, who might have destroyed him with much less loss had they had 1 vessel with great guns. But they were obliged to use small vessels, because the holes and places he lurked in would not admit of others of greater draught. And it was no small difficulty for this gentleman to get to him, having grounded his vessel at least a hundred times, in getting up the river, besides other discouragements enough to have turned back any gentleman without dishonour who was less resolute and bold than this lieutenant. The broadside that did so much mischief before they boarded, in all probability saved the rest from destruction; for before that, Teach had little or no hopes of escaping, and therefore had posted a resolute fellow, a negro whom he had bred up, with a, lighted match in the powder room, with commands to blow up, when he should give him orders, which was as soon as the lieutenant and his men could have entered, that so he might have destroyed his conquerors; and when the negro found how it went with Blackbeard, he could hardly be persuaded from the rash action by two prisoners that were then in the hold of the sloop.

Now that we have given some account of Teach's life and actions, it will not be amiss that we speak of his beard, since it did not a little contribute towards making his name to terrible in those parts.

Plutarch and other grave historians have taken notice that several great men amongst the Romans took their surnames from certain odd marks in their countenances, as Cicero from a mark or vetch on his nose. So our, hero, Captain Teach, assumed the cognomen of Black-beard, from that large quantity of hair which, like a frightful meteor, covered his whole face and frightened America more than any comet that has appeared there a long time.

This beard was black, which he suffered to grow of an extravagant length; as to breadth, it came up to his eyes. He was accustomed to twist it with ribbons, in small tails, after the manner of our Ramillies wigs, and turn them about his ears. In time of action he wore a sling over his shoulders, with three brace of pistols, hanging in holsters, like bandoliers; and stuck lighted matches, under his hat, which, appearing on each side of his face, his eyes naturally looking fierce and wild, made him altogether such a figure that imagination cannot form an idea of a Fury from Hell to look more frightful.

If he had the look of a Fury, his humours and passions were suitable to it. We shall relate two or three more of his extravagances which we omitted in the body of his history, by which it will appear to what a pitch of wickedness human nature may arrive, if its passions are not checked.

In the commonwealth of Pirates he who goes the greatest length of wickedness is looked upon with a kind of envy amongst them, as a person of a more extraordinary gallantry, and is thereby entitled to distinguished by some post. And if such a one has but courage, he must certainly be a great man. The hero of whom we are writing was thoroughly accomplished this way, and some of his frolics of wickedness were so extravagant as if he aimed at making his men believe he was a Devil incarnate. For being one day at sea, and a little flushed with drink, *Come,* says he, *let us make a hell of our own, and try how long we can bear it.* Accordingly he, with two or three others went down into the hold and closing up all the hatches, filled several pots full of brimstone and other combustible matter, and set it on fire, and so continued until they were almost suffocated, when some of the men cried out for air. At length, he opened the hatches, not a little pleased that he held out the longest.

The night before he was killed he sat up and drank till the morning with some of his own men and the master of a merchant-man; and having had intelligence of the two sloops coming to attack him, as has been before observed, one of his men asked him in case anything should happen to him in the engagement with the sloops, whether his wife knew where he had buried his money? He answered, *That nobody but himself and the Devil knew where it was, and the longest liver should take all.*

Those of his crew who were taken alive told a glory which may appear a little incredible; however, we think it will not be fair to omit it, since we had it from their own mouths. That once, upon a cruise, they found out that they had a man on board more than their crew. Such a one was seen several days amongst them, sometimes below, and sometimes upon deck; yet no man in the ship could give an account who he was, or from whence he came, but that he disappeared a little before they were cast away in their great ship. But, it seems, they verily believed it was the Devil.

One would think these things should induce them to reform their lives; but so many reprobates together encouraged and spirited one another up in their wickedness, to which a continual course of drinking did not a little contribute. For in Blackbeard's journal which was taken, there were several memorandums of the following nature, found writ with his own hand: *Such a day, rum all out:—Our company somewhat sober:—A damn'd confusion amongst us!—Rogues a-plotting:—Great talk of separation—so I looked sharp for a prize:—Such a day took one, with a great deal of liquor on board, so kept the company hot, damned hot; then all things went well again.*

FROM *THE NAVAL WAR OF 1812*
OR THE HISTORY OF THE UNITED STATES NAVY DURING
THE LAST WAR WITH GREAT BRITAIN TO WHICH IS APPENDED
AN ACCOUNT OF THE BATTLE OF NEW ORLEANS
1882

Theodore Roosevelt

When 26-year-old Lt. Thomas Macdonough was sent to Lake Champlain in up-state New York in the fall of 1812, his orders were simple. He was to take command of a squadron of boats, and use it to control the lake and the water route from Canada down into New York. Simple, but not easy. He found, upon his arrival, that his "squadron" consisted of two gunboats. One had opened its seams to the point where he could stick his hand through the gaps in the planks. The other hadn't dried out quite so badly, because it was on the bottom of the lake.

He began by requisitioning six small sloops from the army. After rebuilding and refitting the gunboats and the sloops to carry cannon, things no doubt started looking a little better. But the British were beginning to put together a rival squadron on the

Richelieu River that flowed north out of Champlain to the St. Lawrence River. Macdonough sent two sloops to station themselves on the north end of the lake at the head of the Richelieu to prevent any British ships from entering the lake. Their commander, Lt. Smith, though under strict orders not to enter British territory, nevertheless sailed down the river chasing a couple of enemy gunboats. At three o'clock in the morning Lt. Smith found the galleys had taken refuge under the guns of a British fort at Isle Aux Noix. A fairly large British force had gathered to welcome him, and the daring officer discovered that it is hard to sail back up a river against the current with the wind on his nose and ended up surrendering both sloops and the 110 precious men in them after a four-hour battle.

The British, grateful for the blunder, which at a stroke gave them overwhelming force, quickly assembled a flotilla and spent the rest of the summer raiding up and down the lake. Macdonough retreated 10 miles up Otter Creek to the town of Vergennes, near the southern end of the lake.

He and the fledgling United States were lucky. At the time, Vergennes was home to eight forges, a blast furnace, a rolling mill, a wire factory, and a sawmill. Otter Creek could be protected by a battery at its mouth, and it was probably the only town on the lake that was both defensible and capable of providing Macdonough with the raw materials he needed to try to rescue the situation by building a new squadron.

In January 1814, Macdonough received authorization to build a ship, and after finding carpenters got down to work. On March 2, his men began what would become the 734-ton ship Saratoga. *Her keel was laid on the 7th, and when she was finished just 40 days later she was 143 feet long and carried 26 guns. In their spare time, the men under Macdonough also converted a steamboat into the schooner* Ticonderoga, *350 tons and 16 guns and saw to repairs on a half dozen gunboats about 75 feet long, each with two masts carrying lateen sails in addition to their 40 oars.*

As work continued on the U.S. squadron into the summer, Macdonough was aware of the growing strength of the British squadron, notably the construction of the 1200-ton frigate Confiance.

On July 23, he set to work on another brig, the Eagle. *When it took its place on Otter Creek among the others on August 11, it weighed in at 500 tons and mounted 20 guns. They had built a brig, about 120 feet long, in 20 days. It was all just in time. The carpenter and bosun must have just been putting the finishing touches on the masts, guns, and rigging when word came that an army of some 11,000 British troops, many of them battle-hardened from fighting Napoleon in Spain, was marching down from Canada to invade the United States.*

THE BATTLE OF LAKE CHAMPLAIN

This lake, which had hitherto played but an inconspicuous part, was now to become the scene of the greatest naval battle of the war. A British army of 11,000 men under Sir George Prevost undertook the invasion of New York by advancing up the western bank of Lake Champlain. This advance was impracticable unless there was a sufficiently strong British naval force to drive back the American squadron at the same time. Accordingly, the British began to construct a frigate, the *Confiance*, to be added to their already existing force, which consisted of a brig, two sloops, and 12 or 14 gun-boats.

The British army advanced slowly toward Plattsburg, which was held by General Macomb with less than 2,000 effective American troops. Captain Thomas Macdonough, the American commodore, took the lake a day or two before his antagonist, and came to anchor in Plattsburg harbor. (*The titles of captain and commodore here were apparently courtesies due Lieutenant Macdonough because of his responsibility for captaining a ship and commanding a squadron*) The British fleet, under Captain George Downie, moved from Isle-aux-Noix on Sept. 8th, and on the morning of the 11th sailed into Plattsburg harbor.

Macdonough and Downie were hurried into action before they had time to prepare themselves thoroughly; but it was a disadvantage common to both, and arose from the nature of the case, which called for immediate action.

Macdonough's squadron

Name.	Tons.	Crew.	Broadside.	Metal from long or short guns.
Saratoga,	734	240	414 lbs.	long, 96—short, 318
Eagle,	500	150	264 "	long, 72—short, 192
Ticonderoga,	350	112	180 "	long, 84—short, 96
Preble,	80	30	36 "	long, 36
6 gun-boats,	420	246	252 "	long, 144—short, 108
4 gun-boats,	160	104	48 "	long, 48

In all, 14 vessels of 2,244 tons and 882 men, with 86 guns throwing at a broadside 1,194 lbs. of shot, 480 from long, and 714 from short guns.

Downie's Squadron

Name.	Tons.	Crew.	Broadside.	Metal from long or short guns.
Confiance,	1200	325	480 lbs.	long, 384—short, 96
Linnet,	350	125	96 "	long, 96
Chubb,	112	50	96 "	long, 6—short, 90
Finch,	110	50	84 "	long, 12—short, 72
5 gun-boats,	350	205	254 "	long, 12—short, 72
7 gun-boats,	280	182	182 "	long, 54—short, 128

In all, 16 vessels, of about 2,402 tons, with 937 men, and a total of 92 guns, throwing at a broadside 1,192 lbs., 660 from long and 532 from short pieces.

Macdonough saw that the British would be forced to make the attack in order to get the control of the waters. On this long, narrow lake the winds usually blow pretty nearly north or south, and the set of the current is of course northward; all the vessels, being flat and shallow, could not beat to windward well, so there was little chance of the British making the attack when there was a southerly wind blowing. So late in the season there was danger of sudden and furious gales, which would make it risky for Downie to wait outside the bay till the wind suited him; and inside the bay the wind was pretty sure to be light and baffling. Young Macdonough (then but 28 years of age) calculated all these chances very coolly and decided to await the attack at anchor in Plattsburg Bay, with the head of his line so far to the north that it could hardly be turned; and then proceeded to make all the other preparations with the same foresight. Not only were his vessels provided with springs, but also with anchors to be used astern in any emergency. The *Saratoga* was further prepared for a change of wind, or for the necessity of winding ship, by having a kedge planted broad off on each of her bows, with a hawser and preventer hawser (hanging in bights under water) leading from each quarter to the kedge on that side. There had not been time to train the men thoroughly at the guns; and to make these produce their full effect the constant supervision of the officers had to be exerted. The British were laboring under this same disadvantage, but neither side felt the want very much, as the smooth water, stationary position of the ships, and fair range, made the fire of both sides very destructive.

Plattsburg Bay is deep and opens to the southward; so that a wind which would enable the British to sail up the lake would force them to beat when entering the bay. The east side of the mouth of the bay is formed by Cumberland Head; the entrance is about a mile and a half across, and the other boundary, southwest from the Head, is an extensive shoal, and a small, low island. This is called Crab Island, and on it was a hospital and one six-pounder gun, which was to be manned in case of necessity by the strongest patients. Macdonough had anchored in a north-and-south line a little to the south of the outlet of the Saranac, and out of range of the shore batteries, being two miles from the western shore. The head of his line was so near Cumberland Head that an attempt to turn it would place the opponent under a very heavy fire, while to the south the shoal prevented a flank attack. The *Eagle* lay to the north, flanked on each side by a couple of gun-boats; then came the *Saratoga*, with three gun-boats between her and the *Ticonderoga*, the next in line; then came three gun-boats and the *Preble*. The four large vessels were at anchor; the galleys being under their sweeps and forming a second line about 40 yards back, some of them keeping their places and some not doing so. By this arrangement his line could not be doubled upon, there was not room to anchor on his broadside out of reach of his carronades, and the enemy was forced to attack by standing in bows on.

The morning of September 11th opened with a light breeze from the northeast. Downie's fleet weighed anchor at daylight, and came down the lake with the wind nearly aft, the booms of the two sloops swinging out to starboard. At half-past seven, the people in the ships could see their adversaries' upper sails across the narrow strip of land ending in Cumberland Head, before the British doubled the latter. Captain Downie hove to with his four large vessels when he had fairly opened the Bay, and waited for his galleys to overtake him. Then his four vessels filled on the starboard tack and headed for the American line, going abreast, the Chubb to the north, heading well to windward of the *Eagle,* for whose bows the *Linnet* was headed, while the *Confiance* was to be laid athwart the hawse of the *Saratoga;* the Finch was to leeward with the twelve gun-boats, and was to engage the

rear of the American line.

As the English squadron stood bravely in, young Macdonough, who feared his foes not at all, but his God a great deal, knelt for a moment, with his officers on the quarter-deck; and then ensued a few minutes of perfect quiet, the men waiting with grim expectancy for the opening of the fight. The *Eagle* spoke first with her long 18's, but to no effect, for the shot fell short. Then, as the *Linnet* passed the *Saratoga,* she fired her broadside of long 12's, but her shot also fell short, except one that struck a hen-coop which happened to be aboard the *Saratoga*. There was a game cock inside, and, instead of being frightened at his sudden release, he jumped up on a gun-slide, clapped his wings, and crowed lustily. The men laughed and cheered; and immediately afterward Macdonough himself fired the first shot from one of the long guns. The 24-pound ball struck the *Confiance* near the hawse-hole and ranged the length of her deck, killing and wounding several men. All the American long guns now opened and were replied to by the British galleys.

The *Confiance* stood steadily on without replying. But she was baffled by shifting winds, and was soon so cut up, having both her port bow-anchors shot away, and suffering much loss, that she was obliged to port her helm and come to while still nearly a quarter of a mile distant from the *Saratoga*. Captain Downie came to anchor in grand style—securing every thing carefully before he fired a gun, and then opening with a terribly destructive broadside. The *Chubb* and *Linnet* stood farther in, and anchored forward the *Eagle*'s beam. Meanwhile the *Finch* got abreast of the *Ticonderoga,* under her sweeps, supported by the gunboats. The main fighting was thus to take place between the vans, where the *Eagle, Saratoga*, and six or seven gunboats were engaged with the *Chubb, Linnet, Confiance,* and two or three gunboats; while in the rear, the *Ticonderoga,* the *Preble,* and the other American galleys engaged the *Finch* and the remaining nine or ten English galleys. The battle at the foot of the line was fought on the part of the Americans to prevent their flank being turned, and on the part of the British to effect that object. At first, the fighting was at long range, but gradually the British galleys closed up, firing very well. The American galleys at this end of the line were chiefly the small ones, armed with one 12-pounder apiece, and they by degrees drew back before the heavy fire of their opponents. About an hour after the discharge of the first gun had been fired the *Finch* closed up toward the *Ticonderoga,* and was completely crippled by a couple of broadsides from the latter. She drifted helplessly down the line and grounded near Crab Island; some of the convalescent patients manned the six-pounder and fired a shot or two at her, when she struck, nearly half of her crew being killed or wounded. About the same time the British gunboats forced the *Preble* out of line, whereupon she cut her cable and drifted inshore out of the fight. Two or three of the British gun-boats had already been sufficiently damaged by some of the shot from the *Ticonderoga*'s long guns to make them wary; and the contest at this part of the line narrowed down to one between the American schooner and the remaining British gun-boats, who combined to make a most determined attack upon her. So hastily had the squadron been fitted out that many of the matches for her guns were at the last moment found to be defective. The captain of one of the divisions was a midshipman, but sixteen years old, Hiram Paulding. When he found the matches to be bad he fired the guns of his section by having pistols flashed at them, and continued this through the whole fight. The *Ticonderoga*'s commander, Lieut. Cassin, fought his schooner most nobly. He kept walking the taffrail amidst showers of musketry and grape, coolly watching the movements of the galleys and directing the guns to be loaded with canister and bags of bullets, when the enemy tried to board. The British galleys were handled with determined gallantry, under the command of Lieutenant Bell. Had they driven off the *Ticonderoga* they would have won the day for their side, and they pushed up till they were not a boat-hook's length distant, to try to carry her by boarding; but every attempt was repulsed and they were forced to draw off, some of them so crippled by the slaughter they had suffered that they could hardly man the oars.

Meanwhile the fighting at the head of the line had been even fiercer. The first broadside of the *Confiance,* fired from 16 long 24's, double-shotted, coolly sighted, in smooth water, at point-blank range, produced the most terrible effect on the *Saratoga.* Her hull shivered all over with the shock, and when the crash subsided nearly half of her people were seen stretched on deck, for many had been knocked down who were not seriously hurt. Among the slain was her first lieutenant, Peter Gamble; he was kneeling down to sight the bow-gun, when a shot entered the port, split the quoin, and drove a portion of it against his side, killing him without breaking the skin. The survivors carried on the fight with undiminished energy. Macdonough himself worked like a common sailor, in pointing and handling a favorite gun. While bending over to sight it a round shot cut in two the spanker boom, which fell on his head and struck him senseless for two or three minutes; he then leaped to his feet and continued as before, when a shot took off the head of the captain of the gun and drove it in his face with such a force as to knock him to the other side of the deck. But after the first broadside not so much injury was done; the guns of the *Confiance* had been leveled to point-blank range, and as the quoins were loosened by the successive discharges they were not properly replaced, so that her broadsides kept going higher and higher and doing less and less damage. Very shortly after the beginning of the action her gallant captain was slain. He was standing behind one of the long guns when a shot from the *Saratoga* struck it and threw it completely off the carriage against his right groin, killing him almost instantly. His skin was not broken; a black mark, about the size of a small plate, was the only visible injury. His watch was found flattened, with its hands pointing to the very second at which he received the fatal blow. As the contest went on the fire gradually decreased in weight, the guns being disabled. The inexperience of both crews partly caused this. The American sailors overloaded their carronades so as to very much destroy the effect of their fire; when the officers became disabled, the men would cram the guns with shot till the last projected from the muzzle. Of course, this lessened the execution, and also gradually crippled the guns. On board the *Confiance* the confusion was even worse: after the battle the charges of the guns were drawn, and on the side she had fought one was found with a canvas bag containing two round of shot rammed home and wadded without any powder; another with two cartridges and no shot; and a third with a wad below the cartridge.

At the extreme head of the line the advantage had been with the British. The *Chubb* and *Linnet* had begun a brisk engagement with the *Eagle* and American gun-boats. In a short time the *Chubb* had her cable, bowsprit, and main-boom shot away, drifted within the American lines, and was taken possession of by one of the *Saratoga*'s midshipmen. The *Linnet* paid no attention to the American gun-boats, directing her whole fire against the *Eagle,* and the latter was, in addition, exposed to part of the fire of the *Confiance*. After keeping up a heavy fire for a long time her springs were shot away, and she came up into the wind, hanging so that she could not return a shot to the well-directed broadsides of the *Linnet*. Henly accordingly cut his cable, started home his top-sails, ran down, and anchored by the stern between and inshore of the *Confiance* and *Ticonderoga,* from which position he opened on the *Confiance*. The *Linnet* now directed her attention to the American gun-boats, which at this end of the line were very well fought, but she soon drove them off, and then sprung her broadside so as to rake the *Saratoga* on her bows.

Macdonough by this time had his hands full, and his fire was slackening; he was bearing the whole brunt of the action, with the frigate on his beam and the brig raking him. Twice his ship had been set on fire by the hot shot of the *Confiance;* one by one his long guns were disabled by shot, and his carronades were either treated the same way or else rendered useless by excessive overcharging. Finally but a single carronade was left in the starboard batteries, and on firing it the naval-bolt broke, the gun flew off the carriage and fell down the main hatch, leaving the Commodore without a single gun to oppose to the few the *Confiance* still presented. The battle would have been lost had not Macdonough's foresight provided the means of retrieving it.

The anchor suspended astern of the *Saratoga* was let go, and the men hauled in on the hawser that led to the starboard quarter, bringing the ship's stern up over the kedge. The ship now rode by the kedge and by a line that had been bent to a bight in the stream cable, and she was raked badly by the accurate fire of the *Linnet*. By rousing on the line the ship was at length got so far round that the aftermost gun of the port broadside bore on the *Confiance*. The men had been sent forward to keep as much out of harm's way as possible, and now some were at once called back to man the piece, which then opened with effect. The next gun was treated in the same manner; but the ship now hung and would go no farther round. The hawser leading from the port quarter was then got forward under the bows and passed aft to the starboard quarter, and a minute afterward the ship's whole port battery opened with fatal effect. The *Confiance* meanwhile had also attempted to round. Her springs, like those of the *Linnet,* were on the starboard side, and so of course could not be shot away as the *Eagle*'s were; but, as she had nothing but springs to rely on, her efforts did little beyond forcing her forward, and she hung with her head to the wind. She had lost over half of her crew, most of her guns on the engaged side were dismounted, and her stout masts had been splintered till they looked like bundles of matches; her sails had been torn to rags, and she was forced to strike, about two hours after she had fired the first broadside. Without pausing a minute the *Saratoga* again hauled on her starboard hawser till her broadside was sprung to bear on the *Linnet,* and the ship and brig began a brisk fight, which the *Eagle* from her position could take no part in, while the *Ticonderoga* was just finishing up the British galleys.

The shattered and disabled state of the *Linnet*'s masts, sails, and yards precluded the most distant hope of Capt. Pring's effecting his escape by cutting his cable; but he kept up a most gallant fight with his greatly superior foe, in hopes that some of the gun-boats would come and tow him off, and dispatched a lieutenant to the *Confiance* to ascertain her state. The lieutenant returned with news of Capt. Downie's death, while the British gun-boats had been driven half a mile off; and, after having maintained the fight single-handed for fifteen minutes, until, from the number of shot between wind and water, the water had risen a foot above her lower deck, the plucky little brig hauled down her colors, and the fight ended, a little over two hours and a half after the first gun had been fired. Not one of the larger vessels had a mast that would bear canvas, and the prizes were in a sinking condition.

On both sides the ships had been cut up in the most extraordinary manner; the *Saratoga* had 55 shot-holes in her hull, and the *Confiance* 105 in hers, and the *Eagle* and *Linnet* had suffered in proportion. The number of killed and wounded can not be exactly stated; it was probably about 200 on the American side, and over 300 on the British.

Captain Macdonough at once returned the British officers their swords. Captain Pring writes: "I have much satisfaction in making you acquainted with the humane treatment the wounded have received from Commodore Macdonough; they were immediately removed to his own hospital on Crab Island, and furnished with every requisite. His generous and polite attention to myself, the officers, and men, will ever hereafter be gratefully remembered." The effects of the victory were immediate and of the highest importance. Sir George Prevost and his army at once fled in great haste and confusion back to Canada, leaving our northern frontier clear for the remainder of the war; while the victory had a very great effect on the negotiations for peace.

LETTERS TO JEFFERSON

1803

Meriwether Lewis

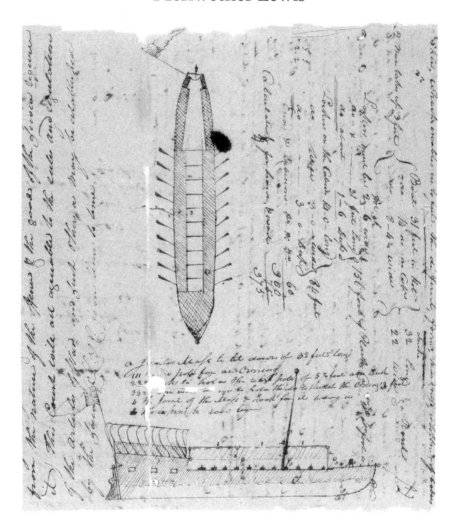

At the behest of President Thomas Jefferson, U.S. Army Captain Meriwether Lewis and Lt. William Clark set off to explore the newly purchased Louisiana Territory in 1803. The expedition was a wonder—three years and something like 6,000 miles up the Missouri River over the Rocky Mountains and down the Columbia to the Pacific Ocean through what was more or less terra incognita. And it was all done without communications with, or support from, the U.S. and Jefferson. It is no surprise that when they arrived back in St. Louis in September of 1806 they found they had mostly been given up for dead.

The story of the expedition has been told many times. But the story of Lewis building the specially designed 55-foot keel boat and an iron-framed folding long boat is both less familiar, and a good read in itself. It will also be familiar to anyone who has ever had grand plans for building or fixing up a boat and making an ambitious voyage. In 1803, like today, one has to make a very generous estimate of the time the preparations, shakedown cruise, and voyage will take, then double it—and even then you can be sure that Murphy's Law will kick in at some point. For most of us, it doesn't matter much. But imagine poor Lewis, coping with drought and drunken boatbuilders, and having to explain to the president of the United States why he is in Cincinnati in the autumn of 1803 and not looking for a winter camp halfway up the Missouri River.

To keep the story moving I have taken out many of the administrative details, such as consideration and appointment of personnel, and in one place an interesting but lengthy description of the excavation of a mammoth skeleton near Cincinnati. Also, note that his spelling was not perfect, and I haven't corrected it.

Lancaster, Apl. 20th 1803.

Sir,

With a view to forward as much as possible the preparations which must necessarily be made in the Western country previous to my final departue, as also to prevent the delay, which would attatch to their being made after my arrival in that quarter, I have taken the following measures, which I hope will meet your approbation; they appear to me to be as complete as my present view of the subject will admit my making them and I trust the result will prove as favorable as wished for . . .

My detention at Harper's Ferry was unavoidable for one month, a period much greater than could reasonably have been calculated on; my greatest difficulty was the frame of the canoe, which could not be completed without my personal attention to such portion of it was would enable the workmen to understand the design perfectly; other inducements seemed with equal force to urge my waiting the issue of a full experiment, arising as well from a wish to incur no expence unnecessarily, as from an unwillingness to risk any calculation on the advantages of this canoe in which hereafter I might possibly be deceived; experiment was necessary also to determine it's dementions: I therefore resolved to give it a fair trial, and accordingly prepared two sections of it with same materials, of which they must of necessity be composed when completed for servise on my voyage; they were of two discriptions, the one curved, or in the shape necessary for the stem and stern, the other simicilindrical, or in the form of those sections which constitute the body of the canoe. The experiment and it's result wer as follow.

Dementions

Curved Section

Length of Keel from junction of section to commencement of curve   1'2"
Length of curved section   4'6"

(Note—The curve of the body was formed by a suspended cord)

Width of broad end   4'10"

Debth of D.D.   2'2"

Simicilindrical Section

Length of keel   4'6"

Ditto beam   4'10"

Debth of Hole   2'2"

Weight of the Materials

Curved Section. . . . lbs. . . . Semicilindrical Section

Iron . . . 22 . . .   Iron . . . 22

Hide . . . 25   Hide . . . 30

Wood . . . 10   Wood . . . 12

Bark . . . 21   Bark . . . 25

Total . . . 78   Total . . . 89

Competent to a

Burthen of 850 lbs.   Burthen of 920 lbs.

Necessary to be transported by land.

Iron and Hide of Curved Section . . . 47

Iron and Hide of Simicilindrical Do. 52 . . . 99 lbs.

Burthen of Curved Section . . . 850

Do. Do. Simicilindrical . . . 920 . . .

Total: 1,770 lbs.

Thus the weight of this vessel competent to the burthen of 1,770 lbs. amount to no more than 99 lbs. The bark and wood, when it becomes necessary to transport the vessel to any considerable distances, may be discarded; as those articles are reaidily obtained for the purposes of this canoe, at all seasons of the year, and in every quarter of the country, which is tolerably furnished with forest trees. When these sectons were united they appeared to acquire an additional strength and firmness, and I am confident that in cases of emergency they would be competent to 150 lbs. more than the burthen already stated. Altho' the weight of the articles employed in the construction of a canoe on this plan, have considerably exceeded the estimat I had previously made, yet they do not weigh more than those which form a bark canoe of equal dementions, and in my opinion is much preferable to it in many respects; it is much stronger, will carry its burthen with equal ease, and greater security; and when the Bark and wood are discarded, will be much higher, and can be transported with more safety and ease. I was induced from the result of this experiment to direct the iron frame of the canoe to be completed.

It is hard to picture the boat from Lewis's description—perhaps he and Jefferson had roughed out some plans for it together before Lewis left Washington so he figured Jefferson could follow. Just reading from the text of the letter, it seemed that he was talking about a double-ended boat about 16' long, with a beam of 4'10" and a depth from keel to gunwale of 2'2". With a little help from my engineer wife on the geometry, I calculated a total displacement for the boat of about 6,300 lbs. So if one figures on about 25 percent of that as a safe working load, Lewis's figure of 1,770 lbs. capacity sounds just about right. But Lewis writes in the letter that after the success of his experiment, he directed the rest of the boat to be constructed, and when it came time to build the boat at the Great Falls of the Missouri, Lewis wrote "the iron frame of my boat is 36 feet long 4 1/2 f. in the beam and 26 Inches in the hole. . . ."

At Great Falls in late June of 1805, Lewis found that assembling the boat was not anywhere near as easy as he had thought. Timber suitable to make thwarts was apparently in short supply, and shooting enough elk and buffalo for the skin covering also took longer than he thought. In the end, Lewis wrote that it took twenty-eight elk skins and four buffalo skins to cover it. But when they had managed those things, their problems were not over. After the skins were stitched together, Lewis found that the holes made in the skins in the course of sewing them enlarged as the skins dried and stretched out, and so the skins leaked. They tried to plug the holes with a mixture of tallow and ground charcoal, but that didn't work, and there were no pines in the area from which he could make pitch. He noted the buffalo skins worked better, but said that as the buffalo had left the area, he had no choice but to abandon the boat.

My Rifles, Tomahawks & knives are preparing at Harper's Ferry, and are already in a state of forwardness that leaves me little doubt of their being in readiness in due time.

Being fully impressed with the necessity of seting out as early as possible, you may rest assured that not a moment shall be lost in making the necessary preparations. I still think it practicable to reach the mouth of the Missouri by the 1st of August. I am Sir, with much esteem and regard Your Most Obt. Servt.

Meriwether Lewis

Pittsburgh July 22nd 1803.

Dear Sir

Yours of the 11th & 15th Inst. were duly recieved, the former on the 18th inst., the latter on this day. For my pocketbook I thank you: the dirk could not well come by post, nor is it of any moment to me, the knives that were made at Harper's ferry will answer my purposes equally as well and perhaps better; it can therefore be taken care of untill my return: the bridle is of no consequence at all. After the reciept of this letter I think it will be best to direct to me at Louisville, Kentuckey.

The person who contracted to build my boat engaged to have it in readiness by the 20th inst.; in this however he has failed; he pleads his having been disappointed in procuring timber, but says he has now supplyed himself with the necessary materials, and that she shall be completed by the last of this month; however in this I am by no means sanguine, nor do I believe from the progress he makes that she will be ready before the 5th of August; I visit him every day, and endeavour by every means in my power to hasten the completion of the work: I have prevailed on him to engage more hands, and he tells me that two others will join him in the morning, if so, he may probably finish the boat by the time he mentioned: I shall embark immediately the boat is in readiness, there being no other consideration which at this moment detains me.

The Waggon from Harper's ferry arrived today, bringing every thing with which she was charged in good order. *(Rifles, powder, shot, many other odds and ends of supplies)*

The party of recruits that were ordered from Carlisle to this place with a view to descend the river with me, have arrived with the exception of one, who deserted on the march, his place however can be readily supplyed from the recruits at this place enlisted by Lieut. Hook.

The current of the Ohio is extreemly low and continues to decline, this may impede my progress but shall not prevent my proceeding, being detemined to get forward though I should not be able to make a greater distance than a mile pr. day. I am with the most sincere regard Your Obt. Servt.

Meriwether Lewis

Wheeling, September 8th 1803.

Dear Sir,

It was not until 7 O'Clock on the morning of the 31st Ultmo. that my boat was completed, she was instantly loaded, and at 10. a.m. on the same day I left Pittsburgh, where I had been moste shamefully detained by the unpardonable negligence of my boat-builder. On my arrival at Pittsburgh, my calculation was that the boat would be in readiness by the 5th of August; this term however elapsed and the boat so far from being finished was only partially planked on one side. In this situation I had determined to abandon the boat, and to purchase two or three perogues and descend the river in them, and depend on purchasing a boat as I descended, there being none to be had at Pittsburgh; from this resolution I was dissuaded first by the representations of the best informed merchants at that place who assured me that the chances were much against my being able to procure a boat below; and secondly by the positive assureances given me by the boat-builder that she should be ready on the last of the then ensuing week, (the 13th): however a few days after, according to his usual custom he got drunk, quarrelled with his workmen, and several of them left him, nor could they be prevailed on to return: I threatened him with the penalty of his contract, and exacted a promise of greater sobriety in future which, he took care to perform with as little good faith, as he had his previous promises with regard to the boat, continuing to be constantly either drunk or sick. I spent most of my time with the workmen, alternately presuading and threatening, but neither threats, presuasion or any other means which I could devise were sufficient to procure the completion of the work sooner than the 31st of August; by which time the water was so low that those who pretended to be acquainted with the navigation of the river declared it impracticable to descend it; however in conformity to my previous determination I set out, having taken the precaution to send a part of by baggage by a waggon to this place, and also to procure a good pilot. My days journey have averaged about 12 miles, but in some instances, with every exertion I could make was unable to exceed 4 1/2 & 5 miles pr. day. This place is one hundred miles distant from Pittsburgh by way of the river and about sixty five by land.

When the Ohio is in it's present state there are many obstructions to it's navigation, formed by bars of small stones, which in some instances are intermixed with, and partially cover large quntities of driftwood; these bars frequently extend themselves entirely across the bed of the river, over many of them I found it impossible to pass even with my emty boat, without geting into the water and lifting her over by hand; over others my force was even inadequate to enable me to pass in this manner, and I found myself compelled to hire horses or oxen from the neighbouring farms and drag her over them; in this way I have passed as many as five of those bars, (or as they are here called riffles) in a day, and to unload as many ore more time. The river is lower than it has ever been known by the oldest settle in this country. I shall leave this place tomorrow morning, and loose no time in geting on.

I have been compelled to purchase a perogue at this place in order to transport the baggage which was sent by land from Pittsburgh, and also to lighten the boat as much as possible. On many bars the water in the deepest part dose not exceed six inches. I have the honour to be with the most perfect regard and sincere attatchment Your Obt. Servt. . . .

Meriwether Lewis, Capt.

On board my boat opposite Marietta September 13th 1803.

Dear Sir

I arrived here at 7. p.m. and shall pursue my journey early tomorrow. This place is one hundred miles distant from Wheeling, from whence in descending the water is reather more abundant than it is between that place and Pittsburgh, insomuch that I have been enabled to get on without the necessity employing oxen or horses to drag my boat over the ripples except in two instances; tho' I was obliged to cut a passage through four or five bars, and by that means past them; this last operation is much more readily performed that you would imagin; the gravel of which many of these bars are formed, being small and lying in a loose state is readily removed with a spade, or even with a wooden shovel and when set in motion the current drives it a considerable distance before it subsides or again settles at the bottom; in this manner I have cut a passage for my boat of 50 yards in length in the course of an hour; this method however is impracticable when driftwood or clay in any quantity is intermixed with the gravel; in such cases Horses or oxen are the last resort: I find them the most efficient sailors in the present state of the navigation of this river, altho' they may be considered somewhat clumsey. I have the honour to be with much respect Your Obt. Servt.

Meriwether Lewis, Capt.

1st U.S. Regt. Infty.

Cincinnati, October 3rd 1803.

Dear Sir,

I reached this place on the 28th Ult.; it being necessary to take in a further supply of provisions here, and finding my men much fatiegued with the labour to which they have been subjected in descending the river, I determined to recruit them by giving them a short respite of a few days, having now obtained the distance of five hundred miles. On the evening of the 1st inst. I again dispatched my boat with orders to meet me at the Big Bone lick, to which place I shall pass by land, it being distant from hence only seventeen miles while by water it is fifty three, a distance that will require my boat in the present state of the water near three days to attain.

The late reserches of Dr. William Goforth of this plase at that Lick has made it a place of more interesting enquiry than formerly, I shall therefore seize the present moment to visit it, and set out early tomorrow morning for that purpose.

(I have removed here a lengthy description of excavating mammoth bones and teeth from Big Bone salt lick near Cincinnati. —ed.)

So soon Sir, as you deem it expedient to promulge the late treaty, between the United States and France I would be much obliged by your directing an official copy of it to be furnished me, as I think it probable that the present inhabitants of Lousiana, from such an evidence of their having become the Citizens of the United States, would feel it their interest and would more readily yeald any information of which, they may be possessed relative to the country than they would be disposed to do, while there is any doubt remaining on that subject.

As this Session of Congress has commenced earlyer than usual, and as from a variety of incidental circumstances my progress has been unexpectedly delayed, and feeling as I do in the most anxious manner a wish to keep them in good humour on the subject of the expedicion in which I am engaged, I have concluded to make a tour this winter on horseback of some hundred miles through the most interesting portion of the country adjoining my winter establishment; perhaps it may be up the Canceze River and towards Santafee, at all events it will bee on the South side of the Missouri. Should I find that Mr. Clark can with propiety also leave the party, I will prevail on him also to undertake a similar excurtion through some other portion of the country: by this means I hope and am pursuaded that by the middle of February or 1st of March I shall be enabled to procure and forward to you such information relative to that Country, which, if it dose not produce a conviction of the utility of this project, will at least procure the further toleration of the expedition.

It will be better to forward all letters and papers for me in future to Cahokia.

The water still continues lower in the Ohio that it was ever known. I am with every sentiment of gratitude and respect Your Obt. Servt.

Meriwether Lewis. Capt.

lst. U.S. Regt. Infty

Mark Twain

" BESIEGING THE PILOT."

Samuel Langhorne Clemens spent a couple of decades wandering the American West in the mid-1800s, often living rough and finding work where he could. In 1857, he traveled down the Mississippi to New Orleans in the hope of finding a ship to take him to Brazil so he could travel up the Amazon. The project didn't work out, but the trip down the river struck a chord with the young writer, and he ended up apprenticing himself to be a river pilot.

A CUB-PILOT'S EXPERIENCE

What with lying on the rocks four days at Louisville, and some other delays, the poor old *Paul Jones* fooled away about two weeks in making the voyage from Cincinnati to New Orleans. This gave me a chance to get acquainted with one of the pilots, and he taught me how to steer the boat, and thus made the fascination of river life more potent than ever for me.

It also gave me a chance to get acquainted with a youth who had taken deck passage—more's the pity; for he easily borrowed six dollars of me on a promise to return to the boat and pay it back to me the day after we should arrive. But he probably died or forgot, for he never came. It was doubtless the former, since he had said his parents were wealthy, and he only traveled deck passage because it was cooler.

I soon discovered two things. One was that a vessel would not be likely to sail for the mouth of the Amazon under ten or twelve years; and the other was that the nine or ten dollars still left in my pocket would not suffice for so imposing an exploration as I had planned, even if I could afford to wait for a ship. Therefore it followed that I must contrive a new career. The *Paul Jones* was now bound for St. Louis. I planned a siege against my pilot, and at the end of three hard days he surrendered. He agreed to teach me the Mississippi River from New Orleans to St. Louis for five hundred dollars, payable out of the first wages I should receive after graduating. I entered upon the small enterprise of "learning" twelve or thirteen hundred miles of the great Mississippi River with the easy confidence of my time of life.

If I had really known what I was about to require of my faculties, I should not have had the courage to begin. I supposed that all a pilot had to do was to keep his boat in the river, and I did not consider that that could be much of a trick, since it was so wide.

The boat backed out from New Orleans at four in the afternoon, and it was "our watch" until eight. Mr. Bixby, my chief, "straightened her up," plowed her along past the sterns of the other boats that lay at the Levee, and then said, "Here, take her; shave those steamships as close as you'd peel an apple." I took the wheel, and my heart-beat fluttered up into the hundreds; for it seemed to me that we were about to scrape the side off every ship in the line, we were so close. I held my breath and began to claw the boat away from the danger; and I had my own opinion of the pilot who had known no better than to get us into such peril, but I was too wise to express it. In half a minute I had a wide margin of safety intervening between the *Paul Jones* and the ships; and within ten seconds more I was set aside in disgrace, and Mr. Bixby was going into danger again and flaying me alive with abuse of my cowardice.

I was stung, but I was obliged to admire the easy confidence with which my chief loafed from side to side of his wheel, and trimmed the ships so closely that disaster seemed ceaselessly imminent. When he had cooled a little he told me that the easy water was close ashore and the current outside, and therefore we must hug the bank, up-stream, to get the benefit of the former, and stay well out, down-stream, to take advantage of the latter. In my own mind I resolved to be a down-stream pilot and leave the up-streaming to people dead to prudence.

Now and then Mr. Bixby called my attention to certain things. Said he, "This is Six-Mile Point." I assented. It was pleasant enough information, but I could not see the bearing of it. I was not conscious that it was a matter of any interest to me. Another time he said, "This is Nine-Mile Point." Later he said, "This is Twelve-Mile Point." They were all about level with the water's edge; they all looked about alike to me; they were monotonously unpicturesque. I hoped Mr. Bixby would change the subject. But no; he would crowd up around a point, hugging the shore with affection, and then say:

"The slack water ends here, abreast this bunch of China-trees; now we cross over." So he crossed over. He gave me the wheel once or twice, but I had no luck. I either came near clipping off the edge of a sugar plantation, or I yawed too far from shore, and so dropped back into disgrace again and got abused.

The watch was ended at last, and we took supper and went to bed. At midnight the glare of a lantern shone in my eyes, and the night watchman said:—

"Come! turn out!"

And then he left. I could not understand this extraordinary procedure; so I presently gave up trying to, and dozed off to sleep. Pretty soon the watchman was back again, and this time he was gruff. I was annoyed. I said:—

"What do you want to come bothering around here in the middle of the night for? Now as like as not I'll not get to sleep again to-night."

The watchman said:—"Well, if this an't good, I'm blest."

The "off-watch" was just turning in, and I heard some brutal laughter from them, and such remarks as "Hello, watchman! an't the new cub turned out yet? He's delicate likely. Give him some sugar in a rag and send for the chambermaid to sing rock-a-by-baby to him."

About this time Mr. Bixby appeared on the scene. Something like a minute later I was climbing the pilot-house steps with some of my clothes on and the rest in my arms. Mr. Bixby was close behind, commenting. Here was something fresh—this thing of getting up in the middle of the night to go to work. It was a detail in piloting that had never occurred to me at all. I knew that boats ran all night, but somehow I had never happened to reflect that somebody had to get up out of a warm bed to run them. I began to fear that piloting was not quite so romantic as I had imagined it was; there was something very real and work-like about this new phase of it.

It was a rather dingy night, although a fair number of stars were out. The big mate was at the wheel, and he had the old tub pointed at a star and was holding her straight up the middle of the river. The shores on either hand were not much more than half a mile apart, but they seemed wonderfully far away and ever so vague and indistinct. The mate said:—

"We've got to land at Jones's plantation, sir."

The vengeful spirit in me exulted. I said to myself, I wish you joy of your job, Mr. Bixby; you'll have a good time finding Mr. Jones's plantation such a night as this; and I hope you never *will* find it as long as you live.

Mr. Bixby said to the mate:—

"Upper end of the plantation, or the lower?"

"Upper."

"I can't do it. The stamps there are out of water at this stage. It's no great distance to the lower, and you'll have to get along with that."

"All right, sir. If Jones don't like it he'll have to lump it, I reckon."

And then the mate left. My exultation began to cool and my wonder to came up. Here was a man who not only proposed to find this plantation on such a night, but to find either end of it you preferred. I dreadfully wanted to ask a question, but I was carrying about as many short answers as my cargo-room would admit of, so I held my peace. All I desired to ask Mr. Bixby was the simple question whether he was ass enough to really imagine he was going to find that plantation on a night when all plantations were exactly alike and all the same color. But I held in. I used to have fine inspirations of prudence in those days.

Mr. Bixby made for the shore, and soon was scraping it, just the same as if it had been daylight. And not only that, but singing—"Father in heaven, the day is declining," etc. It seemed to me that I had put my life in the keeping of a peculiarly reckless outcast. Presently he turned on me and said:—

"What's the name of the first point above New Orleans?"

I was gratified to be able to answer promptly, and I did. I said I didn't know.

"Don't *know*?"

This manner jolted me. I was down at the foot again, in a moment. But I had to say just what I had said before.

"Well, you're a smart one," said Mr. Bixby. "What's the name of the *next* point?"

Once more I didn't know.

"Well, this beats anything. Tell me the name of *any* point or place I told you."

I studied a while and decided that I couldn't.

"Look here! What do you start out from, above Twelve-Mile Point, to cross over?"

"I—I—don't know."

"You—you—don't know?" mimicking my drawling manner of speech. "What *do* you know?"

"I—I—nothing, for certain."

"By the great Caesar's ghost, I believe you! You're the stupidest dunder-head I ever saw or ever heard of, so help me Moses! The idea of *you* being a pilot—*you!* Why, you don't know enough to pilot a cow down a lane."

Oh, but his wrath was up! He was a nervous man, and he shuffled from one side of his wheel to the other as if the floor was hot. He would boil a while to himself, and then overflow and scald me again.

"Look here! What do you suppose I told you the names of those points for?"

I tremblingly considered a moment, and then the devil of temptation provoked me to say:—"Well—to—to—be entertaining, I thought."

This was a red rag to the bull. He raged and stormed so (he was crossing the river at the time) that I judge it made him blind, because he ran over the steering-oar of a trading-scow. Of course the traders sent up a volley of red-hot profanity. Never was a man so grateful as Mr. Bixby was: because he was brim full, and here were subjects who could *talk back*.

He threw open a window, thrust his head out, and such an irruption followed as I never had heard before. The fainter and farther away the scowmen's curses drifted, the higher Mr. Bixby lifted his voice and the weightier his adjectives grew. When he closed the window he was empty. You could have drawn a seine through his system and not caught curses enough to disturb your mother with. Presently he said to me in the gentlest way:—

"My boy, you must get a little memorandum-book, and every time I tell you a thing, put it down right away. There's only one way to be a pilot, and that is to get this entire river by heart. You have to know it just like A B C."

That was a dismal revelation to me; for my memory was never loaded with anything but blank cartridges. However, I did not feel discouraged long. I judged that it was best to make some allowances, for doubtless Mr. Bixby was "stretching." Presently he pulled a rope and struck a few strokes on the big bell. The stars were all gone now, and the night was as black as ink. I could hear the wheels churn along the bank, but I was not entirely certain that I could see the shore. The voice of the invisible watchman called up from the hurricane deck:—

"What's this, sir?"

"Jones's plantation."

I said to myself, I wish I might venture to offer a small bet that it isn't. But I did not chirp. I only waited to see. Mr. Bixby handled the engine bells, and in due time the boat's nose came to the land, a torch glowed from the fore-castle, a man skipped ashore, a darky's voice on the bank said, "Gimme de k'yarpet-bag, Mars' Jones," and the next moment we were standing up the river again, all serene. I reflected deeply a while, and then said,—but not aloud,—Well, the finding of that plantation was the luckiest accident that ever happened; but it couldn't happen again in a hundred years. And I fully believed it *was* an accident, too.

By the time we had gone seven or eight hundred miles up the river, I had learned to be a tolerably plucky upstream steersman, in daylight, and before we reached St. Louis I had made a trifle of progress in night-work, but only a trifle. I had a note-book that fairly bristled with the names of towns, "points," bars, islands, bends, reaches, etc.; but the information was to be found only in the note-book—none of it was in my head. It made my heart ache to think I had only got half of the river set down; for as our watch was four hours off and four hours on, day and night, there was a long four-hour gap in my book for every time I had slept since the voyage began.

My chief was presently hired to go on a big New Orleans boat, and I packed my satchel and went with him. She was a grand affair. When I stood in her pilot-house I was so far above the water that I seemed perched on a mountain; and her decks stretched so far away, fore and aft, below me, that I wondered how I could ever have considered the little *Paul Jones* a large craft. There were other differences, too. The *Paul Jones*'s pilot-house was a cheap, dingy, battered rattle-trap, cramped for room: but here was a sumptuous glass temple; room enough to have a dance in; showy red and gold window-curtains; an imposing sofa; leather cushions and a back to the high bench where visiting pilots sit, to spin yarns and "look at the river;" bright, fanciful "cuspadores" instead of a broad wooden box filled with sawdust; nice new oil-cloth on the floor; a hospitable big stove for winter; a wheel as high as my head, costly with inlaid work; a wire tiller-rope; bright brass knobs for the bells; and a tidy, white-aproned, black "texas-tender," to bring up tarts and ices and coffee during mid-watch, day and night. Now this was "something like;" and so I began to take heart once more to believe that piloting was a romantic sort of occupation after all.

The moment we were under way I began to prowl about the great steamer and fill myself with joy. She was as clean and as dainty as a drawing-room; when I looked down her long, gilded saloon, it was like gazing through a splendid tunnel; she had an oil-picture, by some gifted sign-painter, on every state-room door; she glittered with no end of prism-fringed chandeliers; the clerk's office was elegant, the bar was marvelous, and the bar-keeper had been barbered and upholstered at incredible cost. The boiler deck (*i.e.,* the second story of the boat, so to speak) was as spacious as a church, it seemed to me; so with the forecastle; and there was no pitiful handful of deck-hands, firemen, and roust-abouts down there, but a whole battalion of men. The fires were fiercely glaring from a long row of furnaces, and over them were eight huge boilers! This was unutterable pomp. The mighty engines—but enough of this. I had never felt so fine before. And when I found that the regiment of natty servants respectfully "sir'd" me, my satisfaction was complete.

CHAPTER VII. DARING DEED.

When I returned to the pilot-house St. Louis was gone and I was lost. Here was a piece of river which was all down in my book, but I could make neither head nor tail of it: you understand, it was turned around. I had seen it when coming up-stream, but I had never faced about to see how it looked when it was behind me. My heart broke again, for it was plain that I had got to learn this troublesome river *both ways*.

The pilot-house was full of pilots, going down to "look at the river." What is called the "upper river" (the two hundred miles between St. Louis and Cairo, where the Ohio comes in) was low; and the Mississippi changes its channel so constantly that the pilots used to always find it necessary to run down to Cairo to take a fresh look, when their boats were to lie in port a week; that is, when the water was at a low stage. A deal of this "looking at the river" was done by poor fellows who seldom had a berth, and whose only hope of getting one lay in their being always freshly posted and therefore ready to drop into the shoes of some reputable pilot, for a single trip, on account of such pilot's sudden illness, or some other necessity. And a good many of them constantly ran up and down inspecting the river, not because they ever really hoped to got a berth, but because (they being guests of the boat) it was cheaper to "look at the river" than stay ashore and pay board. In time these fellows grew dainty in their tastes, and only infested boats that had an established reputation for setting good tables.

All visiting pilots were useful, for they were always ready and willing, winter or summer, night or day, to go out in the yawl and help buoy the channel or assist the boat's pilots in any way they could. They were likewise welcome because all pilots are tireless talkers, when gathered together, and as they talk only about the river they are always understood and are always interesting. Your true pilot cares nothing about anything on earth but the river, and his pride in his occupation surpasses the pride of kings.

We had a fine company of these river-inspectors along, this trip. There were eight or ten; and there was abundance of room for them in our great pilot-house. Two or three of them wore polished silk hats, elaborate shirt-fronts, diamond breastpins, kid gloves, and patent-leather boots. They were choice in their English, and bore themselves with a dignity proper to men of solid means and prodigious reputation as pilots. The others were more or less loosely clad, and wore upon their heads tall felt cones that were suggestive of the days of the Commonwealth.

I was a cipher in this august company, and felt subdued, not to say torpid. I was not even of sufficient consequence to assist at the wheel when it was necessary to put the tiller hard down in a hurry; the guest that stood nearest did that when occasion required—and this was pretty much all the time, because of the crookedness of the channel and the scant water. I stood in a corner; and the talk I listened to took the hope all out of me. One visitor said to another:—

"Jim, how did you run Plum Point, coming up?"

"It was in the night, there, and I ran it the way one of the boys on the *Diana* told me; started out about fifty yards above the wood pile on the false point, and held on the cabin under Plum Point till I raised the reef—quarter less twain—then straightened up for the middle bar till I got well abreast the old one-limbed cotton-wood in the bend, then got my stem on the cotton-wood and head on the low place above the point, and came through a-booming—nine and a half."

"Pretty square crossing, an't it?"

"Yes, but the upper bar's working down fast."

Another pilot spoke up and said:—

"I had better water than that, and ran it lower down; started out from the false point—mark twain—raised the second reef abreast the big snag in the bend, and had quarter less twain."

One of the gorgeous ones remarked:—

"I don't want to find fault with your leadsmen, but that's a good deal of water for Plum Point, it seems to me."

There was an approving nod all around as this quiet snub dropped on the boaster and "settled" him. And so they went on talk-talk-talking. Meantime, the thing that was running in my mind was, "Now if my ears hear aright, I have not only to get the names of all the towns and islands and bends, and so on, by heart, but I must even get up a warm personal acquaintanceship with every old snag and one-limbed cotton-wood and obscure wood pile that ornaments the banks of this river for twelve hundred miles; and more than that, I must actually know where these things are in the dark, unless these guests are gifted with eyes that can pierce through two miles of solid blackness; I wish the piloting business was in Jericho and I had never thought of it."

At dusk Mr. Bixby tapped the big bell three times (the signal to land), and the captain emerged from his drawing-room in the forward end of the texas, and looked up inquiringly. Mr. Bixby said, "We will lay up here all night, captain."

"Very well, sir."

That was all. The boat came to shore and was tied up for the night. It seemed to me a fine thing that the pilot could do as he pleased, without asking so grand a captain's permission. I took my supper and went immediately to bed, discouraged by my day's observations and experiences. My late voyage's note-booking was but a confusion of meaningless names. It had tangled me all up in a knot every time I had looked at it in the daytime. I now hoped for respite in sleep; but no, it reveled all through my head till sunrise again, a frantic and tireless nightmare.

Next morning I felt pretty rusty and low-spirited. We went booming along, taking a good many chances, for we were anxious to "get out of the river" (as getting out to Cairo was called) before night should overtake us. But Mr. Bixby's partner, the other pilot, presently grounded the boat, and we lost so much time getting her off that it was plain the darkness would overtake us a good long way above the mouth. This was a great misfortune, especially to certain of our visiting pilots, whose boats would have to wait for their return, no matter how long that might be. It sobered the pilot-house talk a good deal. Coming up-stream, pilots did not mind low water or any kind of darkness; nothing stopped them but fog. But down-stream work was different; a boat was too nearly helpless, with a stiff current pushing behind her; so it was not customary to run down-stream at night in low water.

There seemed to be one small hope, however: if we could get through the intricate and dangerous Hat Island crossing before night, we could venture the rest, for we would have plainer sailing and better water. But it would be insanity to attempt Hat Island at night. So there was a deal of looking at watches all the rest of the day, and a constant ciphering upon the speed we were making; Hat Island was the eternal subject; sometimes hope was high and sometimes we were delayed in a bad crossing, and down it went again. For hours all hands lay under the burden of this suppressed excitement; it was even communicated to me, and I got to feeling so solicitous about Hat Island, and under such an awful pressure of responsibility, that I wished I might have five minutes on shore to draw a good, full, relieving breath, and start over again. We were standing no regular watches. Each of our pilots ran such portions of the river as he had run when coming up-stream, because of his greater familiarity with it; but both remained in the pilot-house constantly.

An hour before sunset, Mr. Bixby took the wheel and Mr. W— stepped aside. For the next thirty minutes every man held his watch in his hand and was restless, silent, and uneasy. At last somebody said, with a doomful sigh,—

"Well yonder's Hat Island—and we can't make it."

All the watches closed with a snap, everybody sighed and muttered something about its being "too bad, too bad—ah, if we could *only* have got here half an hour sooner!" and the place was thick with the atmosphere of disappointment. Some started to go out, but loitered, hearing no bell-tap to land. The sun dipped behind the horizon, the boat went on. Inquiring looks passed from one guest to another; and one who had his hand on the door-knob and had turned it, waited, then presently took away his hand and let the knob turn back again. We bore steadily down the bend. More looks were exchanged, and nods and nods of surprised admiration—but no words. Insensibly the men drew together behind Mr. Bixby, as the sky darkened and one or two dim stars came out. The dead silence and sense of waiting became oppressive. Mr. Bixby pulled the cord, and two deep, mellow notes from the big bell floated off on the night. Then a pause, and one more note was struck. The watchman's voice followed. "Labboard lead, there! Stab-board lead!"

The cries of the leadsmen began to rise out of the distance, and were gruffly repeated by the word-passers on the hurricane deck.

"M-a-r-k three! . . . . M-a-r-k three! . . . . Quarter-less-three! . . . . Half twain! . . . . Quarter twain! . . . . M-a-r-k twain!"

FROM *SHANTYBOAT: A RIVER WAY OF LIFE*
1953

Harlan Hubbard

Shantyboat *was another of the good surprises that came my way while editing this book. Hubbard was one of those all-American characters, in this case kind of a more sustainable (and married, does the second add to the first?) Thoreau. There are certainly more of them around then we will ever know, but then most do not write as well as Hubbard.*

A painter and writer who lived on the banks of the Ohio River for most of his life, he and his wife, Anna, built an engineless shantyboat in the early 1940s and spent eight years slowly cruising down the Ohio and Mississippi Rivers and then on into the bayous of Louisiana. They would find a likely spot to lay up for the summer, plant a garden, fish, and gather wild foods. When the harvest was in, they would cast off and spend the winter slowly drifting downstream on the current.

Today there are entire cookbooks dedicated to wild foods, innumerable books, pamphlets, even DVDs on how to build and survive in a house out in the forest somewhere, and on "sustainable living" in general. But in the 1940s and '50s, when the Hub-bards started doing it, that sort of life was still pretty common, and was usually known as being dirt poor. Hubbard writes as if his choice was the most natural thing in the world, but it must have raised some eyebrows in those go-go times as to why a couple of educated middle-class people would choose to step off the prosperity escalator to live among the shantyboaters and small farmers who were even then fading from that part of the world.

But in reading Shantyboat, *it quickly becomes clear that* dirt poor *does not even begin to describe the Hubbards' life, if it ever described anything very well. The book has much more music and art than hardscrabble and manual labor. When research-ing this introduction, I stumbled across some photos of the house and studio they built and lived in for thirty-five years in Trimble County, Kentucky, as described in the book* Payne Hollow: Life on the Fringe of Society. *They remind me of nothing so much as the traditional Japanese houses I came to know while living in Tokyo. Elegant simplicity, in wood and stone, full of light, but with lots of loaded bookshelves. Later of course a lot of people caught up with the Hubbards, and no doubt for many his work helped show them the way. It is a luminous book.*

THE JOHNBOAT

It was one of Sadie's country sayings that half of February should be good weather. After the passing of the ice we thought that perhaps winter had used up the days assigned to it, and made ready to build our johnboat.

A johnboat is a rowboat usually fourteen or sixteen feet long, square at both ends, and flat-bottomed. With this fundamental design, it may be lit-tle more than a box or a trough. Some of them are just about that. On the other hand, if it is built by a craftsman who has a feeling for good design, a johnboat is a beautiful, easy-running boat. It is to be found the length of the river, and in every tributary and creek big enough to float one. Its name changes, if not its appearance. As we drifted from one section to another our johnboat was called flatboat, joeboat, footboat, dinkyboat, paddleboat and on the Lower Mississippi, bateau.

Every shantyboater has one johnboat at least. It answers all his needs. It can carry a heavy load; its square ends make it easy to step into from the deck of a shantyboat; its scow bow is good for running up on a bank; and it is better for fishing than a skiff, being more steady and roomier. With the shantyboater the johnboat corresponds to the farmer's wagon or the yachts-man's dinghy. Also it can be used as a temporary fish box. When the river is muddy the shantyboater bails out the rainwater from the johnboat for his wife to wash clothes in; "johnboat water" is a common term with us. In addition, we often use ours as a temporary bridge to shore. We take a bath from it and climbing into it after a swim is easy. The johnboat is often abused and can have little care out in the sun and rain. Ice and snow fill it; it freezes in the ice. I have seen ours a solid cake, inside and out.

In former years I had built two johnboats, but neither had been well de-signed. This new one I hoped would be more successful. To that end I stud-ied and made measurements of boats which were trim and easy to row, asking questions of their builders. As ours was not to be used with an outboard motor, ease of rowing was a first requirement. To achieve this, we planned its great-est beam well forward, yet with little difference in the width of the bottom: thus there would be no drag from bulging sides or flaring stern. The boat would have a long rake, a high bow to ride the waves, and the sides flaring out sharply at the point of greatest beam would give stability. We were not much concerned about appearance, trusting that a boat which was seawor-thy and easy-running would also have good lines and proportions.

Suitable lumber to build it was hard to find. The brash new poplar of-fered by the Brent lumberyard could not be trusted. The best we could find was redwood, two fourteen-foot planks one inch by twelve, which was not quite wide enough. For the bottom we obtained some cypress but not in long enough pieces to be put on lengthways. Our neighbor, Al Edwards, hauled it all out from town in his little truck, one rainy spring-like day, on his way home from work.

High up in our clearing, where the river would not interfere, we set up some trestles to work on. The first day we fashioned the rakes on bow and stern, set in a stout headlog and stern piece, spread the sides to their proper width. There is no doubt that all our boatbuilding, and our telling about it too, is the work of amateurs. After all, we are amateurs at shantyboating. Even now when we met a genuine river man, one who was "born in a john-boat with the catfish," and who has never been far from the river, we real-ize that we are still novices. Perhaps it is for this very reason that our river life has continued to hold the same fascination as it had in the beginning.

At any rate, the building of the johnboat was a pleasant occupation. We stopped our sawing, planing, and hammering now and then to look across the river or to sniff the mild air. The sweet smell of the shavings that we made combined with the fragrance of the sun-warmed earth, and the boat with its curving lines harmonized with the natural forms around it as if still related to the trees from which it came. These mild days were not of spring but the weary end of winter; yet they anticipated the coming season. Unseen bluebirds softly whistled as they went by and the faint tinkling of song sparrows was heard now and then. A south wind overtaking the current ruffled the golden water. One day was so warm that Andy ventured over to see how we were getting along. As he talked of the boats he had built in his younger days, we recalled a picture of him seated at the oars—such a vigorous and aggressive young man that the tales he told could well be believed.

We worked all day in this good weather, knowing that it would not last. Even so, we kept an eye on the river which could be seen through an opening in the trees. Our work stopped whenever a boat went by. In the hazy air, even the color of the white boats and red barges seemed changed. Once we heard a full-toned whistle, familiar yet not to be identified. Then as we watched, the old, almost forgotten towboat *W. C. Mitchell* steamed past, panting and clanking, putting forth clouds of smoke and steam. It was a boat from the past, not like the new white boats, but ancient and gray, in harmony with the sunset reflected in the eastern sky and water. In the following weeks the *W. C. Mitchell* passed frequently; then after an interval of absence, its total loss was reported.

The expected return of winter weather came before the johnboat could be finished. More snow fell. We again had icy banks, frozen lines, and fires of the best-heating wood. Then followed rains and a rising river. It came up fast and surpassed the first predicted crest. A stage of forty-one feet was then forecast, and we moved up into our clearing again, where the outlook was as novel as if we had never been there before. Work was pushed on the incomplete johnboat which was now just outside our windows. Anna and I could be sociable as we worked at our different tasks. Our new boat was well along now. Extra width had been added to the sides to give a good freeboard. A skeg was placed on the stern rake. This is a sort of permanent rudder or fin which makes the boat run in a straight line. The boat was turned right side up again, and about all that remained was to put in decks and seat.

With a stout ring in each end, and oars and oarlocks, it would be ready for service. It was a handsome boat, at once sturdy and graceful, as it rested there on the trestles, dreaming perhaps fo rough, swift water, the oars' pull, and the thrust of the wave.

Toward the end of February the weather became warm again. Heavy rains fell for days. There was no sky, only water dripping and pouring from an overhanging mist. Muddy streams cascaded down the bank in unexpected places to be swallowed up by the unheeding river. Its level was unchanged at first, but when Donald came over and said that a stage of from fifty-six to fifty-eight feet was forecast, we were prepared for it. The Detisches were floating now, and Donald wanted me to help him move the *Bozo* closer inshore to be out of the wind's path.

The rising water soon floated our johnboat but it was only an incident in the excitement of the flood. We were tied to the swaying tops of small elms, and more trees above us must be cut to allow for our upward passage. Only a scanty fringe of the locusts remained between us and the railroad. We waved at the engineers as the trains roared by almost overhead, and the trainmen looked down at the firelight in our cabin. In this new position the familiar landmarks were all changed. The angle of the railroad and the river's bend seemed different, the distant hills were lower. Being higher up, we saw unfamiliar lights at night. House lights across the river, and headlights of cars on highways which we could never see before. The Four Mile Bar navigation light, once so far above us, now flashed in our windows. The upbound boats ran close to the willows on the opposite shore, seeking easier water. As the river rose higher, their course was behind the outermost willows, of which only the tall tips were above water. On the wide, swift river floated drift of all sorts, islands of matted branches, great trees with all their roots, and many an inviting plank or timber.

Our life went on in its usual way in spite of the different surroundings, for we had already learned to adapt ourselves to constant change. There was considerable work on the wet shore. One task was to move our loose property farther up the bank. We had already collected some plunder, and even a worthless scrap of driftwood or a worn-out basket if it is once tossed out on shore, will be cared for and moved ahead of rising water until at last above the crest of the flood—where it is more likely abandoned after all. Firewood was a problem too. The area of the riverbank was restricted, and the bleached piles of driftwood which were now floating on the high water like rafts. Old railroad ties were our reserve of fuel, and they made good fires in the wettest weather. They were not desirable, though—Anna objected to the smoke and the soot which the burning creosote made, almost as bad as coal, and I did not like to saw the ties on account of the gravel imbedded in them.

Most pleasant it was after a bout with some rough work in the cold and wet to come back to the warmth of our cabin. Each time I marveled again— how neat and clean it was, so insulated from the chaos of the riverbank. What good living there in that small enclosure, floating on the wild river, against the inhospitable shore.

As soon as the planking had swelled enough to make the seams tight we rowed the johnboat for the first time. It promised to fulfill all our hopes, and soon became our mainstay on the river. In it I was a new animal, as a man on horseback is conceived to be. The johnboat was so useful that we wondered how we had ever managed without it. Now I could go out on the river or down the shore, looking for drift. We had a view of our boat and landing from the water for the first time. It made us feel like real shantyboaters to call on our neighbors by water, tying up at their deck and climbing aboard. We were becoming part of the river fraternity now, and as we sat in Sadie's cheery kitchen, with perhaps half a dozen others, we ventured a few words about our own doings and opinions.

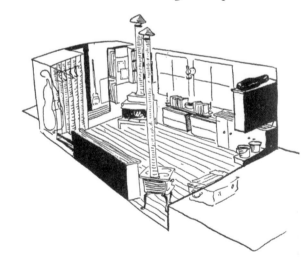

illustration by Harlan Hubbard

FROM *THE RIDDLE OF THE SANDS*
1903

Erskine Childers

I was surprised, in reading through early articles and literature on cruising in small boats at how often I ran across references to Erskine Childers' The Riddle of the Sands *as an inspiration for the idea that one does not have to have a small ship, built in mahogany and teak, a liveried army of sailors and servants, and of course a funny hat, white pants, and a blue blazer, to enjoy the sea.*

Joshua Slocum had of course become famous for his world cruise in a small oyster smack a few years before Childers wrote Riddle. *But he was a professional, born and raised to the sea. Given how commonplace pleasure boating has become, it was interesting to realize that Childers' character Arthur Davies was something rather new when the the book was published in 1903—a more or less middle-class guy who had bought an old wooden lifeboat that had been converted into a yacht, and was cruising on a shoestring for the pure hell of it.*

Childers (1870-1922) was, in himself, an enormously interesting man. Born in London, he was educated at Cambridge, worked as a clerk in Britain's House of Commons, and was wounded fighting in the Boer War. While recovering from his wounds, he wrote Riddle, *which was based in part on his cruises along the German coast.*

His mother was Irish, though; he had in part been raised by an uncle in Ireland, and was drawn to the cause of Irish nationalism and Home Rule. In 1910 he re-signed his post in the House of Commons and returned to Ireland to write and work for Irish independence. Days before the start of World War I, he smuggled a shipment of arms from Germany to Ireland aboard his 44-foot sailing yacht, Asgard. *The start of the war saw him back in the service of Britain, and he received a Distinguished Service Cross for his intelligence work. But after the war, he returned to Ireland and rose through the ranks of Sinn Féin to, among many other services, represent the Na-tionalists at the Versailles Conference in Paris and become a member of the Irish par-liament, or Dáil, in 1921.*

But the political ferment devolved into civil war between the Irish Republican Army and Sinn Féin, and Childers was caught up in the turmoil. On November 24, 1922, Childers was executed by firing squad in Dublin. His last words were "Take a step or two forward, lads. It will be easier that way."

Riddle *is also perhaps the first spy thriller. The protagonist, Davies, cruising Ger-many's North Sea coast, comes to suspect that Germany is building a series of shal-low-water harbors and ships in preparation for an invasion of Britain in the war that everybody, even in 1903, knew was coming. In its time it had far more influence than most works of fiction. Winston Churchill later credited it as a major reason that the Admiralty decided to establish naval bases at Invergordon, the Firth of Forth, and Scapa Flow.*

In this part Davies has talked an old school friend, Carruthers, into spending his vacation duck hunting and sailing on the Dulcibella, *Davies' yacht. Carruthers, ex-pecting a* yacht, *is somewhat let down to find himself scrabbling his way down a slimy wharf in the dark to be rowed out to a centerboard yawl, a little over 30 feet long. After a few days of leaking decks, salt beef, hardtack, barked shins, and no ducks, he has had enough and demands an explanation.*

THE SPY

I'll tell you,' said Davies, 'I'll tell you the whole thing. As far as you're concerned it's partly a confession. Last night I had made up my mind to say nothing, but when Bartels turned up I knew it must all come out. It's been fearfully on my mind, and perhaps you'll be able to help me. But it's for you to decide.'

'Fire away!' I said.

'You know what I was saying about the Frisian Islands the other day? A thing happened there which I never told you, when you were asking about my cruise.'

'It began near Norderney,' I put in.

'How did you guess that?' he asked.

'You're a bad hand at duplicity,' I replied. 'Go on.'

'Well, you're quite right, it was there, on 9th September. I told you the sort of thing I was doing at that time, but I don't think I said that I made inquiries from one or two people about duck-shooting, and had been told by some fishermen at Borkum that there was a big sailing-yacht in those waters, whose owner, a German of the name of Dollmann, shot a good deal, and might give me some tips. Well, I found this yacht one evening, knowing it must be her from the description I had. She was what is called a "barge-yacht", of fifty or sixty tons, built for shallow water on the lines of a Dutch galliot, with lee-boards and those queer round bows and square stern. She's something like those galliots anchored near us now. You sometimes see the same sort of yacht in English waters, only there they copy the Thames barges. She looked a clipper of her sort, and very smart; varnished all over and shining like gold. I came on her about sunset, after a long day of exploring round the Ems estuary. She was lying in—'

'Wait a bit, let's have the chart,' I interrupted.

Davies found it and spread it on the table between us, first pushing back the cloth and the breakfast things to one end, where they lay in a slovenly litter. This was one of the only two occasions on which I ever saw him postpone the rite of washing up, and it spoke volumes for the urgency of the matter in hand.

'Here it is,' said Davies and I looked with a new and strange interest at the long string of slender islands, the parallel line of coast, and the confusion of shoals, banks, and channels which lay between. 'Here's Norderney, you see. By the way, there's a harbour there at the west end of the island, the only real harbour on the whole line of islands, Dutch or German, except at Terschelling. There's quite a big town there, too, a watering place, where Germans go for sea-bathing in the summer. Well, the *Medusa,* that was her name, was lying in the Riff Gat roadstead, flying the German ensign, and I anchored for the night pretty near her. I meant to visit her owner later on, but I very nearly changed my mind, as I always feel rather a fool on smart yachts, and my German isn't very good. However, I thought I might as well; so, after dinner, when it was dark, I sculled over in the dinghy, hailed a sailor on deck, said who I was, and asked if I could see the owner. The sailor was a surly sort of chap, and there was a good long delay while I waited on deck, feeling more and more uncomfortable. Presently a steward came up and showed me down the companion and into the saloon, which, after *this,* looked—well, horribly gorgeous—you know what I mean, plush lounges, silk cushions, and that sort of thing. Dinner seemed to be just over, and wine and fruit were on the table. Herr Dollmann was there at his coffee. I introduced myself somehow—'

'Stop a moment,' I said; 'what was he like?'

'Oh, a tall, thin chap, in evening dress; about fifty I suppose, with grey-ish hair and a short beard. I'm not good at describing people. He had a high, bulging forehead, and there was something about him—but I think I'd bet-ter tell you the bare facts first. I can't say he seemed pleased to see me, and he couldn't speak English, and, in fact, I felt infernally awkward. Still, I had an object in coming, and as I was there I thought I might as well gain it.'

The notion of Davies in his Norfolk jacket and rusty flannels harangu-ing a frigid German in evening dress in a 'gorgeous' saloon tickled my fancy greatly.

'He seemed very much astonished to see me; had evidently seen the *Dul-cibella* arrive, and had wondered what she was. I began as soon as I could about the ducks, but he shut me up at once, said I could do nothing here-abouts. I put it down to sportsman's jealousy—you know what that is. But I saw I had come to the wrong shop, and was just going to back out and end this unpleasant interview, when he thawed a bit, offered me some wine, and began talking in quite a friendly way, taking a great interest in my cruise and my plans for the future. In the end we sat up quite late, though

I never felt really at my ease. He seemed to be taking stock of me all the time, as though I were some new animal.' (How I sympathized with that German!) 'We parted civilly enough, and I rowed back and turned in, meaning to potter on eastwards early next day.

'But I was knocked up at dawn by a sailor with a message from Dollmann asking if he could come to breakfast with me. I was rather flabbergasted, but didn't like to be rude, so I said, "Yes." Well, he came, and I returned the call—and—well, the end of it was that I stayed at anchor there for three days.' This was rather abrupt.

'How did you spend the time?' I asked. Stopping three days anywhere was an unusual event for him, as I knew from his log.

'Oh, I lunched or dined with him once or twice—with *them,* I ought to say,' he added, hurriedly. 'His daughter was with him. She didn't appear the evening I first called.'

'And what was she like?' I asked, promptly, before he could hurry on.

'Oh, she seemed a very nice girl,' was the guarded reply, delivered with particular unconcern, 'and—the end of it was that I and the *Medusa* sailed away in company. I must tell you how it came about, just in a few words for the present.

'It was his suggestion. He said he had to sail to Hamburg, and proposed that I should go with him in the *Dulcibella* as far as the Elbe, and then, if I liked, I could take the ship canal at Brunsbüttel through to Kiel and the Baltic. I had no very fixed plans of my own, though I had meant to go on exploring eastwards between the islands and the coast, and so reach the Elbe in a much slower way. He dissuaded me from this, sticking to it that I should have no chance of ducks, and urging other reasons. Anyway, we settled to sail in company direct to Cuxhaven, in the Elbe. With a fair wind and an early start it should be only one day's sail of about sixty miles.

'The plan only came to a head on the evening of the third day, 12th September.

'I told you, I think, that the weather had broken after a long spell of heat. That very day it had been blowing pretty hard from the west, and the glass was falling still. I said, of course, that I couldn't go with him if the weather was too bad, but he prophesied a good day, said it was an easy sail, and altogether put me on my mettle. You can guess how it was. Perhaps I had talked about single-handed cruising as though it were easier than it was, though I never meant it in a boasting way, for I hate that sort of thing, and besides there *is* no danger if you're careful—'

'Oh, go on,' I said.

'Anyway, we went next morning at six. It was a dirty-looking day, wind W.N.W., but his sails were going up and mine followed. I took two reefs in, and we sailed out into the open and steered E.N.E. along the coast for the Outer Elbe Lightship about fifty knots off. Here it all is, you see.' (He showed me the course on the chart.) 'The trip was nothing for his boat, of course, a safe, powerful old tub, forging through the sea as steady as a house. I kept up with her easily at first. My hands were pretty full, for there was a hard wind on my quarter and a troublesome sea; but as long as nothing worse came I knew I should be all right, though I also knew that I was a fool to have come.

'All went well till we were off Wangeroog, the last of the islands—*here*— and then it began to blow really hard. I had half a mind to chuck it and cut into the Jade River, *down there,* but I hadn't the face to, so I hove to and took in my last reef.' (Simple words, simply uttered; but I had seen the operation in calm water and shuddered at the present picture.) 'We had been about level till then, but with my shortened canvas I fell behind. Not that that mattered in the least. I knew my course, had read up my tides, and, thick as the weather was, I had no doubt of being able to pick up the lightship. No change of plan was possible now. The Weser estuary was on my starboard hand, but the whole place was a lee-shore and a mass of unknown banks—just look at them. I ran on, the *Dulcibella* doing her level best, but we had some narrow shaves of being pooped. I was about *here,* say six miles south-west of the lightship, when I suddenly saw that the *Medusa* had hove to right ahead, as though waiting till I came up. She wore round again on the course as I drew level, and we were alongside for a bit. Dollmann lashed the wheel, leaned over her quarter, and shouted, very slowly and distinctly so that I could understand; "Follow me—sea too bad for you outside— short cut through sands—save six miles."

'It was taking me all my time to manage the tiller, but I knew what he meant at once, for I had been over the chart carefully the night before. You see, the whole bay between Wangeroog and the Elbe is encumbered with sand. A great jagged chunk of it runs out from Cuxhaven in a north-westerly direction for fifteen miles or so, ending in a pointed spit, called the

Scharhorn. To reach the Elbe from the west you have to go right outside this, round the lightship, which is off the Scharhorn, and double back. Of course, that's what all big vessels do. But, as you see, these sands are intersected here and there by channels, very shallow and winding, exactly like those behind the Frisian Islands. Now look at this one, which cuts right through the big chunk of sand and comes out near Cuxhaven. The *Telte* it's called. It's miles wide, you see, at the entrance, but later on it is split into two by the Hohenhörn bank: then it gets shallow and very complicated, and ends in a mere tidal driblet with another name. It's just the sort of channel I should like to worry into on a fine day or with an off-shore wind. Alone, in thick weather and a heavy sea, it would have been folly to attempt it, except as a desperate resource. But, as I said I knew at once that Dollmann was proposing to run for it and guide me in.

'I didn't like the idea, because I like doing things for myself, and, silly as it sounds, I believe I resented being told the sea was too bad for me. Which it certainly was. Yet the short cut did save several miles and a devil of a tumble off the Scharhorn, where two tides meet. I had complete faith in Dollmann, and I suppose I decided that I should be a fool not to take a good chance. I hesitated. I know; but in the end I nodded, and held up my arm as she forged ahead again. Soon after, she shifted her course and I followed. You asked me once if I ever took a pilot. That was the only time.'

He spoke with bitter gravity, flung himself back, and felt his dramatic pause, but it certainly was one. I had just a glimpse of still another Davies— a Davies five years older throbbing with deep emotions, scorn, passion, and stubborn purpose; a being above my plane, of sterner stuff, wider scope. Intense as my interest had become, I waited almost timidly while he mechanically rammed tobacco into his pipe and struck ineffectual matches. I felt that whatever the riddle to be solved, it was no mean one. He repressed himself with an effort, half rose, and made his circular glance at the clock, barometer, and skylight, and then resumed.

'We soon came to what I knew must be the beginning of the Telte channel. All round you could hear the breakers on the sands, though it was too thick to see them yet. As the water shoaled, the sea, of course, got shorter and steeper. There was more wind—a whole gale I should say.

'I kept dead in the wake of the *Medusa,* but to my disgust I found she was gaining on me very fast. Of course I had taken for granted, when he said he would lead me in, that he would slow down and keep close to me. He could easily have done so by getting his men up to check his sheets or drop his peak. Instead of that he was busting on for all he was worth. Once, in a rain-squall, I lost sight of him altogether; got him faintly again, but had enough to do with my own tiller not to want to be peering through the scud after a runaway pilot. I was all right so far, but we were fast approaching the worst part of the whole passage, where the Hohenhörn bank blocks the road, and the channel divides. I don't know what it looks like to you on the chart—perhaps fairly simple, because you can follow the twists of the channels, as on a ground-plan; but a stranger coming to a place like that (where there are no buoys, mind you) can tell nothing certain by the eye—unless perhaps at dead low water, when the banks are high and dry, and in very clear weather—he must trust to the lead and the compass, and feel his way step by step. I knew perfectly well that what I should soon see would be a wall of surf stretching right across and on both sides. To *feel* one's way in that sort of weather is impossible. You must *know* your way, or else have a pilot. I had one, but he was playing his own game.

'With a second hand on board to steer while I conned I should have felt less of an ass. As it was, I knew I ought to be facing the music in the offing, and cursed myself for having broken my rule and gone blundering into this confounded short cut. It was giving myself away, doing just the very thing that you can't do in single-handed sailing.

'By the time I realized the danger it was far too late to turn and hammer out to the open. I was deep in the bottle-neck bight of the sands, jammed on a lee shore, and a strong flood tide sweeping me on. That tide, by the way, gave just the ghost of a chance. I had the hours in my head, and knew it was about two-thirds flood, with two hours more of rising water. That meant the banks would be all covering when I reached them, and harder than ever to locate; but it also meant that I *might* float right over the worst of them if I hit off a lucky place.' Davies thumped the table in disgust. 'Pah! It makes me sick to think of having to trust to an accident like that, like a lubberly cockney out for a boozy Bank Holiday sail. Well, just as I foresaw, the wall of surf appeared clean across the horizon, and curling back to shut me in, booming like thunder. When I last saw the *Medusa* she seemed to be charging it like a horse at a fence, and I took a rough bearing of her position by a hurried glance at the compass. At that very moment I *thought* she seemed to luff and show some of her broadside; but a squall blotted her out and gave me hell with the tiller. After that she was lost in the white mist that hung over the line of breakers. I kept on my bearing as well as I could, but I was already out of the channel. I knew that by the look of the water, and as we neared the bank I saw it was all awash and without the vestige of an opening. I wasn't going to chuck her on to it without an effort; so, more by instinct than with any particular hope, I put the helm down, meaning to work her along the edge on the chance of spotting a way over. She was buried at once by the beam sea, and the jib flew to blazes; but the reefed stays'l stood, she recovered gamely, and I held on, though I knew it could only be for a few minutes, as the centre-plate was up, and she made frightful leeway towards the bank.

'I was half-blinded by scud, but suddenly I noticed what looked like a gap, behind a spit which curled out right ahead. I luffed still more to clear this spit, but she couldn't weather it. Before you could say knife she was driving across it, bumped heavily, bucked forward again, bumped again, and—ripped on in deeper water! I can't describe the next few minutes. I was in some sort of channel, but a very narrow one, and the sea broke everywhere. I hadn't proper command either; for the rudder had crocked up somehow at the last bump. I was like a drunken man running for his life down a dark alley, barking himself at every corner. It couldn't last long, and finally we went crash on to something and stopped there, grinding and banging. So ended that little trip under a pilot.

'Well, it was like this—there was really no danger'—I opened my eyes at the characteristic phrase. 'I mean, that lucky stumble into a channel was my salvation. Since then I had struggled through a mile of sands, all of which lay behind me like a breakwater against the gale. They were covered, of course, and seething like soapsuds; but the force of the sea was deadened. The *Dulce* was bumping, but not too heavily. It was nearing high tide, and at half ebb she would be high and dry.

'In the ordinary way I should have run out a kedge with the dinghy, and at the next high water sailed farther in and anchored where I could lie afloat. The trouble was now that my hand was hurt and my dinghy stove in, not to mention the rudder business. It was the first bump on the outer edge that did the damage. There was a heavy swell there, and when we struck, the dinghy, which was towing astern, came home on her painter and down with a crash on the yacht's weather quarter. I stuck out one hand to ward it off and got it nipped on the gunwale. She was badly stove in and useless, so I couldn't run out the kedge'—this was Greek to me, but I let him go on—'and for the present my hand was too painful even to stow the boom and sails, which were whipping and racketing about anyhow. There was the rudder, too, to be mended; and we were several miles from the nearest land. Of course, if the wind fell, it was all easy enough; but if it held or increased it was a poor look-out. There's a limit to strain of that sort—and other things might have happened.

'In fact, it was precious lucky that Bartels turned up. His galliot was at anchor a mile away, up a branch of the channel. In a clear between squalls he saw us, and, like a brick, rowed his boat out—he and his boy, and a devil of a pull they must have had. I was glad enough to see them—no, that's not true; I was in such a fury of disgust and shame that I believe I should have been idiot enough to say I didn't want help, if he hadn't just nipped on board and started work. He's a terror to work, that little mouse of a chap. In half an hour he had stowed the sails, unshackled the big anchor, run out fifty fathoms of warp, and hauled her off there and then into deep water. Then they towed her up the channel—it was dead to leeward and an easy job—and berthed her near their own vessel. It was dark by that time, so I gave them a drink, and said good-night. It blew a howling gale that night, but the place was safe enough, with good ground-tackle.

'The whole affair was over; and after supper I thought hard about it all.'

The Theory

Davies leaned back and gave a deep sigh, as though he still felt the relief from some tension. I did the same, and felt the same relief. The chart, freed from the pressure of our fingers, rolled up with a flip, as though to say, 'What do you think of that?' I have straightened out his sentences a little, for in the excitement of his story they had grown more and more jerky and elliptical.

'What about Dollmann?' I asked.

'Of course,' said Davies, 'what about him? I didn't get at much that night. It was all so sudden. The only thing I could have sworn to from the first was that he had purposely left me in the lurch that day. I pieced out the rest in the next few days, which I'll just finish with as shortly as I can. Bartels came aboard next morning, and though it was blowing hard still we managed to shift the *Dulcibella* to a place where she dried safely at the mid-day low water, and we could get at her rudder. The lower screw-plate on the stern post had wrenched out, and we botched it up roughly as a make-shift. There were other little breakages, but nothing to matter, and the loss of the jib was nothing, as I had two spare ones. The dinghy was past repair just then, and I lashed it on deck.

'It turned out that Bartels was carrying apples from Bremen to Kappeln (in this fiord), and had run into that channel in the sands for shelter from the weather. To-day he was bound for the Eider River, whence, as I told you, you can get through (by river and canal) into the Baltic. Of course the Elbe route, by the new Kaiser Wilhelm Ship Canal, is the shortest. The Eider route is the old one, but he hoped to get rid of some of his apples at Tönning, the town at its mouth. Both routes touch the Baltic at Kiel. As you know, I had been running for the Elbe, but yesterday's muck-up put me off, and I changed my mind—I'll tell you why presently—and decided to sail to the Eider along with the *Johannes* and get through that way. It cleared from the east next day, and I raced him there, winning hands down, left him at Tönning, and in three days was in the Baltic. It was just a week after I ran ashore that I wired to you. You see, I had come to the conclusion that *that chap was a spy.*'

In the end it came out quite quietly and suddenly, and left me in pro-found amazement. 'I wired to you—that chap was a spy.' It was the close association of these two ideas that hit me hardest at the moment. For a sec-ond I was back in the dreary splendour of the London club-room, spelling out that crabbed scrawl from Davies, and fastidiously criticizing its pro-posal in the light of a holiday. Holiday! What was to be its issue? Chilling and opaque as the fog that filtered through the skylight there flooded my imagination a mist of doubt and fear.

'A spy!' I repeated blankly. 'What do you mean? Why did you wire to me? A spy of what—of whom?'

FROM *THE FALCON ON THE BALTIC*
1888

E. F. Knight

Edward Frederick Knight (1852-1925) was another of the early small-boat nuts who sailed and wrote about their adventures in the late 1800s. Born in England but raised in France, Knight learned to sail in a small boat on the River Seine. He was one of those particularly British personalities—a barrister who worked for several British newspapers as a war correspondent, but also found time to make a number of remarkable voyages. He cruised extensively on the British and French coasts, hunted for pirate treasure on an uninhabited island off the coast of Brazil, explored the Amazon River and the South American coast, and wrote several popular books on the voyages. But no less an authority than Arthur Ransome thought The Falcon on the Baltic *the best of the bunch.*

The Falcon *that Knight cruised to the Baltic was small—a 29-foot lifeboat that had been decked over and given a ketch rig. For some reason these boats, double-diagonal planked in teak, were fairly common at the time—perhaps the big shipping* companies were moving to steel for their lifeboats. The Dulcibella in The Riddle of the Sands is another example, and people, looking to maximize their adventure and independence while minimizing their outlay in cash and time, have been following in his footsteps ever since.

Ransome wrote this bit in an introduction to the 1951 Mariner's Library edition of The Falcon on the Baltic, and there is really very little else to be said on the subject:

> There are still ship's lifeboats to be picked up cheaply and, if you are content with good crawling headroom and do not spoil them by some ridiculous superstructure, you can still make reasonable vessels of them, vessels in which you can move from one port to another, sleep and cook aboard, anchor in creeks where you can hear curlews instead of other people's wireless, and at week-ends, and on holidays, live in ecstatic discomfort. To all for whom such vessels are a dream of the future or a happy memory of the past Knight speaks as a personal friend.

This excerpt describes Knight's voyage northward through the Zuider Zee, a giant salt lake near Amsterdam. One of the delights of reading through Falcon on the Baltic is the sense of having a last look at some of the forgotten corners of the old Europe. Radio, the automobile, TV, modern education, and war would change everything within a few decades—it ought to be said in many ways for the good. But it is a window on a time when very little had changed for hundreds of years—when for many people the next town was a foreign land, and customs, dress, and even language could change a great deal in just fifty miles.

THE ZUIDER ZEE

On Wednesday the 15th of June we started at 2 p.m. for the Zuider Zee. As we were getting under weigh we saw a large steam-yacht coming in, flying the R.T.Y.C. burgee. We were told that she was the *Rionag na Mara*.

The Y or harbour of Amsterdam is an inlet of the Zuider Zee. In order to protect the city and its canals from an encroach of the sea, a huge dam has been constructed across the Y at Schellingwoud. This dam (I quote Baedeker) is one and a quarter miles in length, and has five locks, the largest of which is 110 yards in length, and twenty-two in width. There are fifty-six ponderous lock-gates, the two heaviest of which weigh thirty-four tons each. This will give some idea of the gigantic scale on which work of this description is done in Holland.

It was a very hot day with a cloudless sky and a light wind. We drifted slowly to the great dam, and entered one of the locks in the company of several traders. The outer gate was opened, we passed through, and were afloat at last on the Zuider Zee. We were glad to be free of the tedious canals for a time, and to cruise once more on broad water.

What small amount of wind there was came right aft, and we contrived, to the gratification of our pride, to run away from all the schuyts. As we came out of the estuary of the Y, the view of the Zuider Zee was a singular one. The heat had produced a thin haze, which did not obscure but surrounded objects with a golden atmosphere. Seawards only the horizon was not visible; there the sky and water mingled in a beautiful sunlit mist that Turner would have loved to paint, while distant fishing-vessels seemed to be floating in the air. Along the shore we were following, stretched as far as the eye could see the massive grass-grown dyke; above which rose here and there red roof-tops, steeples, and trees. Farther still a tall churchspire stood out of the waters, like an island; the low land round it being beneath the horizon; this, from its bearings, I took to be the church at Hoorn.

I had started from Amsterdam without troubling my head as to what port I should put into for the night, for my chart showed me that there was a large choice of harbours all round the Zuider Zee. True that most of these are silting up, and can only admit fishing-boats and such small fry, but then the draught of the *Falcon* is under three feet, a fact we were grateful for when on this very shallow sea, where the greatest depth in the centre is a little over two fathoms.

We steered to the northward, keeping close under the shore in about six feet of water. The wind, still very light, now headed us, so it was evident that we should not get far before nightfall. At about six o'clock we opened out the little island of Marken. Between this and the mainland is a channel two miles broad, with only four feet of water in it, and at the head of a small bay opposite the island is the town of Monnikendam, which is about fifteen miles from Amsterdam by water. I decided to bring up at this place for the night, so we sailed into the bay, where the water gradually shoaled till we had only two feet under us—a foot less than our own draught; but we contrived to drive the yacht on with oars and quant through the deep mud, which was almost as yielding as the water. This, we discovered, was a common method of navigating the Zuider Zee; there is no possibility of foundering under such circumstances.

The little town presented a pretty picture on this quiet summer's evening, with its quaint gabled houses, its background of green trees, and its flat-bottomed fishing-craft, lying alongside the quay or the canal—of course it has its canal, what Dutch village has not? There came to us from the shore the sweet scent of new-mown hay, and the sound of cackling hens and lowing cattle, and noise of children just let loose from school, that sounded pleasant and homely to our ears.

We pushed on through the soft mud till we reached the quay, which was already crowded with wondering people, and here we stuck comfortably in the slime, with only a foot or so of water round us, so that it was scarcely necessary to take warps on shore. This night our weary pump had a rest, for her bed of mud gave the *Falcon* an excellent Blackwall caulking.

No sooner were we alongside than a man came down to the quay, and spoke volubly to us for some time. We could not understand him at all, so he tried signs, and showing us a handful of stuivers, pointed to the yacht. Had he taken a fancy to our vessel, and was he making a bid for her?

Evidently Wright took this view, for he called out indignantly, "It isn't enough, Mynheer." The man stared at him for a moment, then despairing of our intelligence, he hurried off, and soon returned with a pompous little fellow in spectacles, who, I believe, was the schoolmaster. He was able to speak a little of a language which he called English. I don't know what it was, but it sounded stranger to our ears than the other man's Dutch.

I do not know how it was managed, but between these two individuals and various members of the crowd, who occasionally put in their suggestions, our dull brains did eventually grasp the idea they were so anxious to convey to us. We understood that the first speaker was the harbour-master and that he wanted our wharfage fee, four stuivers. I gave him his fourpence and he departed happy. I think this was the only port we visited in the course of the cruise in which we did not come across someone who spoke English.

We found the small boys somewhat of a nuisance in Monnikendam; but this was nothing to what was before us. As I shall shortly have to explain, the shores of the Zuider Zee produce in large quantities the most troublesome urchins of all Europe. Happily, it is the custom to pack them off early to bed, so at any rate we were able to sleep comfortably through the night. On the following morning we were awakened by a familiar sound on the quay above us, the cry of the milkman—they call it "mulk" here—so we turned out and bought a bucketful. In every Dutch port the vendors of milk and eels, and often the butchers as well, would thus visit us at an early hour to solicit our custom. On studying the chart I perceived a dot right in the middle of the Zuider Zee, and which represented the little island of Urk. A lonely island on the sea he happens to be navigating always has a fascination for a yachtsman, so, having before me as a further inducement the fact of its lying on my way to Zwartsluis, I decided to sail for Urk. The morning was sultry and calm, and there was no wind at all until 11 a.m., when a light air sprang up, but it was right ahead. Seeing that it was not possible to reach Urk that day, and having had enough of Monnikendam, and its boys, we punted the yacht through the mud out of the bay and made for the opposite island of Marken, which was visible about three miles distant. Every tourist who goes to Amsterdam is obliged to visit Marken. This is one of the rules laid down in the tyrant guide-books, and it must be obeyed. In vain I rose in revolt against this law and tried to sail elsewhere. The wind, which was in league with Baedeker, would not have it so, and I had to submit and go perforce to Marken.

The island possesses a small artificial harbour with not more than four feet of water, which, however, is quite enough for its fishing-boats and for our yacht. We tacked across the channel, entered the harbour, and made fast to the quay, which, to our surprise, was deserted. Were there, then, no boys in happy Marken?

I looked round me and saw that there were only two or three houses near the quay, for the village is towards the middle of the island. Marken is inhabited by a race of hardy fishing-folk, the most primitive people in Holland, who still go about in the costume in fashion with their forefathers three hundred years ago. The island has been much written up of late, is often visited by tourists, and has, therefore, become a recognized show place, and its inhabitants run the risk of losing their simplicity and being considerably spoilt.

The natives soon found us out, and first of all the harbour-master came down to us for his wharfage fee of two stuivers per ton. I then left Wright in charge of the yacht and proceeded to explore the island on foot. Marken is rather more than two miles long. It consists of flat pasture-land intersected by little ditches, and it is, of course, surrounded with a dyke. There is a church and a neat little village of tiny old wooden houses huddled up close to each other, with no streets between them, but narrow paths only, a plan conducive to cosiness in the long, hard winters. The men were away fishing, so I only came across women and girls, who were all dressed in the picturesque and becoming style of their great-great-grandmothers, and several of whom, though built much after the model of the native schuyts, having their greatest beam at the waist, were decidedly pretty. The girls of Marken have beautifully fresh and clear complexions, and many a one of these fair plump faces, with its honest blue eyes, and golden curls falling coquettishly on either side of the close-fitting skullcap, would have made a very pretty picture indeed.

I returned to the yacht and found that a schuyt had come into the harbour with a party of Dutch tourists from Amsterdam, who were being personally conducted by what seemed to be a native Cook on a small scale. And now I saw that the primitive islanders had acquired some of the tricks of civilization, even such as are practised by the simple mountaineers of Switzerland. For no sooner had the tourists stepped on shore than down trotted to the quay-side three pretty little maids of eight or nine, with their yellow curls flying behind them. They were not dressed in their everyday clothes, but in the gorgeous Sunday costume peculiar to the island. They had not even completed their toilet before starting from home, for they were assisting each other to arrange a ribbon here, or haul taut a refractory lace there, as they came along. They seemed very much amused and very proud of their finery as they stood hand in hand in a row on the quay, blushing and smiling archly and looking up occasionally with shy eyes at the strangers of the city. The little humbugs! It was so obvious that their mothers had hastily dressed them up, and sent them down for the inspection of the innocent tourists, as specimens of the famous Marken medieval costume, on the chance of earning a few stuivers; and the children certainly did not return empty-handed to their shrewd mammae.

Later on some of the fishing-boats came in, manned by sturdy, clean-shaven men, whose dress, if not so splendid, was as old-fashioned as that of the women. They wore tight-fitting black jackets, black skull-caps, and black knickerbockers of true Dutch voluminousness, while their well-stockinged feet were thrust into loose sabots. Save for the sabots it was a very Oriental-looking get up, and its like can be seen in any Turkish city.

In the evening, after we had finished our dinner, I believe that all the girls in Marken were down at the quay-side, drawing buckets of water to carry home for that last general wash-up of everything, which is never neglected in a Dutch establishment. They stood on the wharf chatting and laughing and peeping into our cabin with the curiosity of their sex, as fresh-featured, pleasant-looking a lot of blonde lasses as one could wish to see, and very smart too in their bright-coloured frocks and snowy linen.

I did not mind the girls. I may as well confess that I rather liked their presence; but by and by school broke up, and down to the quay-side ran all the naughty boys of Marken. We suffered a terrible persecution at their hands, so that the tender-hearted girls pitied us and rebuked, but to no effect, their unruly brothers. The Hollanders spoil their children, never punish them, and allow them—provided they don't play the truant from school, for education is a serious business in this country—to do pretty well as they like. Should a stranger—my authority is one of our consuls over here—take it upon himself to spank one of these little rascals for throwing stones at him or otherwise misbehaving himself, the whole of the parents of the locality would rise in a body and seek that stranger's blood. A Corsican vendetta would be child's play to what he might expect. If you value your life, put up with insult, robbery, blows, torture at the hands of a Hollander infant, but do not venture to chastise him. Of all the children in Europe the Dutch child is most to be feared. Now the Zuider Zee child is the most terrible of Dutch children, and the Marken child the most terrible of the Zuider Zee, and hence of the whole species. Our position can, therefore, be imagined by any father of a large family.

These small ruffians stood on the quay and reviled us in unknown tongues, they hurled stones at us and also bricks from a convenient stack—bricks are very dear in Marken and are imported here by sea, and yet the owner of those bricks, who happened to be standing by, contented himself with a timid remonstrance, but dared take no stronger measures.

As we could not defend ourselves, we dissimulated, pretending to be altogether unconscious of what was going on; then, as our persecutors waxed bolder, we smiled at them with an affectation of amiability we were far from feeling, for infanticide was in our hearts. But the most pathetic smile fails to move the ruthless Marken boy to mercy.

At last a fisherman who spoke a few words of English took compassion on us. He came on board.

"I vill show you vere you was better go," he said, "not to have bad children alongside. Dey vas very dam here, de children."

This good Samaritan piloted us to the other side of the harbour, where we lay moored to some stakes.

"You stop better here," he said, "not many boys throw so long as this was."

But some few of them could throw as far, nevertheless, and worried us occasionally; and let me warn yachtsmen who visit Marken that the boys are not sent early to bed here, as they are in most Dutch villages, but are permitted to stay up and annoy the poor foreigner half the night. Some people pay blackmail to these brigands, but that makes matters worse unless it be done in a scientific manner. Had I been able to speak Dutch, I should have picked out some half-dozen of the strongest boys and offered to give them sixpence each on the morrow in consideration of their thrashing the other boys and keeping them quiet during our stay. I mentioned this to Wright.

"It's a very good plan, sir," he said; "and then, after we'd set them all fighting like Kilkenny cats, we could sail away to-morrow morning without paying them their sixpences."

That would have been a sweet revenge, indeed, for all our ill-treatment at the hands of the children of Marken, but alas! we knew no Dutch, and found it impossible to make delusive promises in pantomime.

But I must do Marken the justice of saying that its women are charming and its men kindly honest fellows, somewhat subdued in manner, perhaps, and sad-visaged; but what else can be expected of a people who are groaning under the heartless tyranny of an infant democracy?

The wind howled dismally through the night, and on turning out the next morning we found that a fresh north-east breeze was blowing. We set all sail and escaped from the island before its demon boys had left their beds. My intention on starting was to cross the Zuider Zee to Urk, but when we got clear of the lea of Marken we encountered a very choppy sea; the water was leaping up round us, not into waves, but into pyramidic lumps like sugar-loaves. Urk was dead to windward of us, and we first put the *Falcon* on the port tack. "She don't seem to be making much way against this lop," remarked Wright, after a while, and she certainly was not.

"It doesn't look much like getting to Urk to-day," I replied; "we'll go about. She'll just lay up the coast on the other tack, and we can put into Hoorn or some other port if the sea and wind don't go down. We'll be well to windward at Hoorn, and if the wind is in the same direction to-morrow we can fetch Urk easily from there."

So we put the *Falcon* on the starboard tack and followed the coast to the northward, travelling very slowly, for each of the short, steep seas slapped the yacht violently in the nose and almost stopped her way altogether. However, we staggered along somehow, with much more noise and motion than speed, our decks constantly wet, and we came to the conclusion that if a moderate breeze like this can raise so nasty a sea on the shallow Zuider Zee it must be a very uncomfortable piece of water when a strong gale is blowing. It has the reputation of being so. Luckily the currents are feeble, the rise and fall of the tide being almost imperceptible hereabouts, else this would be a very dangerous sea indeed.

After two hours or so the wind headed us so that we had to tack, and the sea became so confused that we missed stays several times in getting about. We stumbled on—that is the best term to describe the boat's motion on this day—through the muddy water, past the monotonous stretches of the dykes, until about ~ p.m., when we perceived the town of Hoorn before us, almost hidden by the branches of its many trees tossing in the gusty wind. We passed through one of the two channels that lead to the harbour, and made fast to the quay close to the picturesque old Water Tower, which dominates the town and serves as a landmark to vessels far out to sea.

The usual crowd gathered on the quay above us, and an old woman commenced to address us. She became quite angry when she found that we could not understand her, and she began to scream at us at the top of her voice, heedless of the fact that we were not deaf but merely ignorant of her language. Had it been a man we should have jumped to the conclusion that this was the harbour-master demanding his fee; but what could this irate lady want with us?

Having failed utterly to explain herself, she suddenly ceased her clamour and beckoned me with her bony hand to follow her. Her air of authority was such that I dared not refuse; I crawled on to the quay and did her bidding with a sinking heart. She led me through the street in silence till we reached a small house. The door was open. Again she beckoned. I hesitated. Then she seized me by the hand and dragged me in. A crowd of inquisitive boys had followed us, so she slammed the door in their faces, and I was left alone with this mysterious woman. Her next proceeding was to unlock the drawer of a fine old carved oak bureau, of which I envied her even in that moment of trepidation. From this she took out a small book, which, without saying a word, she placed in my hand. I opened it at the title-page, and lo! it proved to be a French-Dutch dictionary! It was shrewd of the old lady to have thought of so excellent an interpreter between us.

I consulted the pages and pointed out to her the Dutch equivalents for the words "What want you with me?"

She opened the book in her turn, and, following her finger with my eyes, I read in succession the two words *huit sous*.

A light broke on my dull intelligence. I hastily turned over the dictionary again and showed her the uncouth Dutch word that stood for harbour-master. "Ja Ja!" she cried, laughing and slapping me on the back. We understood each other at last; this was the harbour-mistress after all, so I paid her the fourpence and she allowed me to depart.

Hoorn is one of the pleasantest-looking towns I saw in Holland. It is pierced by numerous canals, all crowded with craft and bordered by avenues of fine trees. In its streets are many quaint old gabled houses, and it has preserved all its original medieval appearance without being by any means a sleepy and stagnant place, for it is a garrison town and its public ways are full of life and colour.

And yet Hoorn is one of the famous dead cities of the Zuider Zee. I was prepared to see ruined houses and grass-grown, deserted streets, but there was nothing of the kind in this tidy, busy settlement; it is the most lively "dead city" imaginable. As for the grass-grown streets—tourists in these regions, whose imaginations run away with them after reading Havard, sometimes speak of these—I doubt that they exist in the deadest Dutch city. True that at Urk, which is not a dead city, I saw a tuft of grass in one of the streets. I stood and looked at it in wonder; how could neat Dutchmen tolerate such an eye-sore? Now there happened to be a native sitting in front of his shop, smoking his huge pipe placidly. His eye followed mine; he saw the dreadful thing, started, blushed deeply, and hurrying to it plucked it up by the roots. Then he looked at me sadly, as one who should say: "I would not for many barrels of herrings that you, a stranger, had seen this thing."

But though what remains of Hoorn is alive enough, especially its boys, it is a genuine dead city, for it was once a far more considerable and important place, being the ancient capital of North Holland; and Cape Horn, which was first doubled by Schouten, was named by him after his native town, then a flourishing seaport.

I looked into my Baedeker, and there read that in 1573 a naval engagement took place off Hoorn between the Dutch and Spaniards, when the admiral in command of the latter was taken prisoner. Late in the afternoon I was sitting on deck smoking, and as I gazed across the yellow Zuider Zee I was thinking how ridiculous it seemed to associate the idea of a naval action with that shallow water—only eight feet deep in the neighbourhood of Hoorn—when I saw a sight which made me leap to my feet and rub my eyes. Was I dreaming, or was I looking at phantoms? For I beheld two men-of-war making straight for the harbour. One was a full-rigged ship, and the other a very beamy iron-plated gunboat, with no masts to speak of. The ship was of very old-fashioned build, the other an ugly modern steamer; they approached slowly side by side, good representatives of the old and new styles. The ship furled her sails and came to an anchor off the entrance of the harbour, the gunboat steamed right in and brought up alongside the quay opposite us. These vessels had doubtlessly been constructed expressly for the Zuider Zee defence, and must have a very light draught. The clumsy ship stuck fast in the mud when she got under way the following morning, but the gunboat tugged her off again. Possibly the former always accompanies the latter for this purpose.

I have made no mention of our pump lately, but it must not be supposed that it was at all idle, for the Blackwall caulking of Monnikendam had been washed out in a very short space of time by the choppy waves of the Zuider Zee. This very necessary apparatus had got completely out of order, its india-rubber valves were worn away by much friction, and on this day it definitely refused to pump at all. Now ours was not an ordinary or garden pump—which is as good as any and is easily put to rights—but a patent arrangement, and therefore exceedingly difficult to mend. I doubted whether the tinkers of Hoorn could restore it to its pristine condition, so I thought it best to take the job in hand myself, and, instead of repairing it, convert it into an entirely new pump on the good old garden system. I cut a valve-plate out of a piece of hard wood, and then, as I required leather to complete my job, I sallied forth to procure some.

I soon found a cobbler's shop, entered, and endeavoured to explain my wants—a piece of hard leather for a valve and a soft piece with which to serve the piston.

"Some leather like this, please," I said, pointing to the sole of my boot. The cobbler put on his spectacles, seized my foot, and closely examined the boot, evidently under the impression that I wanted him to repair it. But as there was nothing amiss with it, he looked puzzled and shrugged his shoulders. "Vor de pomp of de ship," I cried; this ought to be good Dutch if it is not.

He seemed to understand me at last, and, motioning to me to wait for him, he went into an inner room and shortly returned, bearing in his arms a great load of every description of foot-covering, ranging from a dandy's patent-leather chaussure to a fisherman's sabot. He threw them on the floor before me with a gesture that said "Take your choice."

"No, no!" I said, shaking my head.

"Then what the deuce do you want?" he cried impatiently.

I don't know Dutch, but I could swear that was the signification of his words.

I was about to retire in despair, when I noticed that a policeman was standing in the doorway smiling grimly to himself. Our eyes met.

"What is it you want, sir?" he asked in English.

An interpreter had arrived very opportunely on the scene, and now the cobbler and myself were able to carry on our negotiations. This policeman had been for many years in the employment of the General Steam Navigation Company, hence his acquaintance with our language. Having procured the leather, I set to work before an admiring crowd, and soon put the pump to rights again.

On the following morning, Saturday, the 18th of June, we started at 8 a.m. for Urk. This island is only twenty-five English miles from Hoorn, but we were so unfortunate with our wind that we must have sailed three times that distance.

The weather was glorious, and only a few small fleecy clouds, very high up, crossed the blue sky. At first the wind was north-west, but it did not remain long in that favourable direction; it gradually freshened up and blew right in our teeth. We put the yacht first on one tack, then on the other; but whenever we went about, the wind would veer round also and head us. We were pursued by Vanderdecken's ill-luck; however, it was very pleasant sailing, and the sea, though choppy, was not nearly so rough as on the previous day.

At midday we were in the centre of the Zuider Zee and out of sight of land. I brought up my sextant and took the latitude, an operation, I imagine, very rarely performed on these waters.

Later on the atmosphere became very clear, so that we were able to distinguish in several directions the summits of far-off steeples and the isolated tops of trees. It was exactly as if we were looking over a country that had been submerged by an immense flood, for no land was anywhere visible.

In the afternoon the wind dropped and there was only a slight ripple on the Zuider Zee. We progressed very slowly until about four o'clock, when we perceived on the horizon, right ahead of us, a group of red lumps which we knew must be the roofs of Urk.

As we approached it, the tiny island—its size is not quite a third that of Marken—presented a curious appearance. There rose, seemingly straight out of the sea itself, a row of little houses dominated by a church and lighthouse. To the right of this village was a dense forest of pole masts, each with its long pennant streaming to the breeze, showing where the fishing-smacks were lying in the commodious haven. And the whole of the shallow, tideless sea was dotted with a vast number of other schuyts, all making for this harbour as fast as they were able with sail and oar.

Urk, diminutive though it be, is a most important fishing-station, and a population of upwards of two thousand is here supported solely by this industry. This was the very day to see Urk at its liveliest, as all the fishermen flock home on Saturday and stay in port till Sunday night. The scene reminded one of a hive on a summer's evening into which all the working bees are hurrying laden with the spoil of the day.

As the harbour seemed to be already full to its mouth I did not care to venture within, for I feared that the boats that came in after me would block up all the available space and prevent my getting out till Monday. Again I preferred to rely on the mercy of an open roadstead than to risk persecution at the hands of diabolical boys; so our anchor was let go some fifty yards from the shore in about eight feet of water. We found that the bottom consisted of hard sand and gravel. This considerably surprised us, for we did not expect to find stones anywhere on the muddy Zuider Zee. I thought that we had anchored over the remains of some ruined dyke or flood-destroyed village—there are many such in Dutch waters. But I believe that Urk is one of the few places in this half-liquid land where the solid earth that lies beneath asserts itself and sends forth stony offshoots to the surface.

As we had only tinned meats on board, I went on shore in the dinghy to buy stores. I pulled between the piers into the harbour and was astonished to see so many fine oak fishing-boats lying in tiers along the quays. The letters on their bows told me that they all belonged to Urk. I do not think that any other place of its size in Europe can boast of so large a fleet.

On landing, I found myself the centre of an admiring crowd of what appeared to me to be the strongest and healthiest people I had ever come across. The men, in their baggy trousers, tight jackets, and broad belts, looked like a race of giants, possessed too of hard and wiry frames that few giants are blessed with. The buxom women were proportionately tall and broad, and the children were far too robust to be otherwise than terribly naughty. When I looked at the boys I was glad that I had left the *Falcon* outside. The men seemed well disposed to strangers. Many of these sturdy fishermen had fraternized with our sailors on the Dogger Bank and understood something of English. Two or three of them piloted me to a little shop where every commodity that the people of Urk require can be purchased. But fresh meat is evidently not considered a necessary here; for they all shook their heads and laughed good-naturedly when I spoke of it. I could have as much salt pork as I liked, but beef was an unknown luxury. Just then, very opportunely, a hen began to cackle, and the sound inspired me to ask for eggs. The good lady of the shop sold me a large number for tenpence; but they were the smallest eggs I have ever seen. I met some of the fowls in the street and saw they were proportionate in size to their island, which the men certainly are not. I now bade Urk farewell, a proceeding that lasted some while, for all those who had joined in the procession that had followed me round the village considered themselves to be my friends and came up to shake hands at parting.

During the night the wind blew on shore so that we tumbled about at our anchorage a good deal. The sky was wild and crossed with mares' tails, and, to all appearance, we were in for an unquiet night. The wind moaned dismally, as it always does in Holland on very small provocation. In this country a stranger finds his meteorologic wisdom much at fault at first; for the weather has a habit of looking worse than it really is, especially when there is any north in the wind; then, even in midsummer, there comes suddenly over a fine sunny day a chilliness, a hazy bleakness, a wintry howling of wind that dismays the imagination and leads one to believe that a storm is imminent.

On the following morning (Sunday, June 19th) we resumed our voyage across the Zuider Zee immediately after breakfast. Bad weather had not followed the threatening signs of the previous evening. It was another sultry, cloudless, and almost calm day, and the light wind was again right in our teeth. We tacked in an easterly direction, intending to sail round the north end of the island of Schokland, which lay between us and our destination, the entrance of Zwarte Water.

For two hours we saw no signs of the land towards which we were sailing; then we perceived a line of yellow sand-hills to the north of us—the mainland near Lemmer. But ahead of us, towards the rising sun, there was a dazzling glare on the water, and a mirage which prevented us from distinguishing anything, save here and there a phantom-like schuyt greatly magnified by the heated atmosphere and appearing to be floating in mid-air. There was a considerable ripple on the sea round us; but it was difficult to say how it was caused. The surface of the shallow Zuider Zee seems to be sensitive to the slightest breath of air. So feeble was the wind that, after tacking with flapping sails for nearly four hours, we had not left Urk more than two miles astern, and the only sound to be heard on this quiet Sunday morning was the persistent cackling of the hens of that island.

But about midday a nice north-west breeze sprang up, and, setting our tanned square-sail, we began to bowl along at a good rate. At last we sighted that commonest landmark of the Zuider Zee, a steeple, bearing south-east, and we ran down towards it under the impression that it belonged to the church of Schokland. But we were mistaken, for Schokland and its low buildings were not yet visible above the horizon, and we were really looking right over the island at some lofty town spire on the mainland far beyond. After running on some way farther we saw three small hummocks, like three separate islands, ahead. Then as we approached we perceived a low sandy coast connecting these three hillocks, and we now had no doubt that this was the island of Schokland before us.

This island is very narrow, but it is three miles long. It seemed to be an almost barren sand-bank, with few houses on it, and not many fishing-boats in its small harbour.

We gave the north corner a wide berth, for the water is very shallow round Schokland, and, indeed, there is but little more than six feet anywhere between it and the mainland. Having passed the point we sailed into an extraordinary labyrinth of tall sticks that puzzled us a good deal. At first we thought they were intended as marks for the different channels; but we soon decided that there were far too many of them for that purpose. These sticks were planted close together in double rows which stretched across the water in every direction as far as the eye could see, like so many streets. There must have been some thousands of them in sight. They were doubtlessly the stakes to which the fishermen attach their nets or lines; but it seemed strange to find such crowds of them stuck right across the fairway of vessels.

We could now plainly distinguish the mainland, and we made out the Kraggenburg lighthouse ahead of us. The Zwarte Water river empties itself into a very shallow bay, across which, from the mouth of the river, a deep channel, known as the Zwolsche Diep, had been dredged for four miles out to sea. This channel is bordered on one side by a pier, at the end of which is the Kraggenburg lighthouse, and on the other side by a submerged embankment of stone marked by big beacons. The wind was now freshening every moment and a nasty sea was rising; but we ran on merrily under all canvas, and at last rushed suddenly into smooth water under the pierhead, and we had done with the Zuider Zee.

FROM *RACUNDRA'S FIRST CRUISE*
1923

Arthur Ransome

Illustration by Brian Anderson

Arthur Ransome is best known for his classic series of childrens' books, Swallows and Amazons. *But his life before his success was a world away from the stories of summer idyls in small boats. Born in 1884, he spent some summers as a child in England's Lake District, where the* Swallows and Amazons *series would later be set. After a short stint at Yorkshire College, he moved to London and worked his way into the literary scene there. Ransome wrote several books on the bohemian demimonde, married, and had a daughter, but his biography of Oscar Wilde got him stuck into an ugly libel suit. While he was eventually exonerated, the trial had apparently taken its toll.*

In 1913 he moved, alone, to Russia, with the idea of learning the language and translating a book of traditional folklore. While he was there, World War I broke out, and then the Russian Revolution came and he ended up writing about it all for a leftist paper, the Daily News, *and later the* Manchester Guardian. *Along the way, he got to know Lenin and Trotsky, did a bit of spying for Britain, and was himself suspected by British authorities of being a Communist sympathizer. To top it all, he made off with Trotsky's personal secretary, Evgenia Petrovna Shelepina, who sailed with him in the Baltic. After* Racundra's First Cruise—*the story of their voyage together—was published, she became his wife.*

Ransome and Evgenia returned to England and settled in the Lake District. He continued to write for the Manchester Guardian, *and then, one summer, he taught the children of some friends to sail.* Swallows and Amazons *followed soon after.*

"The Ship and the Man" was first published in the Manchester Guardian *in 1922, and later included in* Racundra. *It is an odd, haunting story, and very different from the rest of the book—very different in fact than any of the other stories I ran across when researching this book, so I couldn't resist including it.*

THE SHIP AND THE MAN

Sailing from Baltic Port, one of a crew of four in another man's ship, I came to the far end of the Dagorort Peninsula, and there had an experience which I cannot refrain from putting in this book, so full it was of the romance of those rarely visited waters.

We had anchored half a mile from the shore off the place that is called Ermuiste, which means 'the terrible', for it is a place of many wrecks, a rocky point open to the widest sweep of the winds across the Baltic Sea. We had not dared to go nearer, and I was glad we had not, for, as I rowed ashore in the little boat, I passed many rocks awash and saw others a foot or two under water. There were dark purple clouds rising over the sea to the N.W., wind was coming, and we were impatient to be off again, to find shelter, or at least to put some miles of sea between us and that notorious coast. But there was still sunlight on the rocky shore and on the dark pinewoods that ran down almost to the water's edge and on the little wooden pierhead, unmarked on the chart, which, seen through binoculars, had tempted us to run in and look for information and supplies. Beyond the pierhead was a little stretch of beach where I meant to land. But, looking over my shoulder as I pulled in, bobbing over the waves in my little boat, I could see none of the things that a pierhead usually promises. There was no watchman's hut on the pier, no smoke above the trees, no cottages, no loafers, no fishermen, no sign of any kind of life. And then, coming nearer, I saw that the pier was in ruins. Much of its planking had gone, great beams were leaning perilously over from it, and here and there masses of it had actually fallen into the water. I wished to waste no time, and was on the point of turning and pulling back to the ship, when I saw something else more promising than the pier. Just within the forest that stretched down to the beach, almost hidden by the tall pines, was the great golden body of an unfinished ship. Where a ship was building, there, surely, must be men, and I rowed in confidently past the ruined pier, slipped off my shoes, rolled up my trousers and, jumping overboard, pulled the little boat through shallow water and up on a narrow strip of small pebbles.

Then, walking up into the shadow of the trees, I came to the ship, the upper part of which, far above my head, was glowing in the splashes of sunshine that came through the tops of the pines which brushed the sides of the ship as they waved in the gathering wind. There was not a man to be seen, or a hut for men, nor was there sound of hammers or any of the usual accompaniments of shipbuilding. But for the ruined pier and that golden hull in the shadows among those tall trees, the coast might have been that of an undiscovered island. And then I began to notice one or two things about the ship herself which seemed a little odd. She was a very large ship to be building on that bit of coast, where there is no real harbour and the most ambitious launches are those of the twenty-foot fishing-boats which a man builds during the winter to earn his living in the summer months. She seemed even larger than she was, as ships do on land, shut in there among the trees that pressed about her as if they had grown up round her. And her lines were not those of a new ship. There was something a little old-fashioned about them, as though she were an unfinished masterpiece of an older period. A few schooners of her type survive today among those *laibas* that carry timber and potatoes round the Esthonian coast, and they outsail those modern ships in which an obstreperous motor, tucked away in the stern, makes up for the want of the love and thought that went into the lines of the older vessels. And then I saw that I was wrong in thinking that she had been newly planked. The upper planking was new, certainly, ruddy gold where the sun caught it, but lower down her hull was weathered. Only the topmost planks had been freshly put on, and as the eye descended from them it passed imperceptibly from a new to an old piece of shipbuilding. The keel, laid on great stones, was joined to them by moss. There was lichen upon it, and on the foot of the stern-post was a large, bright cluster of scarlet toadstools.

Just then I found a narrow, lightly worn track running from the ship farther into the forest. I walked along it, and only a few score yards away, but quite invisible from the shore, I came out of the silence and the trees into a small clearing and a loud noise of grasshoppers. There was a tiny hayfield, not bigger than a small suburban garden, a cornfield, perhaps three times the size, and an old log cabin with a deep thatched roof, an outhouse or two, a dovecot and pigeons' fluttering about it.

The pigeons fluttered and murmured, but no dog barked and no one answered when I knocked at the low door of the hut. I knocked again, and then, doubtfully, tried the wooden latch, opened it and walked in. A very little light came through the small windows, heavily overhung by the deep thatch. The hut was divided into two rooms. In the first were a couple of spinning-wheels, one very old, black with age, the other quite new, a precise copy of it, the two contrasting like the upper planking and the keel of that still unfinished ship. There was also a narrow wooden bed, a great oak chest and a wooden stool, all made as if to last for ever. A few very clean cooking-things were on the stove, and fishing-lines and nets were hanging from wooden pegs on the walls. The second room held no furniture but a bench and a big handloom for weaving. There was some grand strong canvas being made upon it, and, as I looked at it, I guessed suddenly that here were being made the sails for the ship.

Without knowing why, I hurried out of the cabin into the sunshine. Leaning on the gate into the cornfield, as if he had been there all the time, an old man stood watching me. He had steel-grey curly hair and very dark blue eyes. The skin of his face was clear walnut. He might have been any age from fifty to a hundred. His clothes were of some strong homespun cloth, probably made on the loom where he was making the sails. The shoes on his bare brown feet were of woven string with soles of thick rope. With his arrival the whole place seemed to have sprung to life. He was accompanied by three sheep, and two pigs snuffled in the ground close by. A dog, impassive as his master, lay beside the gate, half opening his eyes, as if he had been waked from sleep.

Somehow I could make no apology for having gone into his cottage. I asked him where to land eastwards along the coast and for the nearest anchorage sheltered from the north-east. He told me what I wanted gravely, and with a curious air of taking his words one by one out of a lumber-room and dusting them before use. I tried to get eggs and butter from him, but he said he had no eggs and never made more butter than he needed. I should get some from the forester at Palli or at Luidja, near the anchorage. I asked him about the pier. Once upon a time there had been people here and timber traffic?

'Yes, but that was a long time ago, and the people have all gone away.'

'Was it then that you began building the ship?'

'Yes; that was when I began building the ship.'

His dark-blue eyes, watching me, but indifferent as the sea itself, invited no more questions. I turned back by the path under the great ship so many times larger than his cottage, and found myself oddly hurried as I pushed our little boat into the water and rowed away. I could just catch the sunlight splashes on the body of the ship among the trees. Would she ever be finished? And what then? What had he planned as he worked at her year after year? Would he die before his dream came true, or before he knew that the dreaming was the better part of it?

FROM **SWALLOWS AND AMAZONS**
1930

Arthur Ransome

THE ENEMY'S BOATHOUSE

Here's a recipe for getting a kid hooked on boats, camping, and quite possibly read-ing in general: Sometime when you are in a bookstore with the child, buy a copy of Arthur Ransome's Swallows and Amazons, *let him or her get a good look at it, and when you get home, put it up on a shelf somewhere, casually suggesting that the child is probably too young to find it interesting and should wait a year or two.*

There are of course some things to remember if this is going to work. The first is that if the child comes to think that it is An Improving Book you are trying to push on her, you are likely to miss stays completely and find yourself wallowing in irons, if not actually making sternway. And so after you tiptoe through the house later that night to "have a quick look" you should read it like these books ought to be read— under the bedclothes with a flashlight—and make sure it is back on the shelf before anybody else is awake. The second is that you might very well find that you have been beaten to the mark; it is unseemly to wrestle with a ten-year-old over one of his books, and so perhaps it would be a good idea to get hold of a copy of Peter Duck *and per-haps* We Didn't Mean to Go to Sea, *as well.*

In this passage, the children are sailing on a large lake in England's Lake District. Their rich imaginations have transformed the lake into "the sea," a local town to "Rio," and much more. Here they are returning from an unsuccessful attempt to capture the Amazon, *a small boat sailed by two girls with whom they're having a mock war.*

SWALLOWS IN THE DARK

No one spoke for some time. The plan had failed, and the cutting-out expedition had come to nothing.

Suddenly they began to feel a little more wind.

"We must have reached the open sea," said Captain John. "You can light up that torch, Mister Mate, and see what you can."

Susan flashed the torch all around them. There were no reeds to be seen. On every side there was nothing but rippled water.

"Hullo," cried Roger. "I can see lights far away."

"Rio lights," said John. "We're out. I'm going to hoist the sail. Hold the torch steady while I reef. Even Daddy used to say, 'Never be ashamed to reef a small boat in the dark.'"

Reefing in the dark, even with the help of a torch held by a willing mate, is not too easy, but it was done at last and John brought the *Swallow* head to wind and hoisted the sail, while Susan took the tiller and the main-sheet.

"Put her on the starboard tack," said John, as soon as she was sailing, "and keep her very full. We want to be sure we are well clear of the rocks off the point."

Even with the reef down there was enough wind to send *Swallow* fast through the water with a steady rippling noise under her bows. "We're sailing due east," said John presently.

"How do you know?" asked Susan.

"Look," said John.

A broad patch of clear sky showed overhead, and in it the larger stars.

"Look," said John, "There's the Saucepan. There's its handle. There's its pot. And those two stars that make the front wall of the pot point to the North Star. There's the North Star. It's broad on our port beam, so we must be sailing east. And Rio lights are broad on the starboard beam away in the south."

"Why do natives always call the Saucepan the Great Bear?" said Susan.

"I don't know," said John. "It isn't like a bear at all. It's more like a giraffe. But you couldn't have a better saucepan."

"She'd go a lot nearer the wind," said Mate Susan.

"Keep her full," said the captain. "Keep her sailing. But we must be well clear of the point now. I'm going to use the compass and chart."

The spirits of the *Swallow*'s crew had risen very much now that they were at sea once more and not fumbling in the dark with reed-beds and water lilies. There is nothing like sea-room to cheer a sailor's heart.

"Are you cold, Roger?" asked the mate.

"Rather," said the look-out.

"Get down below the gunwale and wrap yourself up in this blanket," said the mate, passing a blanket forward by way of the captain.

John, too, crouched in the bottom of the boat. He got out the guidebook, and found the chart in it with the help of his torch. Then he laid his compass on the middle thwart, so that the black line marked on the rim inside it was nearest to the bows. That was no good, because *Swallow* was heeling over and the compass was on a slant so that the compass card could not work. He had to hold it in his hand. Even then the card swung a great deal. He held the compass as steady as he could in one hand, while with the other he threw the light of the torch on it and watched to see what point on he card was opposite the black line. It did not keep still, but swung first one way and then the other.

"Almost exactly east," he said at last. "Now bring her closer to the wind."

The mate put the tiller down a little at a time and *Swallow* pointed nearer and nearer to the wind.

"East, East by South, East South East. South-East by East, South East," he said rapidly.

"She won't go much nearer than that," said the mate.

"Keep her so," said Captain John. "South-East it is, or jolly near it." He looked at the chart in the book. "That'll take her to about here and then she'll go perhaps a bit better than south-west on the other tack. But the trouble is, we don't know how far we go on a tack. We'll just have to sail fairly short tacks and try to keep them about the same length. Then we shan't be going near the shore on either side. We'll be able to see by the Rio lights when we are getting near the islands. I'm going to count a hundred, and then we'll go about. Then I'll count a hundred on the other tack before we go about again."

"Rio lights are going out," said Mate Susan.

They were. One by one the lights on the hill above Rio Bay disappeared.

"It must be awfully late," said Susan.

The clouds swept over the stars again. There were no lights to be seen anywhere. The little *Swallow* rushed along in the darkness, Susan keeping her close to the wind, facing directly forward and putting the tiller up a little when she felt the hint of cold breath on her left cheek.

"Ninety-two, ninety-three, ninety-four, ninety-five, ninety-six, ninety-seven, ninety-eight, ninety-nine, a hundred . . . Ready about," said John. Susan put the *Swallow* about. For a moment the water was silent under her keel, and then, as she gathered speed, the pleasant, galloping noise of the waves began again.

"You take the tiller, John," said the mate, "I want to get out some chocolate for that boy."

John took the tiller, counting steadily and slowly. He had the compass with him, and sometimes lit the torch and fixed it between his knees, and held the compass in its light. But it was really not much good, though he would have liked to think it was. The best he could do was to keep the ship sailing and to see that she sailed about the same distance on each tack. And then—what if the wind had shifted a little?

The mate got out the cake and chocolate. She and the captain found that they could do with some just as well as the boy. The boy, warm in his two sets of clothes and his blanket, was enjoying himself enormously.

"Wouldn't Titty have liked it?" he said.

"Liked what?" said Susan.

"Sailing like this in the dark," said the boy.

Susan said nothing. She did not like thinking of Titty alone on the island for so long.

John said nothing. For one thing, he was counting to himself and getting near a hundred. For another, the light of Susan's torch in the bottom of the boat, where she was cutting hunks of cake and breaking up chocolate, and the light of his own torch, when he used it to look at the compass, made the darkness of the night even darker than it really was. It was better than being stuck in the river, much better, but Captain John knew very well that he could not really tell how near they might be to the shore. He was the captain of the *Swallow,* and must not wreck his ship. Daddy had trusted him not to be a duffer and, sailing in this blackness, he did not feel so sure of not being a duffer as he did by day. And there were no lights in Rio to help him. Everything was black. He could only keep on tacking against the wind, and he was wondering what he should do when *Swallow* came near the islands off the Bay. And how would he know when she was coming near them? It would not do to let his crew know that he was worried. So he said nothing, except that he went on with his counting. Perhaps he counted a little louder than before. He reached a hundred, put *Swallow* about, and began again: "One, two, three," as she went off on he other tack.

Backwards and forwards *Swallow* scurried across the lake in the dark. The islands could not be far away.

Suddenly, John stopped counting.

"Listen," he said. "Trees. I can hear the wind in them. What's that?" He flashed his torch over the side. There was the white splash of water breaking on a rock. The noise of wind in trees was close ahead.

"Let go the halyard," called John. "Down with the sail. Grab the yard as it comes."

Susan was as quick as she could be. She knew by John's voice that there was no time to lose. The sail came down in a rush. She gathered it in as well as she could. Then she flashed her torch into the darkness ahead.

"There's something close here," she said.

Swallow drifted in smooth water. John put out the oars.

"It's here," said Susan. "Close here. Pull, pull your left. It's a landing stage."

Swallow bumped gently against wood.

"Hang onto it, whatever it is," called John. He shipped his oars. Then he scrambled forward. The torch showed the black damp wooden beams of one of the landing stages used by the natives for their rowing boats.

"Hold your torch up, Susan," he said. "I'm going ashore."

Susan held up her torch. John was on the landing stage in a moment.

"All right now," he said. "I've got the painter." He lit his torch, and Susan saw him, as *Swallow* drifted back, standing on the landing-stage and making fast the painter round a post.

"We're all right here, anyhow," he said. "Lucky for us not to hit that rock as we passed. I wonder which island this is."

He walked up the landing stage, lighting himself with his torch. Then he came back.

"There's a notice which says, 'Private. Landing Forbidden.'"

"What are we to do?" said Susan.

"Land," said Captain John. "At least, land if we want to. The natives are asleep anyhow. We'll stay here until there's a little light. There's bound to be some light soon. Only duffers would try to get through the islands in dark as black as this."

"What about Titty?" said Susan.

"Titty's in camp. She's got a tent. She'll be all right. So are we now."

Captain John was extremely happy. Now that the danger was over, he knew very well that they had a nearly as possible been duffers after all, racing around in the dark. And instead of being smashed on a rock, here was the *Swallow* snugly tied up to a landing-stage. Where they were did not matter. Dawn would show that.

SWALLOWS·AND·AMAZONS·FOR·EVER!

From *Swallows and Amazons*, by Arthur Ransome. Reprinted by permission of David R. Godine, Publisher, Inc. Copyright 1986 by Arthur Ransome

FROM *SAILING ALONE AROUND THE WORLD*
1899

Joshua Slocum

In Boston during the winter of 1892, Captain Joshua Slocum was fifty-one and had commanded and been part owner of a number of ships. But bad luck and innovation had washed him ashore and left him broke. One day (I always picture it in a low-ceilinged bar, filled with tobacco smoke, the smell of a working harbor, and sailors cast upon the shore as steamships belching black clouds of smoke took over the seas) a whaling captain offered him a ship, but one that "wants some repairs."

"I was only too glad to accept," Slocum wrote, "for I had already found that I could not obtain work in the shipyard without first paying fifty dollars to a society, and as for a ship to command—there were not enough ships to go round. Nearly all our tall vessels had been cut down for coal-barges, and were being ignominiously towed by the nose from port to port, while many worthy captains addressed themselves to Sailors' Snug Harbor."

Reading between the lines, it was a cruel joke, but one that Slocum shrugged off, building another Spray *essentially from scratch. After sailing his 37-foot oyster sloop around the world and writing a best seller about his adventures, he no doubt enjoyed his oysters, beer, and the last laugh, served cold upon his return to Boston years later.*

BUILDING *SPRAY*

The next day I landed at Fairhaven, opposite New Bedford, and found that my friend had something of a joke on me. For seven years the joke had been on him. The "ship" proved to be a very antiquated sloop called the *Spray,* which the neighbors declared had been built in the year 1. She was affectionately propped up in a field, some distance from salt water, and was covered with canvas. The people of Fairhaven, I hardly need say, are thrifty and observant. For seven years they had asked, "I wonder what Captain Eben Pierce is going to do with the old *Spray?*" The day I appeared there was a buzz at the gossip exchange: at last some one had come and was actually at work on the old *Spray.* "Breaking her up, I s'pose?" "No; going to rebuild her." Great was the amazement. "Will it pay?" was the question which for a year or more I answered by declaring that I would make it pay.

My axe felled a stout oak-tree near by for a keel, and Farmer Howard, for a small sum of money, hauled in this and enough timbers for the frame of the new vessel. I rigged a steam-box and a pot for a boiler. The timbers for ribs, being straight saplings, were dressed and steamed till supple, and then bent over a log, where they were secured till set. Something tangible appeared every day to show for my labor, and the neighbors made the work sociable. It was a great day in the *Spray* shipyard when her new stem was set up and fastened to the new keel. Whaling-captains came from far to survey it. With one voice they pronounced it "A 1," and in their opinion "fit to smash ice." The oldest captain shook my hand warmly when the breast-hooks were put in, declaring that he could see no reason why the *Spray* should not "cut in bow-head" yet off the coast of Greenland. The much-esteemed stem-piece was from the butt of the smartest kind of a pasture oak. It afterward split a coral patch in two at the Keeling Islands, and did not receive a blemish. Better timber for a ship than pasture white oak never grew. The breast-hooks, as well as all the ribs, were of this wood, and were steamed and bent into shape as required. It was hard upon March when I began work in earnest; the weather was cold; still, there were plenty of inspectors to back me with advice. When a whaling-captain hove in sight I just rested on my adze awhile and "gammed" with him.

New Bedford, the home of whaling-captains, is connected with Fairhaven by a bridge, and the walking is good. They never "worked along up" to the shipyard too often for me. It was the charming tales about arctic whaling that inspired me to put a double set of breast-hooks in the *Spray*, that she might shunt ice.

The seasons came quickly while I worked. Hardly were the ribs of the sloop up before apple-trees were in bloom. Then the daisies and the cherries came soon after. Close by the place where the old *Spray* had now dissolved rested the ashes of John Cook, a revered Pilgrim father. So the new *Spray* rose from hallowed ground. From the deck of the new craft I could put out my hand and pick cherries that grew over the little grave. The planks for the new vessel, which I soon came to put on, were of Georgia pine an inch and a half thick. The operation of putting them on was tedious, but, when on, the calk-ing was easy. The outward edges stood slightly open to receive the calking, but the inner edges were so close that I could not see daylight between them. All the butts were fastened by through bolts, with screw-nuts tightening them to the timbers, so that there would be no complaint from them. Many bolts with screw-nuts were used in other parts of the construction, in all about a thousand. It was my purpose to make my vessel stout and strong.

Now, it is a law in Lloyd's that the *Jane* repaired all out of the old until she is entirely new is still the *Jane*. The *Spray* changed her being so gradu-ally that it was hard to say at what point the old died or the new took birth, and it was no matter. The bulwarks I built up of white-oak stanchions four-teen inches high, and covered with seven-eighth-inch white pine. These stanchions, mortised through a two-inch covering-board, I calked with thin cedar wedges. They have remained perfectly tight ever since. The deck I made of one-and-a-half-inch by three-inch white pine spiked to beams, six by six inches, of yellow or Georgia pine, placed three feet apart. The deck-inclosures were one over the aperture of the main hatch, six feet by six, for a cooking-galley, and a trunk farther aft, about ten feet by twelve, for a cabin. Both of these rose about three feet above the deck, and were sunk suf-ficiently into the hold to afford headroom. In the spaces along the sides of the cabin, under the deck, I arranged a berth to sleep in, and shelves for small storage, not forgetting a place for the medicine-chest. In the midship hold, that is, the space between cabin and galley, under the deck, was room for provision of water, salt beef, etc., ample for many months.

The hull of my vessel being now put together as strongly as wood and iron could make her, and the various rooms partitioned off, I set about "calking ship." Grave fears were entertained by some that at this point I should fail. I myself gave some thought to the advisability of a "professional caulker." The very first blow I struck on the cotton with the calking-iron, which I thought was right, many others thought wrong. "It'll crawl!" cried a man from Marion, passing with a basket of clams on his back. "It'll crawl!" cried another from West Island, when he saw me driving cotton into the seams. Bruno simply wagged his tail. Even Mr. Ben J——, a noted authority on whaling-ships, whose mind, however, was said to totter, asked rather confidently if I did not think "it would crawl." "How fast will it crawl?" cried my old captain friend, who had been towed by many a lively sperm-whale. "Tell us how fast," cried he, "that we may get into port in time." However, I drove a thread of oakum on top of the cotton, as from the first I had intended to do. And Bruno again wagged his tail. The cotton never "crawled." When the calking was finished, two coats of copper paint were slapped on the bottom, two of white lead on the topsides and bulwarks. The rudder was then shipped and painted, and on the following day the *Spray* was launched. As she rode at her ancient, rust-eaten anchor, she sat on the water like a swan.

The *Spray*'s dimensions were, when finished, thirty-six feet nine inches long, over all, fourteen feet two inches wide, and four feet two inches deep in the hold, her tonnage being nine tons net and twelve and seventy-one hundredths tons gross.

Then the mast, a smart New Hampshire spruce, was fitted, and likewise all the small appurtenances necessary for a short cruise. Sails were bent, and away she flew with my friend Captain Pierce and me, across Buzzard's Bay on a trial-trip—all right. The only thing that now worried my friends along the beach was, "Will she pay?" The cost of my new vessel was $553.62 for materials, and thirteen months of my own labor. I was several months more than that at Fairhaven, for I got work now and then on an occasional whale-ship fitting farther down the harbor, and that kept me the overtime.

FROM **THE BOY, ME, AND THE CAT**
LIFE ABOARD A SMALL BOAT, FROM MASSACHUSETTS TO FLORIDA AND BACK IN 1912

Henry Plummer

In the fall of 1912, Henry Plummer, recently retired from an insurance firm, set off in a small yacht with his son, Henry, and a cat, Scotty, on a voyage from New Bedford to Florida and back. His account of the voyage through the maze of canals and rivers that would later become the Intracoastal Waterway will be of interest to anyone who knows, or would like to know, the modern version. But at its heart, the story is that of a father who wanted to have a real adventure with a son he had not seen enough of. He writes of their voyage with dry humor, understatement, and a refreshing absence of the kind of self-conscious chest-thumping that one too often finds in more modern examples of the genre.

It was startling and disturbing, though, in such a lovely and otherwise reflective narrative, to run across the word nigger here and there, and a reference or two to "lazy niggers" as a type or a truism. It is especially odd given that a few years after the voyage, he spent a considerable amount of time and money on behalf of a young boy who had sailed from the Cape Verde Islands off the coast of Africa to join his parents who had emigrated to the US. When the boy arrived, he was found to have an eye infection, and the immigration police decreed that he must be deported, possibly never to see his parents again. Plummer read of the situation and, outraged, went down to Washington, DC, and spent days going from one office to another until he finally managed to have the decision overturned. The boy was not white. Those were different times, I guess.

THE CRUISE OF THE *MASCOT*

Sept. 1912 The Mascot is an old-fashioned Cape Cod catboat 30 years old. Her dimensions are, length overall, 24 ft. 6 in., waterline 23 ft., beam 10 ft., draught 3 ft. 6 in. With self-bailing cockpit, she is as safe and able a little ship as a man could want to go to sea in. Cabin accommodations are comfortably ample for two men and include a small shipmate stove near gangway on port side, a well-filled bookcase forward on starboard side, two roomy transoms and plenty of storage room.

Today we hauled out on marine railway to paint and also had a 3-horsepower engine installed in our 15 ft. dory skiff. Mighty busy days settling up business matters and attending personally to every detail of outfitting for Henry is new to the game and can be of very little help at this time.

January 10th to 15th Am not going to write daily log of this time for it would be too tedious reading, but it was by no means tedious living. We became part and parcel of the swamp and marsh. We were of it, in it, and passed through it it like a muskrat or mink, like a snipe or plover. The tide; its set, speed and turning. The wind; its strength and direction. These were what counted and on them we either halted or went on. The ripple of the tide at every bend, the line of foam bubbles on every reach was a matter of constant interest and study. Such days are not for either rich or poor, for those ignorant or wise, but for those only who can cast themselves bodily into nature and be absorbed by it. I don't wonder big launch owners and house boat owners always send their boats south under charge of the crew.

There could be nothing more dreary than just a-setting still and being taken through these twisting rivers that lead for miles and miles through the never ending rice marshes. We saw some ducks and shore birds, but got shots at very few and missed those ingloriously. One morning during a thick fog, H. tried Helen Keller *{a .22 rifle they brought along to shoot game for the pot}* at a cormorant which down here they call a nigger's goose. The bird was on the wing, yet once it sounded as if the bullet had found meat, but the bird did-n't drop. Two or three hundred yards farther on we came across him stone dead with the lead through his heart. The fog was a nuisance and brought us to anchor at the mouth of the river leading into St. Helena's Sound which we wished to cross on our way to Hunting Is. H. went ashore to try and pick up a mess of something to eat, but at 5 PM yelled out of the fog that his boat was high and dry and he would like me to send him his supper on a tray. Foolish little boy. I got him on board again about 7 and mighty glad he was to crawl into the warm cabin and eat a good hearty supper for he had been nearly bogged, was wet through and plastered with mud. A bit seared, too, and I don't believe will try this country again alone. He got seven shore birds, but cooked and ate them on shore himself. Greedy cuss. He brought a present in a match box and when I opened it, out hopped a chameleon lizard right into my lap. What with Scotty trying to catch it and I trying not to, there was a very busy cup of tea. We caught him the next day. Have named him Bill from Alice in Wonderland and added him to ships company.

One morning the fog burned away to as pretty a bit of blue sky and southerly wind as you ever saw. We were off to cross St. Helena's Sound at once. What do you think? In an hour a black, viscous looking squall made up in the west and struck just as we had tied two reefs. A short smother of rain and wind and then cloudy skies and light airs with strong tide and lumpy seas. That Sound is no Massachusetts Bay. All about are 1ft. and 2 ft. spots. I did the best I could, but one spot that should break didn't and everything else did and what with the tide sweeping us about we had a mighty anxious hour or two with the lead giving us from 9 to 10 feet of water on a falling tide. Finally got into our creek and of all dreary sur-roundings these certainly won out over any we have yet seen. For miles and miles the dark brown oyster bars stretched endlessly and the creek with many branches wound about like a maze. It was near night when we took bottom and learnt from some nigger oyster gatherers that we were way out of the main creek and bound for the sticks. So it was snug down for the night. At high tide these oyster bars will be covered and we will be anchored in a great shallow lake through which it would be most dangerous to try to navigate for these bars are simply covered with sharp pointed oyster clusters which differ in my opinion mighty little from rocks. Hundreds of big plover all over and about this afternoon. Big as pigeons, tame as pigeons, too. Went in launch to get some for supper. Missed them sitting, also flying, and came back without one. I am in that delightful stage when I pull the trigger three for four times before I shoot. Flinching? Well, I guess so. H. ain't no better than I am. We have a standing bet of five glasses of Coca-Cola to one that the other fellow doesn't kill. So far we stand even and nobody has hit a thing. Dreary, cold, cloudy, northeast weather. Put launch ashore and repacked stuffing box, but that didn't stop leak which now threatens to almost sink her overnight.

The clouds all rolled away and a morning broke as bright as a new dollar with a waspish northeaster whisking across the marshes. It was off and away "pronto." With single reef we cut things wide open. Slack sheet, down peak and away we rushed the reaches. In sheet, up peak and we beat her up the bends and then repeat with our wake swashing from bank to bank. We kept at it all day and it was one of the sporting sails of my life. Through narrow creeks, down broad rivers, across big sounds we drove and hustled. Just a little slip-up in jibing or tacking and we would have been in the meadows, but we made none. When we shot out of the creek into Port Royal Sound we made just three jumps and landed with a swash in the river on the other shore. Old Mascot only wet her garboards twice in crossing, and the launch never touched water at all. So it was all day and we anchored for the night with Savannah, Ga. but a few miles away. The night came pretty as a picture, but snappy cold and with the highest glass we have yet seen, 30.2. Think must have change soon. When glass is persistently high down here I promptly suspicion trouble. By 4 a.m. I felt sure we were in for another duster for glass began to drop, heavy clouds rolled up from northeast and wind piped on. I lay awake hoping that I wouldn't have to get out anchors until daylight for it was pesky dark and cold. Suddenly all the breeze let go to a dead calm and then came out of the northwest smartly but not troublesome and I got in some handsome winks until seven o'clock when I turned out to an undeniably pretty day and good breakfast. Then it was away under sail once more, and passing for a mile or so through a little winding creek, we entered the Savannah River and by noon were sailing along the waterfront of one of the busiest of southern ports.

Inner Basin at Mowbray Arch Ghent, Norfolk, Virginia

Little engine going finely all day and in the calm of a beautiful spring evening we pushed down the little creek, entered the river, set our lights as darkness fell, and hauling along close to navy yard and the big battleships, we dropped anchor at 7 PM off the Norfolk Rowing Club. We are a total of 50 days from Miami, with 31 sailing days for a distance, as the crow flies, of about 1,000 miles. This means over 30 miles a day *average*, and, the size of boat considered, together with character of water passed through, makes it rather a remarkable record. Day after day we sailed farther than New Bedford to Boston, and with the exception on one night run outside, all runs were made by daylight.

May 1st. Tripped anchor after breakfast and ran through the drawer into a little inner basin like the Charles River one on a small scale. It is called the Mowbray Arch Ghent, though why I have not yet discovered.

May 2nd. Fair and deliciously warm. None of the Cape Cod dampness on any of this trip. Leather shoes tucked away forward for the whole cruise turned out today without any mould whatever. Always a little dust when sweeping the cabin floor.

H. left this afternoon to visit coal mines in West Virginia. It was hard to see him go. When his steamer sailed I was out in the launch to wave him good-bye. I guess it was just as well the steamer's wash came along and gave me all I wanted to do to keep putt-putt right side up. Feelings, like stomach aches, are queer things. Am afraid he won't come back quite my boy again. Sort of making a start on life's cruise I fancy, and somebody else is going to be captain. He'll help me sail home, tie me up to the dock and then spread canvas and away. Quite right. I wouldn't wish it any otherwise and the master that gets him will know he's got a man when the time comes. For H., this cruise has not been all a pleasant summer's outing. Once or twice he has seen the edge of the big shadow not so very far away and has neither batted an eye nor quivered a lip. He'll do. Bene, it is well.

FROM **THE CURVE OF TIME**
1968

M. Wylie Blanchet

This book is one to read all the way through. It must have been something for the salty old sea dogs of Vancouver Island to hash and rehash in the 1920s and 30s. A woman, recently widowed when her husband went missing while on a short voyage in the family runabout, Caprice, *decides to pack her young family of five kids into the 26-foot boat and spend the summer cruising the treacherous waters of the Gulf of Georgia north to Queen Charlotte Straight. Cougars, bears, hermits, killer whales, engine problems, powerful currents, ugly weather: Muriel Wylie Blanchet saw them all and more. With another author these sorts of adventures might have consumed the book. For Blanchet they seem to have been just things to deal with, learn from, and tuck away so as not to interfere with simply having the adventure of a lifetime, every year for fifteen years as her children grew and thrived.*

NORTHWARD TO SEYMOUR INLET

The end of July, we anchored overnight just inside the western entrance of Well's Pass, in Kingcome Inlet. We wanted to make an early morning run up the open coast to Seymour Inlet. The entrance to Seymour Inlet is just south of Cape Caution, and that would be the farthest north we had ever been.

We had crept into Kingcome Inlet two days before in heavy fog—soft, white, insistent fog that shut out all our known world. Our once friendly trees were now menacing shadows that would drift suddenly into sight, hesitate for a moment, then swiftly turn and flee away. Instead of a clear green sea with its colourful, inhabited shallows, there was a misty void, over which we silently moved. Everything took on the unreal silence of the spirit world. Voices that were thrown with more than usual force were caught and divided and muted, reaching us like soft echoes. We were in the world of the little brown dog, and there was no way out.

I woke at about four-thirty and poked my head out of the curtain. The deck was wet with dew—which should mean a fine day. A mother merganser with her brood suddenly caught sight of me. In horror, she turned and fled, her crest streaming out behind her like red hair, her brood paddling desperately after her—on the surface, as though it were mud or snow. A kingfisher started shouting at another one to keep off his territory or he'd split him in two . . . It was time I was up.

Jan in the bow bunk, was still asleep. I would leave her for awhile—we could have breakfast later when we got near Blunden Harbour. Young Peter was scrambling into his clothes. He loved to be mate when no one else was around. I started the engine, pulled up the anchor, and nosed out into the Pacific.

It was almost high tide now. It ebbed north here, and we would have the tide with us most of the morning. We kept the main shore in sight. Over to the south-west, where we should have been able to see the north end of Vancouver Island, it was misty and we could see nothing.

The sea was perfectly calm, not a ripple. But when we rounded the last cape at the outer north point of Well's Pass we struck our first Pacific swells. They were wide apart and perfectly gentle. But we gradually rose . . . and down we gradually sank . . . Up again . . . down again . . . A wondering head poked up through the hatchway and made descriptive motions with its hands.

"Where are we?" demanded John, from his bunk. "Why is the sea so funny?"

"It isn't the sea," explained Peter loftily; "it's the ocean. It's been doing that for ages."

The swells had an entirely different feel about them than the waves. Not dangerous exactly, but relentless—an all-the-way-from-China kind of feeling about them. Whatever the sea was doing, I felt that I should like to locate that inner passage as soon as possible. There were cliffs at the moment, so it probably started farther along. I didn't care for the unexpected breaking and spouting of the breakers on a calm surface—breaking on something we couldn't see. We rounded another cape with a great mass of kelp off it. Then I made out a line of kelp extending along the coast as far as the eye could see. From where we were it looked much too narrow to be the Indian passage. Jan went up into the bow, and I worked in closer. It began to look wider and there was evidently reef underneath or alongside the kelp. Then we came to a gap with no kelp and evidently no reef—nothing that would bother us anyway. We slipped through on top of a swell . . . and here certainly was the Indian channel. It seemed deep right up to the shore and about thirty feet wide. What low water would show we couldn't tell. There might be no room for the boat at all—the Indians might only use it at high tide . . . At least the wide kelp bed broke up the swell and none was breaking on the shore.

This was no dash we were making—it was a crawl. There would be no help in these waters if we ran on a reef. We had a good dinghy, but how humiliating it would be to have to row away from our wrecked boat, with no one to blame but ourselves! The tide was dropping rapidly, still helping us on our way. The reef outside of us was now above water in many places; but that only made our channel more secure. The shore, as we had hoped, shelved very steeply. Evidently we were not going to be squeezed between. Around eight o'clock we came to a small group of islands—the Raynor group. Tucking in behind them out of the swell we had our breakfast. We landed on shore for a run, and found our bodies strangely unstable and hard to adapt to the solidness of the rock.

We knew that there was an Indian village in Blunden Harbor and were very tempted. But it would have been foolish not to take advantage of this sunny, quiet day for the run up to Seymour. We passed the entrance to Blunden Harbor—all necks craning. There was no sigh of any habitation. So the Indian village must be farther in round the bluff. The entrance seemed quite exposed.

It was lunch time when we pushed thankfully into the Southgate Islands—the end of the open run. We hadn't had any wind at all, but the rollers were distinctly alarming at times. Very frightening when they suddenly broke right ahead of you on a completely hidden rock. They would throw a mass of spray high into the air. The reef would show for a moment in the hollow, and it wasn't hard to see what would have happened to our boat if we had been there. The loggers at Simoom had told us that the tugs towing log booms were often held up for as long as two weeks in the Southgates by wind. They would have picked up the booms in Belize or Seymour Inlets and come down with the tide to these islands to wait for favourable weather to make Wells Pass. That is the farthest north from which they would try to bring booms. Above there, they would make up Davis rafts— great mounds of logs all tied up and wound together with heavy steel cable. Like an iceberg they were mostly below water, and waves and rollers could not wash out the logs—the way they can in a boom.

This circle of the Southgates completely protected the enclosed water and made a perfect booming ground. And it was deep right up to the steep sandstone shores. Cables tied round trees were lying across the slopes, ready for the booms that would come.

The names of various tugs, and the dates, were painted in red or white on the low cliffs. Under some of the shallow caves and overhanging ledges in the sandstone we found oil-paintings, on wood, of various tugs. Amateurish, but some of them quite good. Two weeks is a long time to wait for wind to go down.

The tide was very low now, and we fooled around in the shallows looking for abalones. I can never quite bring myself to the point of eating an abalone. These virile animals, which the Norwegian fishermen tell us should be beaten with a stick before cooking, probably taste like beefsteak with a fishy flavour.

Then, calls from the children to come and see. Up on a dry, grassy point they had found dozens of the abalone shells of all sizes—cleaned out by the seagulls. They nested them together in high stacks. Trading was brisk. Then the air was filled with their unspoken longings. I ignored it—swirling around me, beating about my head . . . then I gave in. "All right," I said, "but down the bilge." If I allowed everything they found on board, there would be no room for us.

We had a swim off the smooth rocks. Lay in the sun to get warm and dry. Then started up the engine and wandered on up to Allison Harbour. We had been told that we might get gas there, and somebody else said he thought there was a store. There was neither. There was a float, and a cabin up on the bank. From the sign nailed up on the wall, it was evidently where the fishing inspector for the district lived. His boat, a heavily-built forty-footer with a high bow, was tied up at one end of the float. He came out on deck when he heard us—then came over and sat on the wharf with us.

When we said we were going into Seymour he told us that he had spent most of last night caught in the Nakwakto Rapids in the narrow entrance. He explained that you are only supposed to go through at slack water—and the slack lasts only six minutes. He had been twenty minutes late, but thought he could still make it as the tide would be with him. He had barely got started before he knew he should never have tried it. The current caught his stern and swung him round and rushed his boat against the shelving cliff. That was the end of his propeller. For the rest of the night the rapids that run sixteen knots had played with him. They would rush him along in a back current, swing him out into the through current—then rush him sideways. Then his bow would hit with a splintering crash against the cliff—and the back current would catch him again. Again and again he hit the cliff, and as the tide fell and the contour of the cliff changed, each time he hit in a different part of the stern or bow. Soon he had to pump steadily, three hours of it, as she began to take water. Then, just before slack, when the strength of the current let up and the back currents were not so fierce, Nakwakto Rapids had let go of him. He drifted out of the narrow entrance into Schooner Passage, got out his dinghy and towed his boat into a cove just round the point to the south—a little bay with a shelving beach and an empty Indian shack. He had beached the boat, bow first, which was where the worst damage was, to keep her from sinking, made a hot drink, and fallen into his bunk. He hadn't awakened until the sun was high.

A fish-boat had come through Schooner Passage and he had hailed him. They had patched up the bow a bit, and the fellow had towed him back to Allison Harbour.

He showed us the splintered bow—a major job to be repaired. The stern was almost as bad, not to mention the propeller. Plainly, he himself was badly shaken. He strongly advised us to keep away from the place. Finally he suggested that we spend the night at his wharf, and go up the next morning to the little cove with the shelving beach and the Indian shack. There, if we climbed the steep mound to the side of the shack, we would overlook the rapids. We could watch for a while and see what we would be up against. Then we could go through with the flood at lunch time.

"You'll see the little island in the middle that splits the flood tide in two with its pointed bow—a great wave to either side. The fellows tell me that if you stay on it for a tide, the whole rock shakes and trembles with the force of the waters. Turret Rock, they call it. But don't forget, slack only lasts six minutes," he warned.

The next morning found us lying on top of the high mound above the rapids, watching that fearsome roaring hole in action. Turret Rock was not breasting the current, but bracing itself against it on its tail. It was hard to tell whether our mound was trembling, or if it was just the motion of the rushing water. Probably the air was in motion from such turbulence. I am supposed to look calm and collected at such moments, and my crew watch me furtively to see that all is well. I was busy, furtively arguing with myself. It was stupid lying here, holding onto the ground, working ourselves up into a panic. We were used to all the other narrows on the coast—Yuculta, Surge, Seymour, Hole-in-the-Wall. They were all fearsome, and how flat they were at slack. Six minutes slack, I told myself, is not much worse than twelve minutes. In all the other narrows you don't have to worry about twenty minutes either side of slack. We would be going in on the flood. If all went well we could get past Turret Rock in six minutes. We always tow our dinghy—even if the engine stopped, we could tow the boat past the island in ten minutes and then we would be through the worst. The fishing inspector had been in the dark, and he had lost his propeller at the first hit. Looking at the cliffs below I thought there might be fewer back currents on the flood tide—always supposing you got past the island. If we hadn't met the inspector I wouldn't be thinking of any of this.

"Come along, youngsters," I said. "Let's get lunch over, and get things ready."

"Are we really going?" they asked, as they slid down.

"When it's dead flat," I said.

I left them on the beach and went back to the boat to get an early lunch ready—preparing for the six minutes. While waiting for the kettle to boil I cleaned the sparkplugs and checked the gaps. Then I cleaned the points on the magneto. Then I wished I hadn't touched anything. Far better to leave an engine alone if it is running well. What possessed me to touch it?

Then I called the children out for lunch. I snapped at everybody. Then someone raised the question whether our decrepit-looking clock was right. I hadn't the faintest idea. We usually judged time by the sun. How could anyone judge slack water in a roaring hole by the sun. I should have to go up on top of the mound and watch it. I pulled up all but the last few feet of anchor rope, then rowed ashore, leaving a worried-looking crew behind me. I started whistling to cheer them up. Usually, if I whistle, they know there is nothing to worry about. It was hard to keep in tune . . . a silly, whistling woman, climbing up a mound . . . whistling out of tune.

I watched . . . I saw the current hesitating . . . I threw myself down the mound, I rowed breathlessly to the boat. I tossed the painter to some-body and told them to tie her close. I pulled up the crank. The engine started first pull. I tried to swallow—for some reason I was breathless. I yanked up the anchor, and worked out the bay—stood well out, in case we were pulled in . . .

There was nothing there to pull us in. A still passage lay ahead of us. Turret Rock stood in the middle, looking perfectly quiet and relaxed. We went gently through, resisting the temptation to speed up. The channel opened out into a comparatively wide section. Then the swirls began to form around us—the six minutes must be up. But we were through. I only speeded up because I didn't know where those treacherous back currents might start. How stupid it had all been! Just because we had seen a smashed-up boat, and heard a worn-out man who had had a bad experience.

Peter shook his head sagely, "You were scared, too, weren't you, Mummy?"

I winked at him "Weren't we sillies!" I said.

PLEISTOCENE CREEK
IN WHICH I ALMOST GIVE IT ALL UP AND QUIT
THE BOATBUILDING BUSINESS FOR GOOD
1999

Robb White Jr.

Florida must have been a real slice of Eden before air-conditioning. A whole literary sub-genre has sprung up to denounce most of what the last fifty years has brought to the state. Call it "Florida Lost Lit", or from the tone of the work of Carl Hiaasen, Dave Barry, and Tim Dorsey, among others, maybe "The Cheeseburger That Ate Paradise Lit" might be closer to the mark. To that group, one has to add Robb White, author of How to Build a Tin Canoe *and perhaps better known for his ruminations on boats, life, boatbuilding, and villains and half-wits in Talla-hassee, in magazines like* Messing About in Boats *and* Woodenboat.

White seems to have spent the best part of his life enjoying the coastal waters, wetlands, and forests of Georgia and Florida. He built elegant small boats of tulip poplar harvested on his own land, and was happy to share what he knew, as long as one posed the questions in a letter, and didn't call or show up at the shop. His father, also named Robb White, wrote The Lion's Paw, *one of the all-time classic small boat adventure stories. It is unfortunately out of print, very hard to find, and incredibly expensive when one does run across a copy.*

White studied biology in college. He had an easy and unpretentious style, and the stories he wrote over the years are infused with his love of the natural world, fishing and hunting, and, as one might imagine, both a special rapport with his own neck of the woods, and scorn for those going out of their way to trash it. This story is one of his most popular, a real piece of Florida Lost.

Robb White died unexpectedly in May 2006.

I have a cousin, a little younger than I am, from whom I was inseparable until I joined the Navy. We even invented our own language in which we were both named "Old Eeen." We did a lot of wild things together when we were boys, and his folks said that I was the one who always instigated the worst of those things. After I got out of the Navy, I continued to try to push up some kind of insurrection in the Old Eeen.

One of the things we did when we were boys was to try to live off the "fat of the land" back in the Ochlocknee River swamp like we were some of the wild people of long ago. The land back there, though isolated and wild enough, wasn't as fat to two little new-boys as it had been to the long-gone old hands who had left their sign along the banks of the river. We did manage to live like wild things for weeks at a time, but we were some hard-bitten, filthy, and very hungry little boogers when we finally made the decision to give it up and walk the five miles out to see if there were any cinnamon rolls in the pantry.

I got out of the Navy just before President Kennedy got shot. On that day I had just finished restoring an old bandsaw and I cried on the freshly polished table . . . rusted it up. Not only that, but I found that the Old Eeen had grown up. I was anxious to go wild again, but the Old Eeen was always remodeling the bathroom or hanging Venetian blinds or fooling with his car or some other civilized domestic chore. I missed him, but that didn't keep me out of the bushes, swamps, and wild coastline around where we live. On one of my explorations, I found Pleistocene Creek.

I was down there at the coast messing around in the marshes and rocky shallows where, if you can ignore the contrails of the jets heading to cursed Tallahassee, it is possible to imagine that nothing has changed since the old days. I noticed that in some of the little marsh creeks, even on the rising tide, the water seemed to be running out and it seemed to be a little bit fresh tasting. I wondered if some of those little streams might actually be distributaries of undiscovered rivers that flowed from the abundant limestone cave-springs, which, when the sea level was lower, were home to the people of the Pleistocene . . . the hunters of the mighty mastodon and the long-haired mammoth, eaters of the colossal *Megatherion* and giant bison, savage competition for the great bears and terrible cats whose bones are found around the ancient fire places, wonderfully preserved in the cave-springs ever since the ice-age time. Those are the same springs that made the short little rivers that still bear the names that the people gave them so many thousands of years ago. After the ice melted back about where it is now and the sea came back, the water table rose and filled the caves. The people lived along the banks of the old rivers and spoke the ancient names. These were the cheerful catchers of the lowly oyster, pinfish, blue crab, mullet, scallop, and Seminole killifish, the durable parts of which show up in the kitchen middens from only a thousand years ago. These were the same happy folks who were run off by worried fools like us who roar thoughtlessly around in high-powered machines and don't even know the name of the place where we are or see what it is like . . . people who would starve to death like ignorant pilgrims if they were set down naked in the middle of all that.

Late one fall, I took my lightest little boat way back in the marsh and let myself become stranded by a low spring tide when the north wind blew the water even farther away from the land. Tasting the trickles, I dragged the boat through the little marsh creeks all through the mud and over the rocks and oyster bars looking for a stream running fresh water. It was hard work. When it got to be dark, I squatted in the low tide mud and savagely ate my raw pelecypod snack and lay my skeeter-and-no-see-um-bitten self down in the bottom of my tiny boat, where it was grounded solid in the mud of the creek that I was working my way up right then. Before daylight, I was awakened by the wind singing in the trees-trees that weren't there when I went to sleep.

I found out that the wind had shifted around to the southeast, the tide had turned, and the combination had done, in just a few hours, what I had been trying to do, off and on, for a long, long time. I was drifting in my tiny boat, spinning slowly in the current of a small, limestone-banked river so far from highways, boat landings, and houses, and so hard to get to that it was easy to convince myself that I was the first person to see it since the wild people. After it got to be daylight, I could see what it was like a concise, deep little river maybe thirty feet wide. The solution-hole-riddled limestone banks were almost vertical and there was a layer of black loam overhanging the rock walls. The woods on either side were higher than anything I had seen along this section of coast. There was an overstory of cabbage palm, red cedar, and live oak trees. Except for scattered palmettos, a few yaupon *(Ilex vomitoria)* bushes and leaves, the ground was shaded bare. I could see taller trees farther back from the river which might have been ash, tulip poplar, swamp hickory *(H. aquatica), Magnolia grandiflora,* red bay, and laurel oak. Some places on the bank and little ponds off the river were lower than the rest and there were short, big bald-cypress trees and tupelo. There was a generations-old osprey nest in a cypress snag right on the edge of the creek. It was easy to see potshards sticking out of the dirt along the bank and on the bottom in the shallow nooks of the river. I saw two shell middens that looked untouched since the last person had dumped the last basket of shells a thousand years ago. Though I longed to start looking further, I knew better. Those things didn't belong to me and besides, the tide was already getting ready to go out. I paddled with it, looking at the landmarks as best I could and went to get the Old Eeen.

Things in the modern world are always more complicated than they ought to be and it was a long time before I could get back to that place. My wife and I had two little boys by then, so I was working all week at a paying job and the boatbuilding business took all my weekends. I guess I sort of joined the Old Eeen in the real world for a while. I didn't have time to paddle for days, sleeping in the bottom of the boat at night, just to get to the memorized spot to go into the marsh. One of the outboard skiffs that has become so indispensable to me now would get me down the coast to the go-in place, but that wouldn't have suited my romantic notions, so I put it off until I had the time to paddle all that long, long way. Neither me nor the Old Eeen had time to do things right anymore. That wonderful place was just as safe from us as it was from the TV football fans for a long time.

Finally I managed to shake loose one January when I got laid off at the furniture factory where I was working at that time. I called the Old Eeen. He was just getting ready to paint the house and fix the gutters, but I browbeat him into putting it off for a little while since it was so cold. On the way down in the car, I told him about that place for the first time. I painted a pretty picture, too. Then I said "Eeen . . . we could go wild again. We could stay wild this time. Nobody in the world knows about that place but me. It ain't on the quadrangles and you can't even see it from an airplane. Even if they knew, nobody will drag a boat all that way just to get to a little creek . . . too far from the TV. You could just not show up in your classroom on Monday morning. The doings of the world would get along just fine without either one of us. Your wife could get along just fine without you and, Lord knows, mine's would soar like an eagle if she could drop this old heavy load. We could go back there and just set this damned skiffboat adrift. This norther would take it to Cuba. Somebody would be delighted to find it washed up. We could dug us out a canoe and live off the fat of the land forever. Wouldn't ever have to worry about no insurance or nothing." The Old Eeen sat silently over there on his side trying act like he was looking out the fogged up window. "We could be real savages, too, like the unconquered Calusas," I went on. "We could paddle swiftly but silently out of the marsh in our canoe . . . keep our heads down out of sight behind the grass . . . then we could swoop down on those fishing boats out on the flats, slip up behind them before they knew what was happening, and knock them in the head with a lighter'd knot. We could drink all the beer out of their icebox and smoke up their cigars and then send their boat on off to Cuba, too. Nobody would ever know . . . 'lost at sea.'" The Old Eeen's eyes darted around a little bit, but he still sat there silently. Finally, he reached in his pocket and got him a cigar and gave me one, too. After he got it lit and smoking good, he said, "Eeen, what if there were some women in that boat?" "Well," I said, "if they were plump with pulchritude and cheerful-looking, we could take them back to the creek and indoctrinate them into our ways and smoke up their Kents. If they were mean and bossy-looking, we would just knock them in the head, too." "I ain't too crazy about that," he said, looking worried. "Maybe we could tell in advance? You got your knobblers, ain't you, Eeen? We could spy on them from the marsh grass and just pass up any boat with mean-looking women in it. I wouldn't want to knock no woman in the head." "Naw, Eeen," I scolded. "You cain't have no knobblers back in the naked wild woods. Hell, you cain't even have no matches." "Yeah, but we could light them Viceroys with a coal when we got back to our fire," said the Old Eeen, eagerly smoking hard on his cigar.

Things don't always turn out right, even with the best of plans. Like I said, this creek was a long, long way down the coast from the nearest road. After we had launched the skiffboat at the closest possible place, we had to hurry so we would have time to pole in and take a brief look at that wonderful little place and then make the long, long trip back to the boat ramp before nightfall because that sort of country is not navigable in the dark.

While we were tearing along in the calm, shallow water in the outboard skiff in the north-wind lee of the marsh, I hit a perverse conch (*Busycon perversa*) shell with the foot of the motor and sheared the pin in the propeller. It was freezing cold, so even though the water was shallow enough to get out on the flats to pull the wheel, I decided to lean over the stern to do it. After I got the propeller off, damned if the engine didn't tilt down and flip me over the transom, out of the boat, flat on my back in the cold, cold water. Not only did I get saturated wet, but I disjointed my right middle finger (never did get completely well and sometimes makes people think that I am attempting some sort of communication) and dropped the durn propeller nut and we couldn't find it to save our lives. We had to turn around right there and row all those miles back to the boat ramp. If the Old Eeen hadn't had on two pairs of britches, I would have froze to death.

Epilogue:

I can't remember if the Old Eeen and I ever managed to get back to that little creek. When my sons got old enough to be interested in that kind of thing, my family went back and carefully camped on the ancient bank right where I knew the old people had last slept a thousand years ago. After it was dark, it seems like we heard their spirits out in the woods. Next day, my oldest son and I swam all the way to the little spring that was the headwaters for most of the little river. The clear water bubbled up through big-grained white sand and thousands of salamander larvae and eggs. The banks were thick with poison ivy and other terrible bushes and vines. It was the wildest little place I ever saw. Sometimes we talk about going back, but the boys are grown men now, just about in the same fix as the Old Eeen. I haven't been back there in twenty years. I am sure that the population explosion around here since then has not let even that spot go undiscovered by the damned go-anywhere airboats, jet skis, "go-devils," and other such joy-riding travesties that are so popular among the ignorant and thoughtless. Both my children and the Old Eeen's are long grown up. He is still a schoolteacher-has all Christmas vacation off. He finished digging a pond in his yard and sold his backhoe and I noticed that his house was all painted up and the roof looks sort of new-well maintained. I am just as no-count as I ever was. We are both so old now that the dilemma about what to do with the women has solved itself. We'll just knock them all in the head. What the hell did I do with my phone number book?

THE £200 MILLIONAIRE

1932

Weston Martyr

Weston Martyr was an English yachtsman and writer, and one of the founders of the Fastnet ocean race. He is probably best known though, for "The £200 Millionaire," a story that has inspired generations of long-term cruisers, and certainly sold many thousands of boats. Some of them probably more than once. Reading through it again recently, it reminded me of a man I met sailing in the Mediterranean.

I was sitting in the marina at Port Saint Louis du Rhone, near Marseilles in the south of France, when a medium-sized sloop, single-handed, approached the dock. It being that kind of marina full of that kind of people, a couple of my neighbors and I hopped off our boats and walked over to take lines. But in the time it took us to cross the thirty yards or so, the boat was docked, the bow line cleated off, and the guy, obviously cruising in his retirement, was tying up the stern. The boat was older, but very well kept and seamanlike. It turned out he was an American, and I stayed to talk.

He had come from Rome, taking it easy in day passages. Normally he sailed with his wife, but she had had a stroke, and had gone back to Missouri. They had been schoolteachers, both divorced, and had remarried late in life. She wanted to see Europe, and he had pottered around in small boats in midwestern lakes. So when they retired, they sold their house, bought a boat in England, and ended up spending 25 years cruising the length and breadth of Europe, from the fiords of Norway to Odysseus's old stomping grounds on the coast of Turkey and the Greek islands. Paris, London, Oslo, Marseilles, the Cyclades, Seville, Barcelona were some places, as I recall, he figured he had called home for a while.

When I first saw the man, I figured he was a pretty spry 65. When he said he had been cruising for 25 years, I did the math, and to confirm it asked him how old he was. Eighty-seven. He was heading, alone through the canals of France, to England to put his boat up for sale with the broker he had bought her from so that he could return to the States to be with his wife. The next morning, when I stuck my head out the companionway, he was gone. But I thought at the time, and have often thought since, that the man had lived more in retirement than most do in their whole lives, and one couldn't hope for better than that.

THE £200 MILLIONAIRE

My wife and I were sailing a hireling yacht through the waterways of Zeeland last summer, when one day a westerly gale drove us into the harbour of Dintelsas for shelter. A little green sloop, flying the Red Ensign, followed us into port. She was manned solely by one elderly gentleman, but we noted that he handled the boat with ease and skill. It was blowing hard, and the little yacht ran down the harbour at speed, but when abreast of us she luffed head to wind, her violently flapping sails were lowered with a run, and she brought up alongside us so gently that she would not have crushed an egg. We took her lines and made them fast, while her owner hung cork fenders over the side and proceeded to stow his sails. Urged by a look from my wife which said, 'he is old and all alone. Help him,' I offered to lend the lone mariner a hand. But he refused to be helped. Said he, 'Thank you, but please don't trouble. I like to do everything myself; it's part of the fun. But do come aboard if you will, and look round. You'll see there's nothing here that one man can't tackle easily.'

We went aboard and found the green sloop to be one of the cleverest little ships imaginable. It is difficult to describe her gear on deck and aloft without being technical; suffice it to say, therefore, that everything was very efficient and simple, and so designed that all sail could be set or lowered by the man at the helm without leaving the cockpit. The boat was 30 feet long by 9 feet wide, and my short wife, at any rate, could stand upright in her cabin. Her fore end was a storeroom, full of convenient lockers, shelves and a small but adequate water-closet. Abaft this came the cabin, an apartment 12 feet long, with a broad bunk along one side of it and a comfortable settee along the other. A table with hinged flaps stood in the middle, while in the four corners were a wardrobe, a desk, a pantry and a galley. Abaft all this was a motor, hidden beneath the cockpit floor. A clock ticked on one bulkhead, a rack full of books ran along the other, a tray of pipes lay on the table, and a copper kettle sang softly to itself on the little stove.

'What do you think of her?' said our host, descending the companion. 'Before you tell me, though, I must warn you I'm very house-proud. I've owned this boat for ten years, and I've been doing little things to her all the time. Improving her, I call it. It's great fun. For instance, I made this matchbox-holder for the galley last week. It sounds a trivial thing; but I wish I'd thought of it ten years ago, because during all that time I've had to use both hands whenever I struck a match. Now I have only to use one hand, and you know all that implies in a small boat, especially if she's dancing about and you're trying to hold on and cook and light the Primus at one and the same moment. Then there was the fun of carving the holder out of a bit of wood I picked up, to say nothing of the pleasure it gives me to look at a useful thing I've made with my own hands. The carving brought out the grain of the wood nicely, don't you think? Now I'm going to make tea, and you must stay and have some with me.' We did stay to tea. And we are glad we did. For one thing, it was a remarkably fine tea, and, for another, we listened to the most entertaining and thought-provoking discourse we have ever heard in our lives. That discourse, in fact, was so provocative of thought that it looks as if it were going to change the whole course of our lives for my wife and me. Said our host, 'I hope you will like this tea. It's brick tea, caravan tea. I got hold of it in Odessa, where it was really absurdly cheap. That's one of the advantages of this kind of life, I find. Cruising about all over Europe in my own boat, I can buy luxuries at the source, so to speak, at practically cost prices. There are four bottles of Burgundy, for example, stowed in the bilges under your feet, the remains of a dozen I bought at Cadaujac while cruising along the Garonne canal. I bought the lot for less than twenty shillings, and it's the sort of wine you pay a pound a bottle for in London. When I come across bargains like that it makes me wish this boat was a bit bigger. It's surprising what a lot of stuff I can stow away in her, but I really need more storage space. If I had room I would buy enough cigars, for instance, in this country where they are good and cheap, to last me over the winter. You see, I like the sun, and in two months I shall be going down the Rhone to spend the winter in the south of France, and the tobacco there is horrible and expensive.'

'Do you live aboard here all alone always?' exclaimed my wife, making her eyes very round. 'Most certainly,' replied our host. 'Now do try some of this Macassar redfish paste on your toast. I got it in Rotterdam from the purser of the Java Mail that arrived last week, so it's as fresh as it's possible to get it. It's really a shame to toast this bread, though. It's just the ordinary bread the bargees buy, but I find Dutch bread is the best in all Europe. Some French bread is good, but it won't keep as long as this stuff will. Sailing down the Danube a year or so ago I got some really excellent bread in Vienna, but it was a little sweet and not so good for a steady diet as this Dutch stuff. The worst bread I ever got was in Poland. I was cruising through the East German canals and I thought I would sail up the Vistula via Cracow, with the intention of putting the boat on the railway when I got to the head of the Vistula navigation at Myslowitz, shipping her across the few miles to the Klodnitz canal, and then cruising through Silesia and Brandenburg via Breslau down the Oder. It was a good and perfectly feasible plan, and I fancy it would have been interesting. But that horrible Polish bread defeated me completely. It was about all I could get to eat, and it seemed to consist entirely of straw and potatoes. So I turned back after passing Warsaw, and fled down the Vistula and the Bromberg canal and on by the Netze to Frankfurt. Do have some more tea.'

We had some more tea. It was a marvelous brew, as stimulating as good wine, and while we drank it our curiosity concerning our host and his extraordinary mode of life welled up within us, to drown at last our manners and overflow in a stream of questions.

'Do you really mean,' said we, 'that you live aboard here always? All the year round? And quite alone? And cruise to Odessa? And Warsaw? And how did you get to the Danube? And the Black Sea? And—? And—?' Thus we went on, while our host smiled at us—the kind of smile that told us we had made a new friend.

'I'll tell you,' he said, when we stopped at last for breath. 'You understand boats and this sort of life, I think, so you'll understand me. I've been living aboard this boat for ten years now, and I hope I shall never have to live anywhere else as long as I'm alive. It's a good life. It's the best kind of life a man can lead—or a woman either. It really is life, you see. Yes. And I think I ought to know. I shan't see sixty again, and I've seen a good deal of life—of different kinds. I'm a doctor, or was once. And I've worked very hard all my life trying to be a good doctor, but failing, I fear, on the whole. I married and we had five children, and it meant hard work bringing them up properly and educating them. But I worked and did it. Then I moved to London to try to make some money. That was the hardest work of all. Then the war came, and more hard work in a base hospital. The war killed two of my sons—and my wife. And when it was all over I looked around, and I didn't like the look of the life I saw ahead of me. To go on working hard seemed the only thing left to do, but I found there was no zest left in my work any more. My daughters were married and my remaining son was doing well in a practice of his own. I found my children could get on very well without me. So there was no one left to work for, and I found I was very tired. I sold my practice and retired to Harwich, where I was born. And there I soon found out that having nothing to do at all is even worse that working hard at something you've lost interest in. I did nothing for six months, and I think another six months of that would have been the death of me. By then I feel I should have been glad to die. But this little boat saved me. I began by hiring her from a local boatman for one weekend. We sailed up the Orwell to Ipswich and back again. The weather was fine, the

Orwell is a lovely river, and I enjoyed my little sail. I enjoyed it so much, in fact, that I hired the boat again. I hired her for a week, and this time I left the boatman behind and sailed alone. Of course, I had sailed boats before. As a boy I got myself afloat in something or other whenever I had a chance, and my holidays as a young man were nearly all spent aboard yachts. So I found I could still handle a boat, especially this little thing in those sheltered waters, and I remembered enough seamanship to keep myself out of trouble. I sailed to Pin Mill, and then up the Stour to Manningtree and Mistley. After that I grew bolder, and one fine day with a fair wind for the passage, I coasted along the Essex shore to Brightlingsea. I explored the Colne and its creeks, and the end of my week found me at West Mersea, so I had to write to the boatman and extend the time of hire. While I was about it I chartered the boat for a month. You see, I discovered I was happy, and I could not remember being happy for a very long while. The exercise and the fresh air and the plain food were all doing me good, too. I'd been getting flabby and running to fat, but the work on the boat very soon altered all that. I would turn into my bunk every night physically tired, knowing I would fall fast asleep at once, and looking forward to waking up again to another day of seeing after myself and the boat, and pottering about and enjoying my little adventures. The life, in fact, was making me young again—and I knew it. I would get up in the morning as soon as the light woke me and wash and shave and cook my breakfast. I used to stick pretty faithfully to coffee, bacon and eggs, and bread and marmalade in those first days, I remember. I was not much of a cook then, and I had yet to learn the pleasure one can get out of cooking a really good meal, not to mention eating it. Then I washed the breakfast things, cleaned up the cabin and washed down the deck. Housemaids' work, but there's not much of it needed to keep this small boat clean and tidy. And what little work there is soon became a labour of love. When I had made the boat all ship-shape I would sit in the cockpit and smoke, and look at her with great pride and contentment. I still do that. It gives me pleasure to see my home in perfect order and to feel that I've done it all myself. And I know, now, that if I paid someone else to do the work for me I should be depriving myself of a deal of the charm of life.

'When my morning chores were done, and if the weather was fine and I felt like moving on, I would heave up my anchor and make sail. During that first month I think I must have explored nearly all the rivers and creeks that run into the Thames Estuary. Most of them, as you probably know, are charming. If I wanted company I would bring up in the evening in one of the anchorages frequented by yachts, or alongside some Thames barges. There's a delightful freemasonry amongst sailors, whether yachtsman or bargees, and I'd generally find myself yarning and smoking with some congenial souls in my own or someone else's cabin until it was time to turn in. At other times I would let go my anchor for the night in some quiet creek, with never a human being within miles. I liked that best. I needed peace and quietness and I found them, to perfection, in those little lost Essex creeks.

'When the weather was bad, or the wind and tide did not serve, I would have a major clean-up, perhaps, or merely potter about, doing the little jobs of work a boat can always provide for you. Or I'd put my watertank and a big basket in the dinghy and row to the nearest village to replenish my stores. One thing is certain, I never for a moment found time hanging heavily on my hands. There was always something to occupy me and always something interesting to see or to do. The life suited me and I throve on it, body and mind. And the way I threw off the years and turned into a boy again was perfectly amazing.

'My month was up almost before I knew it, and when it did get time to go back to Harwich and all that meant, I simply could not bear the thought of it. To think of returning to the sort of life I'd been leading on shore was as dreadful as the prospect of having to serve a life sentence in prison. I did not like the thought of it but there did not seem to be anything else I could do. You see, I've not got very much money. I had just enough to allow me to live, very simply, and even the expense of hiring this boat was really more than I could afford. What I wanted to do, of course, was to go on living aboard here, but, to my sorrow, that seemed quite impossible.

'Then, one night, I sat down in this cabin and thought the thing out— right out, in all its bearings. First I considered the question of finance. I don't want to bore you with my private affairs, but the figures are, I think, instructive and valuable, as they show what a lot can be done with very little. My capital amounted to a little over £4,000, and my yearly income just touched £200. The problem I set out to solve was: can I buy the boat out of my capital and still have sufficient income to live aboard her all the year around, and to maintain the boat and myself adequately? The price of the boat I knew already; she was for sale for £200. If I bought her my income would be reduced to £190, or less than £16 a month. Was this enough? It did not look like it, by any means. It meant only £3 17s. a week to cover food, clothing, light and heat, and upkeep and repairs to the boat, to say nothing of depreciation and insurance. The figure seemed so ridiculous that I nearly gave up my idea in despair.

'However, I am, thank goodness, a methodical sort of man, and I'd kept a list of my expenses during the time I'd been living aboard the boat. I analysed that list, and found that my food and oil for the lamps and stove had cost me only £7 15s. for the month. I had also spent 30s. on gear for the boat, such as paint, ropes, shackles and such things, while my bill for petrol and lubricating oil came to 15s. only, as I had sailed as much as possible and used the motor as little as I could. Not counting the cost of hiring the boat, my total expenditure had, therefore, been only £10 for the month, or £120 a year. This left £70 over for repairs, accidents, depreciation and insurance. As far as the finance was concerned, the thing began to look possible after all.

'I was very cheered by this discovery, and I then asked myself: "Can I continue to live aboard this little boat from year's end to year's end in health and comfort of body and mind?" As far as the summers were concerned I knew I could answer that with a whole-hearted "Yes." But what about the winters? Could I endure being shut up in a small confined space while the gales blew and it was cold and wet, and the nights were long and dark? I wondered. And I had to admit to myself, very much against the grain, that I probably would not be able to endure these things. I remember I went to bed after that, feeling very miserable. But when I woke up next morning the first thing I said to myself was "but why stay in England in the winter: Why be cold and wet when all you have to do is to follow the sun and sail your boat (your Home) south?" To cut all this short, I sailed back to Harwich and sent to London for a map of the French canals. And when it came I found my idea of following the sun south was entirely feasible. All I had to do was to choose a fine day in early autumn and sail across the Channel from Dover to Calais. From Calais the map showed me a network of canals and navigable rivers spreading over the whole face of France, and I discovered that a boat of this size and draught could proceed through those inland waterways right through the heart of France to the Mediterranean. I bought this boat that same day. I had a few small alterations made to her, and the following week I sailed from Harwich, bound south—for Ramsgate, Dover, Calais, Paris, Lyons, and the Riviera.'

'Well done!' I cried. And my wife said, 'Hush! And then? Then?' Our new friend smiled at us again. 'Yes,' he said. 'You're right. It was a bit of a rash proceeding—at my age. But I've never regretted it. That first cruise was perfectly delightful and, on the whole, a very simple affair. I had my troubles, of course. I got to Dover easily enough by coasting all round the Thames Estuary and putting in somewhere snug every night. But I stayed in Dover for ten days before I judged the weather was fine enough for me to sail to Calais. The truth is, I was rather scared. The passage is only twenty-one miles, but I felt a regular Christopher Columbus when I ventured across the Channel at last. It was a fine day, with a light north-east wind, and under sail and motor I got across in four hours. But I assure you Columbus was nothing to me when I sailed into Calais harbour! I felt I had triumphantly accomplished a most tremendous adventure, and I was immensely pleased and proud. And I can assure you it's rather remarkable for anything to make a cynical and disillusioned old man of my age feel like that.

'From Calais onward it was all canal and river work. It took me two months to get to Marseilles, because I went a round-about way and took my time over it. I had no need to hurry, of course, but I don't think anything could have made me hurry through the lovely country in which I found my-self. I wandered down the Oise to Paris, where I stayed a week, moored in the Seine almost in the shadow of the Champs- Elysees' tree. It was amusing and comfortable, too, living in the middle of Paris like that. I could dine ashore if I wanted to and go to a theatre, and then walk back and go to bed in my own floating hotel without any fuss or bother. And when I got tired of the city I just moved on, hotel and all. I went up the Marne to Chalons, along the canals to Bar-le-Duc and Epinal, and down through the Haute-Saone and Cote d'Or country to Macon and Lyons. I mention these towns to show you the route I took, but it was all the little out-of-the-world places between them that I used to stop at and which I found so interesting. I met all sorts of people and everyone was very helpful and kind, and by the time I got to Lyons I could speak about four different brands of French quite well.

'The passage down the Rhone to Arles was rather strenuous. The current is very strong and I had to take a pilot, which spoilt my fun; but it was soon over, and I got to Marseilles without any more bother. I had got as far south then as I could get, so I spent the rest of the winter in most of those delightful little harbours which sprinkle the coast between Marseilles and Frejus. I found practically no winter along that stretch of coast, which is much better, I think, than the Riviera proper. I can recommend Porquerolles if ever you find yourselves down that way, while Port Cros must be one of the loveliest places there are on this earth. I enjoyed every minute of that first winter, and by the time the spring came round I knew I had discovered the perfect life. I was happier than I ever hoped to be, and healthier than I had ever been. I found myself looking forward to each day, and every day had some new interest. Life was, without exaggeration, nearly perfect. If I found myself anywhere or amongst people I did not care for, all I had to do was to heave up my anchor and go somewhere else. That's one of the many advantages of living aboard a boat. When you want to go away there's no packing, no taxis, no tips, no trains and no bother. And you haven't got to find a place to lay your head when you get to your journey's end. In a boat you just move on, and your sitting-room, your kitchen, your bedroom and all your little personal comforts and conveniences move on with you. And when you get to your destination there you are, at Home.

'It added to my peace of mind, too, to find I was living well within my income, in spite of the fact that I was living very well and doing myself a great deal better than I had, for instance, in my Harwich lodgings. Of course I had to be careful and not go in for too many luxuries, but I lived as I wanted to live, and it surprised me to find how little it cost me to do it. I'll show you my account book, if it will interest you, but first I'll show you where I've been during these last ten years.

'Look at this! It's the official French canal map, showing all the canals and navigable rivers in the country. You'll notice there's very little of France you can't get at by water. It's almost unbelievable where you can go; everywhere, practically, except to the tops of the mountains. It's the same in Belgium and Holland, and in Germany, too, and until I got these canal maps I had no idea of the extraordinary manner the inland waterways of Europe have been developed. The ordinary maps don't give the details, so perhaps it's not surprising that people in England don't realise they can travel in a yacht from Calais through every country in Europe, except Spain and Italy, entirely by river and canal. It sounds incredible, doesn't it? But I've done it myself, in this boat. Including Switzerland!'

'Switzerland!' cried my wife. 'How did you?' 'There are two ways of getting there,' said our extraordinary friend. 'Up the Rhine Lateral canal, or the way I went—up the Rhine-Rhone canal from Strassburg to Mulhause and along the Huningue canal to Basle. That was as far as I could conveniently get then, but I believe the new canal is open now, running right through to Lake Constance and Bregenz. But I'm ahead of my yarn. When the spring came round that first year I went from Marseilles by canal all the way to Bordeaux. I spent that summer cruising up the coast to L'Orient and from there along the canals, right through Central Brittany from Brest to Nantes. Then I came south again, away from the cold, and spent the winter exploring South-West France, along the Dordogne and the Garrone and its tributaries. I saw most of that lovely country between Perigueux and Bordeaux in the north, Floirac and Albi in the east, and from Carcassonne in the south to Lacave, which is pretty well on the Spanish border. The whole country down there flows with milk and honey, to say nothing of the wine and the scenery. I had a good time. 'Then I went up north via the Midi canal and the Rhone, got into the Rhine at Strassburg, sailed all down that river to Rotterdam, and spent the summer in Holland. I liked this country and the people so much that I stayed here all that winter. Then I branched out. I was beginning to see the possibilities of this game by then, and I had gained confidence in myself and the boat. I won't bore you with all the details of my travels, but I went through North Germany to the Mecklenburg lakes. You ought to go there. More lakes than you could explore in two years, set in a park-like country. Perfect. But take a mosquito-net. Then I sailed south to Dresden and Prague, then north to the Danish archipelago and the Swedish islands. I wintered in the Moselle valley, explored Central France and tried to go through the Loire country, but found a difficulty there owing to the shallowness of those particular rivers. After that I pottered about in Belgium and up the Rhine to Mainz, and from there up the Main and through the Ludwigs canal into the headwaters of the Danube. I can recommend Bavaria and all the lost country around there. It's the Middle Ages. And, of course, once I got on the Danube I had to go down it. And I am glad I did, because it's a wonderful river and the scenery is magnificent. I drifted down it, taking my time and meaning to go as far as Vienna, or maybe Budapesth. But you know how it is. There was the river, going on and on all across Europe, so I went on too—to Belgrade, the Iron Gates,

Rustchuck and Galatz, until I came to Sulina and the Black Sea.

'I turned back that time, because I did not like the idea of venturing into Russian waters, the political situation being what it was. So I went up the Danube again. It took me two years to get to Passau on the German border. The Danube runs very swiftly, so progress was slow, and at times I had to take a tow, but the real reason I took so long was the number of side trips I felt I simply had to take up the various tributaries. I could write a book about it all, and some day I think I must, but so far I've been so busy moving about and enjoying life that I never have time for writing. And I wonder if my book would be readable if I wrote it? You see, I've had few "interesting adventures" or things like that. I got thoroughly lost once on the willow swamps on the lower Tisza, and went down with a bad go of fever in the middle of it. But I got out all right. And some Bulgarians above Sistove fired at me one day, but it turned out they were Customs guards and thought I was a smuggler, and we finished up the best of friends. Beyond that, and a little unpleasantness with a Ruthenian gentleman who tried to steal my dinghy, nothing much out of the ordinary happened. But I met a lot of very strange and interesting people. I had a wonderfully good time. In fact the country and the people along the Danube fascinated me; so much so that, after sailing about over Eastern Germany and a little of Poland, I went down the Danube again. This time I went as far as Odessa. I wanted to go on, either up the Dnieper, or through the Sea of Azoff, up the Don, through the Katchalinskay canal, and then either up the Volga to Nijni Novgorod, or down river to Astrakhan and the Caspian. Unfortunately I could not get permission from the Russians to make either of those trips. Perhaps it is just as well, as the country was rather disturbed and I might have got into trouble. But one of these days, when things have settled down, I intend to make that trip yet, because, bar politics, there's absolutely nothing to prevent it.'

I remember it was at this point in our friend's discourse that I interrupted him by crying out in a loud voice, 'By God!' and hitting the cabin table hard with my fist. My wife said nothing, but there was a look in her eyes and a light in them that showed me she understood and approved the wild and fascinating thought that had flashed into my mind. And our friend, it appeared, understood me also, for said he, 'Yes. Why not? All you need is a boat drawing less than four feet, with a motor in her for choice and her mast in a tabernacle. That and the—well, let's call it courage; the courage to step out of your rut. It looks hard; but a mere step does it—as I found out. Of course, it costs money. Following the seasons all over Europe in your own home is a millionaire's life; but I've managed to live it at an average cost, over the last ten years, of less than £150 per annum. Look at this!'

He put an open book before us on the table. It was his account book, and it contained, in full detail, his daily expenditures during all the years he had been living aboard his boat. It was, I can assure you, a most engrossing work, and was full of items such as these, which I found on a single page and copied there and then. And I shall regret it till I die that I had no time to copy any more:—

'Sept. 5. Capdenac. 8 duck eggs and 1 duck (cooked), 3s. 1d. 7th. 10 lb. grapes in fine willow basket, gratis. 6 boxes matches, 2s.! Sulphur at that! Note: Smuggle in big stock of matches when next I come to France. 8th. Very hard cheese, 1 ft. in dia., 1 basket peaches, 1 jeroboam peach brandy, 1 kiss on both cheeks, gratis, or perhaps fee for removing flint from farmer's eye. 9th. Mule hire, 10d. Alms to leper, 1s., interesting case. Castets, 15th. 6 feet of bread, 1s., 1 pint turps, i/:d. 16th. 2 gallons turps, 8d. Castelsarrasin. Oct. 2nd Bribe to gendarme, Sd.' I should dearly love to publish that account book, just as it stands, without any comment or explanation. It would, I think, make fascinating and suggestive reading.

'Look here,' said our friend, turning over the unique pages and exposing the following figures to our devouring eyes. 'This is a summary of my first twelve months' income and outgoings:—

	£ (pounds)	s. (shillings)	d. (pence)
Income	190	0	0
Expenditure:			
Upkeep of boat (at 9s. per week)			
	23	8	0
Petrol and oil (distance covered under motor 1220 miles)			
	10	4	0
Charts, canal dues			
	13	8	0
Food, drink, clothes, light and heat (at just under £2 a week)			
	100	0	0

Total:

147	0	0

Balance

43	0	0
£190	0	0

'I managed to save £43, you see, that first year, enough to buy a new boat like this one, every five years, if I continued to save at the same rate. I was extra careful that year. I didn't spend much on myself, but I bought the boat all she needed and kept her up in first-class shape. I painted her inside once and three times outside, doing it all myself, and I had her sails tanned to preserve them. The tanning was done by a fisherman I made friends with in Toulon. He did a good job. In the end he wouldn't let me pay for anything except the cost of the materials, because he said we were amis and he liked English sailors. And one day I came across a broken-down motorboat, drifting off Cape Camaret, and towed her into port. Her owner was scared to death, and very grateful accordingly. He was no sailor, but he was a mighty good mechanic, and he insisted on giving my little engine a first-class overhaul, just to show his gratitude.

'My fuel bill was very small, because I never use the motor if I can sail. The £13 odd for dues, etc., was mostly spent on maps and charts, not that many charts are necessary, but I simply can't resist buying the things. I spend hours poring over them, and planning more voyages than I shall ever have time to make. As for the canal and harbour dues—they're ridiculous; generally some fraction of a penny per ton. And this boat's registered tonnage is only two ton. The only expensive piece of water to travel over in Europe is the Rhone. It's got a terrific current, pilotage is compulsory, and to get up it you have to be towed. But everywhere else the only trouble about the charges is to find change small enough to pay them with. £2 a week for food and so on sounds very little, but all I can say is I live well on that sum. You see, if I want, say, vegetables I don't go to a shop in a city for them. No. Perhaps I see a good-looking garden on the river bank. I stop and have a yarn with the owner, and when I depart I'm richer by a basket full of fresh vegetables, and maybe a chicken and some eggs and fruit as well, while the gardener is left with a fair price for his produce and something to talk about for weeks. He's pleased and I'm pleased. I've paid less than I would if I bought from a shop, and he's received more than he would if he sold to a dealer. And when I say I've got fresh vegetables I mean fresh—which is something you can't get from a shop.

'Clothes don't bother me much. It's not essential to dress in the latest style, living this life. I keep my go-ashore clothes in that tin uniform case, and when I get to a city and want to see the sights I put on a civilised suit. Otherwise I use soft shirts, jerseys and flannel trousers. I do my washing myself; half an hour a fortnight does it, which is nothing to grumble about. I use paraffin oil for light and cooking in the summer, and in the winter I keep that little stove going on coal and wood. I find I burn wood mostly, because I've got a passion, apparently, for collecting any odd pieces I find drifting about. There must be a strain of longshoreman blood in me somewhere, I think, for I can't resist picking up bits of driftwood, even though I have to throw most of them overboard again, and I generally have a bigger collection of the stuff on deck than I can ever hope to burn.

'So you see, one way and another, my expenses are very small. The £30 or £40 I save every year I put by for accidents, major repairs, depreciation and a sort of insurance fund. I've bought a new suit of sails and had the whole boat surveyed and recaulked and the engine practically renewed, all out of the fund, and I've still got enough left to buy a new boat if I want one. I'm getting so rich, in fact, that I don't know what to do with all my money. I tried to get rid of some of it by buying extra fine gear for the boat, but I found that scheme merely saved me more money in the long-run. For instance, I scrapped my Manilla running rigging and replaced it with best hemp at twice the cost, but I'll be bothered if the hemp hasn't lasted four times as long as the Manilla already! And to make it worse, people will persist in giving me things, bless 'em. I've made a lot of friends in pretty well every corner of Europe. Can't help it, living this sort of life, it seems. And most of them have an idea that, living as I do, I am to be regarded with compassion. A poor old man, living all alone aboard a little boat—that's how they seem to feel about me, I fear. So, whenever I turn up, my compassionate friends appear, bearing gifts! It's quite embarrassing sometimes. And sometimes it's a real nuisance. The Middelburg canal is barred to me, for instance, because the keeper of one of the swing bridges refuses to let me through until he's been aboard to greet me and give me a box of cigars or a jar of schnapps; which things he really can't afford, as he's a poor man with a very large family. He does it, it seems, because I'm leading just the kind of life he'd like to lead if he hadn't been blessed with a wife, his mother-in-law and nine children. The result is I have to go round now by Terneuzen, instead of through Middelburg, whenever I want to pass from Holland into Belgium. And I always have to go through Strassburg by night to dodge a dear old gentleman, who invariably presses on me about a stone of the smelliest cheese on earth whenever he catches sight of me. He calls me his brave ancient ami so lonely. Lonely! Why, I should think I must have a larger and more varied assortment of friends than any man in Europe. And I keep on making more all the time. For instance, I hope I've made two today.'

He had; and we are glad to say he dined with them that evening, entrancing them with his talk until far into the night. He talked of gentle rivers wandering through valleys of everlasting peace; of a quiet canal, lost amongst scented reeds and covered with a pink-and-white carpet of water-lilies; of a string of tiny lakes, their blue waters ringed with the green of forest pines; of a narrow canal, built by old Romans, but navigable still, that climbs up through clouds into the high mountains; of aqueducts spanning bottomless ravines and a view from the yacht's deck of half Southern Germany; of a Red Ensign flying at the peak and a Black Forest eagle's screamings at that sight; of the Croatian mayor who had never heard of a certain country called England; of a thousand square miles of blood-red swamp, studded with giant willows; of Wallachian water-gipsies and their cats who catch fish; of the mile-long log raft commanded by a Russian ex-admiral; of a spiked helmet dredged from out the Meuse by the yacht's anchor; of the warm-hearted kindliness of Bulgarian brigands and the barbarous fines of Frs. 25,000 extorted (unsuccessfully) by 'the most civilised country in Europe'; of pack-ice and ice-breakers in the heart of old Amsterdam; of the 1000 ton motor-barge that trades each year between Groningen and Sulina; of the 300-ton barge proceeding from Bruges to Dunkerque in tow of a jolly old lady of seventy; of a spilliken-like traffic jam in the old moat at Furnes and the Fordson tractor that extricated twenty-eight barges; of the Flemish barge named No. 27 Park Lane, because the wounds of her skipper had been succoured at that address in 1914; of pig-manure, chem-

ical fumes and rotting flax on the Lys, and the barge with a deckload of pot-
ted hyacinths that outdid all those scents; of the ten-knot currents on the
Rhone and the silent waters of the Oude Ryn that ebb and flow no more; of
the charm of this old earth and the fun of living on it, if only you understand
the proper way to live. Said our friend, 'I've found one good way to live and
be happy. There must be other ways, too, but I don't know 'em, so I mean
to stick to my way—till I come to the end of it. The secret seems to be, to
do everything you can yourself. It's difficult to explain, but take an example.
Take travel. Allow yourself to be carried about the world in Wagon-Lits and
cabins-deluxe, and what do you get out of it? You get bored to death. Everything is done for you and you don't even have to think. All you have to do
is to pay. You're carried about with the greatest care and wrapped up and fed
and insulated from—from everything. You see about as much of life as a
suckling in the arms of its nurse. No wonder you get bored! But get yourself about the world, on your own feet, or in your own boat, and you're
bound, you're bound to fill your life with interest and charm and fun—and
beauty. You'll have your disagreeable and uncomfortable times, of course,
but they merely serve to make the good times taste better. "Sleep after toyle,
port after stormie seas." Old Spenser knew. He'd been through it. Sail all
day in the wet and cold, then bring up in some quiet harbour and go below
and toast your feet before the galley fire and you'll realise what bliss means.
Travel in a steam-heated Pullman and then put up at the Ritz and see if you
find any bliss there! You see what I mean? Stewart Edward White put it all
much better than I can. He wrote, "I've often noted two things about trees:
the stunted little twisted fellows have had a hard time, what with wind and
snow and poor soil; and they grow farthest up on the big peaks."'

Next morning our friend must have risen with the sun, and we were still
beneath our blankets when the incense of his coffee and bacon drifted down
our cabin hatch. Presently the sound of ropes falling on deck warned us he
was getting under weigh, and we arose to say goodbye to him. 'Good morning,' said he. 'I'm sorry to disturb you so early, but I want to catch the first
of the flood. With luck it'll carry me into the Rhine and I'll be in Germany
by evening. Now I'll cast off and go—and see what this good day's got in
store for me. A fair tide and a fair wind is a fine beginning, anyway. Good-
bye, you two. We'll meet again somewhere, for certain, if only you follow
that impulse you had last night. I don't want to influence you unduly; but,

remember—one step does it and you're out of the rut for good. Good-bye. God bless you both.'

He set his jib and the little green yacht fell off before the wind and headed for the harbour entrance. She sailed away with the sun shining bright upon her, and upon the white head of the man at her helm. Presently she entered the broad river, and we saw our friend look back and wave his hand in farewell. Then the boat was hidden by a bank of golden sand, and the last we saw of her was her little Red Ensign, a tiny flame outlined against the sky.

This seems to be the end of the story, but I do not know. I am not sure. I am not sure, because the words of that elderly adventurer seem to have set us thinking. I notice we do not say very much, but I know we think a lot. For, at intervals during the cold and fogs of this last winter, there have passed between my wife and me some detached but significant utterances—such as: 'I don't see why I couldn't get on with my writing aboard a boat just as well as I can inside this flat.'

'Only £200 a year! Hang it! We ought to be able to earn that much between us, you'd think?' 'I think, my dear, one of those steam-cookers would be a splendid thing to have if we, for anyone living aboard a small boat.' 'What a foul fog! It hurts to think of the sun shining, now, in the south of France.'

'May the Devil run away with that damned loudspeaker next door. You know, if this flat was a boat, we could move it out of hearing.' 'If I get bronchitis again next winter. My dear, I don't think I could stand another winter here.'

Also we have purchased a monumental work entitled, *Guide Officiel de la Navigation Interieure,* published by the Ministere des Travaux Publiques. This is a fascinating work, heartily to be recommended. It has a lovely map.

Also we have just heard of a little boat. In fact, we have been to look at her. She is sound and very strong. She has two good berths and a galley and lots of stowage space. Also she has a little auxiliary motor. And her mast is in a tabernacle. And she is for sale. And we have fallen in love with her. So perhaps this is not the end of this story. In fact, we hope and we pray this story has only just begun.

FROM **PRINCESS NEW YORK**
1953

Joe Richards

The Friendship sloop is one of the classic working boats of the American North-east. They were shippy-looking little gaff-rigged workboats, with a clipper bow and a long bowsprit, simple, sea-kindly, built to take it for people who knew what they needed, and handy enough to be sailed alone if need be. The kind of boat in other words, to set some people's head to spinning. Joe Richards stumbled across one in a small yard in New York in 1938. She was a converted fishing boat, 26 feet long by 9 feet 6 inches in the beam, and constructed in the yard of none other than Wilbur A. Morse, in about 1888. Many thousands of them were built over the years by many people, but it was the Morse yard in Friendship, Maine, that became known for building the best. Richards, a well-known artist in New York at the time, was 29, the romantic type, and had a little money in his pocket . . .

FINDING *PRINCESS*

I looked the other way when I first saw her. Something told me, "This girl is not for you."

I was looking over a little weekender with bilges like a coffin, a dead-rise dog with an ugly wooden outboard rack bolted to her flat stern that had recently come off the forms of a local yard. She too was for sale. I had climbed up to inspect her when I caught another glance of *Princess*. It was perhaps the sheer of her deck, the clipper bow, the gentle reverse curve of her forefoot or the well-fed look of her fat-bellied chine that did it. I was a goner.

The negotiations for the transfer of title to *Princess* were straightforward and simple. I found the owner through the yard manager. Over a cup of coffee I asked for the truth. Then I handed over pieces of green paper, backed up by the Government of the United States, for a sloop which I was told was "as sound as a dollar." I went home and fell into a beautiful sleep with the title to *Princess* under my pillow.

You know where you could have found me the next morning. I sat on her port bunk and feasted my eyes. I remembered tales I had heard as a child in Maine of the uncanny sailing qualities of a Friendship sloop, and this was the real McCoy—built by Wilbur A. Morse, twenty-six feet long, over nine feet of beam, deep in the water and balanced like a bird in flight.

There were little lockers under the stove. I found a hammer with one claw, a sailmaker's palm stiff with salt, odds and ends. It was fun to poke around and find the evidence of voyages made, departures and landfalls, leaves of an old log, rusty fishhooks and sinkers, beer openers and bobby pins. She had lived!

It was a lovely morning. I sat with the hammer dangling in my hand, leaned back against the ceiling and gave the old girl an affectionate rap. "Holy Cow!"

The hammer went through her ceiling like a one-inch auger bit through cheese. There were four eyes now. The eye on the transom, the hole in the ceiling and both of mine, now wide open. I rapped her again and there were five. I dug up the floor boards in a frenzy like a man looking for money that had been stolen. I was that man all right, there were no frames in sight. I began to tear away at the ceiling. It came off in black, rotten masses. In an agony of frustration and despair, I ripped away with that crippled hammer at the pristine whiteness of the ceiling till the whole story of corruption and fraud lay exposed to the light of the clean spring sky. Never did a young crusading D.A. attack the substrata of entrenched vice with more ferocity than I set to on that poor cancerous old frump.

The pitiful evidence of framing came loose in long sections to the touch or broke apart like toasted muck. The ceiling was out, lying alongside in a pile that rose to the waterline. The white icebox and the black stove were perched on top like carrion birds on a crazy nest when, brandishing the lone claw of the hammer, I went after the yard manager with blood and flecks of dry rot in my eye.

The yard manager was deaf. I am not joking. He was really deaf! He wore a faraway smile and an earphone which I suspected was tuned into KDKA. Somehow I managed to convey my state of mind.

"Well, I thought you paid a mite too much for her," said the yardman, who had some sort of anonymous name like Smith, "but you have a fine model there, and we will give you a hand if you want to rebuild her." I began to take heart. "You should have looked into her before you bought her." The yard manager Smith puffed his pipe.

The words "dry rot" had meant very little to me. I had heard the phrase in pompous speeches by politicians in connection with the decay of the moral fiber of society. So this is where they got the word. My head was spinning like an outboard prop. I could see myself on the floor of the Senate, waving a rotten rib and shrieking, "See what happens!"

"Whatever held her together up till now?"

"Force of habit and a little paint," said Smith. "As a matter of fact, they took her down to Montauk last fall in a gale so strong that all three of them had to hang onto the tiller to keep her from coming about."

"Clean her out, and we'll give you a hand," said Smith. "Frame her up, and she'll give you a lot of pleasure."

I went back to the *Princess*. She still looked beautiful on the surface. It took a few days to get started. What bits and pieces of frames still clung to her belly were left undisturbed. They were used as a pattern to bend new ones. The steam box used to soften oak for bending was stoked up.

The following weekend, there were thirty frames bent over a form that followed the curve of *Princess*. They cost a dollar apiece. There's a strip of deck planking along the edge of the boat called a waterway. I might have pried it up and made it easy to slide the frames into place, but let's face it, I'm an artist not a boat-builder. I learned the hard way.

Each frame was dragged down into the damp hull and set into a notch in the keel. The curve of the contour was a great big beautiful S. The frames were bent to fit perfectly amidships, and as I moved forward a different part of the S fitted into place. There seemed to be a reason for it.

Suddenly there in the dark I knew. This was calculus. S was a symbol, a mathematical thing. The pieces I cut off from the bottom of the S to make it fit were longer as I moved forward. But always by the same amount. Then it hit me. The boat itself was a slide rule, the granddaddy of all slide rules, and still a better one than most. Small wonder that this was one of the finest designs for a hull that man has ever known.

What with her years and odd bulges, Princess was a little out of line. The curved frames, like whalebone stays of a lady's corset, had to be pressed into position. I rigged automobile jacks to do the job, and broke half a dozen in the process. Like the man said, "Anything for progress."

The old nail holes in the planks were cleaned out, and bronze screws were used to lock the frames in place. The new wood was slightly green for bending, and the screws were driven home without drilling. I have muscles to prove it but no brains. When I released the jacks, they went off like the crack of doom. Four hours I was as deaf as Mr. Smith.

That weekend I installed two frames. There was an unbelievable difference in the feel of her when you climbed aboard. After I pulled the ceiling out, she shivered like a jellyfish when you went near her. Now she began to stiffen up. I began to stiffen up too. Lying in that damp hull was giving me rheumatism, but I was back at it the following weekend.

Working all day Saturday and most of Sunday, I broke my record, the Sabbath, and all of my fingernails. I installed three frames. That made five. I had only twenty-five to go.

It was getting along toward July, about the time I was getting suspicious of a patch of cement on the inside of her stem, that a beautiful little red seaplane landed in the bay and taxied up to the water's edge. The flyer got a can of gas from the yard, filled his tank, and buzzing me good-bye, disappeared into the heavenly sky. I went back to the mines. Probing pay dirt in the stem, I reached clear through and felt the warm sunlight on my empty hand. You can find some funny sights around an old boatyard—like me lying disconsolately in the dank bottom of a half-rotten vessel with my arm poked though the stem in the place of a figurehead.

The fourth of July found me with a pick and shovel digging a big hole in the rock-studded earth under the bow. I had to have room to drive out the iron drift pins that held her stem to the keel. The planks had been pried loose from the stem at a tremendous cost of time and patience and were stretched out fore and aft, creating an enormous maw with festoons of caulking cotton caught in its teeth. The bowsprit, still dangling by the forestay, was loose and hung alongside the shrouds. The knightheads were rotten and fell apart to the touch.

When I had dug a big enough hole to turn around in, one of the boys in the yard came by. "So you're going to bury her after all!" I threw the shovel at him.

As it got later in the season I began to play hooky in the middle of the week. I was desperate. I had to get that stem out. The very next day I came out and cut the tie rods that held the stem to the first deck beams, and the dry weather helped me drive the drift pins out.

As I worked along, and old man employed by the yard sat on a barrel near *Princess* during his lunch hour and shot the breeze. He had actually worked for Morse, and he would tell me about the yard in Friendship, Maine—how they went out into the woods and cut the timbers for the vessels; how they fed their steam-driven sawmills with the scraps of wood around the yard; about the disgruntled cousins and relatives who broke away and tried to build real Friendship sloops but could never make it. "There was no one like Wilbur A. Morse, except an old hunchback feller who used to do all the designing for him," said my friend.

It does seem incredible now that one man could have known so much about a boat. They are all gone now, gathered to their fathers, but they knew how to fashion a vessel, God bless them.

I showed my friend the rotten stem that finally came loose.

"You'll never find one like that around here," he said. "That one we got right off the tree." But the old man helped me build a new one. We scarfed it together. "This will be better than the original," he said. "It'll never warp." I looked at the old stem. It was warped an inch or two out of line. I paid the yard thirty dollars for the oak, bolts and the old man's time, and I took the stem out and set it in place. Everything cost thirty dollars in those days.

The stem fell into place. I borrowed a big auger and lay in the bottom of the hole and drilled up for the bolts. Then I cut new knightheads and fastened them to the stem. There didn't seem to be anything you couldn't do on a boat if your back was as strong as the obsession.

That night at home, hammering and sawing and pounding in my imagination, as boat people do for hours after the tools have been put away, I remembered the slightly cruddy ends of the planks that I had planned to refasten to the stem. Would the screws hold them? I had visions of the bow opening up in a seaway and gulping down a bellyful of salt water.

The more time you spend working in a boatyard, the more fearful you become of the power of the sea. You are really at war with the sea, armed with a puny caulking iron and a silly-looking, long-headed mallet, and the longer you make war without actually coming in contact with your adversary, the more fearful you become. "You build 'em and I'll sail 'em," says the hearty mariner.

Yet there is plenty to say for the sailor who knows his vessel. Among seafaring people that knowledge is called sea savvy. I was getting plenty of savvy and damn little sea!

Washers! I said to myself in the middle of the night. That will do it! I'll put washers on all the screws that hold the planks to the stem. Washers by God!

Next day I bought washers, a whole gross of them, all shiny and made of brass. They would teach that old devil sea a lesson. I got hold of an electric drill and spent the whole evening counter-sinking the holes in them. In the morning I set out for the yard. It was getting to be August.

I started with the garboard and pulled her into place. The washers were fine. Tremendous strength in those washers. No danger of splitting wood. About that time the old man who had served his apprenticeship in the boatyard of Wilbur A Morse hobbled over to see how I was getting along with the new stem.

"Washers!" he growled.

"What's wrong with washers?" I asked. "Nice and strong."

"Washers," he said with a spurt of tobacco juice. There was a wild look in his eye. I waited.

There may be a code of etiquette that makes yachting pleasant, and there are unchanging customs that rule all men who go to sea. But the code of the boat-builder is a law that permits no infraction, that will tolerate no variation. It is as unyielding as North.

"Take 'em off, or I'll never talk to you again," said the old man. I took them off. Years later I was still finding washers in the bilge, all countersunk. I bought a smile for myself with every one.

My affair with *Princess* became a marriage of convenience. Every hour spent traveling out to the boatyard, every moment spent digging out dry rot, even the time spent trying to figure out what to do next, froze the knot a little tighter. I had married for money—my money.

The fever that drives a man to rebuild a fifty-year-old vessel can make him lose sight of the reason for doing it. The surge of the tide down along the water's edge was lost on me. The clean westerly tugged at the shrouds and I heard nothing. A new part added to the vessel made the old parts look worse. The accomplishment of one day became a command for the next. I fell into a panic lest the cycle would take so long that I would have to start on the first again by the time the last was job was done. I would be doomed, caught in an endless chain of dry rot and disintegration.

Then I discovered Cuprinol. I filled a bucket with the stuff, and swabbed her every hour on the hour. The boat smelled of Cuprinol, I smelled of Cuprinol, my studio smelled of Cuprinol, even my English bulldog smelled of Cuprinol. "What is that smell?" my friends would ask.

"Cuprinol," I would answer. "I love it!"

Princess began to perk up. The planks were drawn into place. She looked like a boat again. Now I could return to the business of reframing her. I fell into the easy rhythm with which I am sure she was first put together in the Downeast boatyard of Wilbur A. Morse. When I got off the bus in Flushing, I was back in the days of canvas.

I tried to drag my friends into the world of knightheads, king planks, driftpins, stringers and rabbets. They looked at me. One real pal I had known since those days up on the hill when as kids we had scooped out a giant sea among the rocks. When the rain came, we built a navy powered by rubber bands. He alone consented to come along and help me work on the boat. Being a man with the greatest reverence for tools, he didn't like the way I leaned a handsaw on its head, or the way I put a plane down on its blade. The way I tossed a chisel around had him frothing. He was a purist. He liked things clean. I caught him with a stiff wire brush gouging away at the soft wood planking, and talked him out of it. Then I went around and drove more screws into the last of the frames. I had her reframed now from the forward end of the bridge deck right up to her bow. I didn't like the way she looked aft, but I wanted to feel her in the water. Here it was the middle of August. I had my sights on Labor Day. All at once I heard a sharp rapping and tapping on the other side of the vessel. My friend had got hold of a flat file, inserted it between two planks at the bow, and was driving it aft with a hammer. I caught him about three feet abaft the chainplates. "What are you doing, Mac?"

"I'm cleaning out her seams." The inner lips of those planks were gone forever. For years and years it was always a little wet along the bunk on the port side, no matter how hard I caulked her. It came to be known as McLennan's Leak.

The hardest thing about rebuilding an ancient ark is the decision you have to make about the things you are not going to do. There were some strange repairs made years before which I just had to show the old man who had worked for Morse.

He shook his head, unbelieving. Some of that reconstruction employed everything from cardboard to little blocks tacked together. From the inside it looked like a mock-up boat, the kind you see on a TV stage for a Sunday afternoon show.

The sternpost, for instance, a structural member as important to a vessel as a ridgepole is to a roof, had been cut clear though to provide additional space for the cockpit floor. The whole keel must have swung like a barn door in a seaway. There is a special God who takes care of those who go down to the sea with ignorance and with faith.

And then someone had gone to considerable pains to figure out the worst way to mount the engine, the forward end of which was supported by a timber laid athwartships with its ends resting neatly on plank ends and doing double duty as butt blocks. This created a bovine condition on the underbelly of *Princess*. I left buckets under her on both sides in the earnest expectation of getting a little milk.

The old boat-builder's reaction was fine. "Well," he said, "some poor fisherman did the best he could, had to earn a living for his wife and kids, couldn't afford to hire anybody, did it himself."

"Was this boat really used for fishing?"

"Was she?" He stared. "Why I've seen her coming home heeled over in a gale in the dead of winter, men hanging on, covered with ice and full of fish."

They were sailed hard, these Friendship sloops. There was money in fish. Then they were sold to yachtsmen when power became the thing. They were tough. The deck beams, now riddled with rot, were fashioned with incredible perfection. Mortised at every joint and flowing from the king plank along into the lovely oval of her transom, they were stout enough to sustain the weight of barrels of fish. I became more and more determined to match her bit by bit, new wood for old, when it happened like a bolt out of the blue.

In fact it was a bolt out of the blue. I was so deep in work that I hardly noticed the later summer sky cloud overhead. When the rain came, I made a break for the shed. There was not much shelter under deck planks that had shrunk like dry string beans. I had just about closed the door of the office when the place lit up with a shaft of lightning and rocked with a simultaneous crack of thunder. It struck *Princess*.

The yard was flooded. Then the sun came out as if nothing had happened. Nothing had. *Princess* was unharmed. The lighting had been grounded by the sloppy shrouds and stays that were dangling all around. I was lucky, but it got me thinking that if I had to die I would rather drown than be fried by lightning in a boatyard. I went back to the office and with sound and motion indicated I planned to launch *Princess* by the first of September. Mr. Smith had heard the lightning strike even without his earphone, and he understood.

From that day on I gave up the incidental business of making a living as an artist. Back from their nest of discarded rotten ceiling with the stove and the icebox. A couple of floors fashioned out of two-inch oak were lagged deep into the keel with bronze. Then the bunks were set in place. I brought out a suitcase full of personal gear and a couple of pans and eating tools and set up housekeeping.

It was fun. A long water pipe that stretched far across the surface of the yard picked up the heat of the sun and delivered hot water for three min-utes and twenty-five seconds at full throttle. That was long enough for a bath. Then it became ice water which, if your timing was right, made it just as nice as my studio at the Beaux Arts. My aim seemed to be an eighty-four hour week, no commuting and no salary, which anybody can have if he really wants it.

The working conditions were ideal. It was great to get up at the crack of dawn, do a full day's work before breakfast, and after another long day's work, to loll around in the cool of the evening and do still another day's work by artificial light.

I developed a personal method of caulking that would have got me fired out of any fourth-rate yard. There were lots of old nail holes to be plugged and broken bits of nails to be extracted. A pair of shoemaker's clippers, which I had learned to manipulate, persuaded the most stubborn ones to come out.

A dentist friend came by one day. "You're just the man I'm looking for!" I set him to work with the clippers. I watched him struggle in vain for an hour to extract one little nail. You learn a lot about people from a boat.

My English bulldog came out and made himself at home on the port bunk. He was a creature to whom God and Nature had denied the primary condition of survival. He was completely lacking in the more elementary protective device—he was utterly devoid of fear. His name was Sonny Boy, being no doubt a product of the Jolson era, and he had belonged to a mo-torcycle cop who had trained him to ride the bike and to fight. His reaction to anything that touched bottom with all fours was cataclysmic. He was a social menace. With the acquisition of *Princess* I was beginning to suspect that I had a certain affinity for that kind of thing.

His devotion to me was abject to a point of embarrassment. Unlike most dogs that I have known, he didn't know how to bark or cry. When he was excited he would holler, and when he was sad he would sing. The rest of the time he snored. Every time I went down to do some work on the bottom, Sonny Boy would dive off the deck and land with a crunch that made me fear for his bones. When I went back on deck, he would get hung up on the ladder or fall, time after time, on his back until I carried him up. In this world of boats whatever fear he had was all for me. He had to be right there every minute lest this strange sea creature gobble me up. If I tried to tie him down, he would sing a wild dirge that was calculated to wake the dead. I had my hands full.

My *Princess* really looked lovely with her chain plates and bowsprit back on and a gleaming white coat of gloss on her topsides. I installed the magneto on the motor and filled her gas tank, which looked very much like an old hot-water boiler that had escaped from somebody's kitchen and gone to sea in the engine department. It was not tricky to get the engine going. A couple of turns on the flywheel with the carburetor choked, and she was primed. Another turn and off she went. At least there was no shriek for attention from this quarter. She ran cool and with surprising little vibration at half-throttle. I didn't bother to open her up for fear of shaking apart that section of the vessel that had not been rebuilt. I was contented and grounded her off.

From the early days of spring I had watched the boats go down into the water. One by one the yard had emptied itself of its foul-weather friends. The excitement of launchings, the beer parties, the plans for rendezvous, the high spirits were all consigned to the past. Now the sun beat down and the wind swept dust and chips of wood and bits of caulking cotton across the yard. Only *Princess* was left. She huddled next to the shed as if she were a little afraid of the sea. With a disease like hers I would have been afraid to go swimming myself.

Now at last it was her turn. My heart beat fast. The boys came over, put down the greased planks and snatched her away. It seemed incredible that the thing I had looked forward to for so many months, that I had labored so long and hard to have happen, could take place so quickly and with so little fuss.

There followed a ritual, however, that has persisted down through the years. It is symbolic of the length of work and the shortness of time. It has taken place at every launching of *Princess* since; it has been observed in Flushing, City Island, Edgewater, Cape May, Annapolis, Norfolk, Oxford, Moorhead City, Charleston, St. Augustine, Palm Beach and College Point. It is a simple ceremony unmarked by either frills or dignity. She had me chasing after her into the water with a last brush load of paint.

FROM **HILLS AND THE SEA**
1906

Hilaire Belloc

There is much to be said about Hilaire Belloc (1870-1953). Born in France and raised in Britain, he was one of the most prolific writers of his, or any other, time. Something like 150 books flowed from his pen, as well as a blizzard of essays, articles and poems. It was once said that "Debating Mr. Belloc is like arguing with a hailstorm." He became a member of Parliament and quit in disgust after four years.

Above all he was a lion of the Roman Catholic Church: "The Faith is Europe, and Europe is the Faith" sums up much of what he wrote. One does not need to read very far into his work to detect an icy contempt for rationalism, humanism, Protestantism, socialism, modernism—all of the -isms except Catholicism (and all of the -ists as well). The style in which he writes has gone out of fashion, and on first reading, I was tempted to think, the man is not of this age; they don't make them like him any-more. But in fact they do.

Hills and the Sea is a loose collection of essays centered on the meaning of pilgrimage, and the European Romantic concept of deep culture—the fundamental connections between people, their history, and the land. There are also a few sea stories, which at first glance seem a little out of place. But they actually fit very well, being very much in the tradition of the ancient stories of Irish monks, especially St. Brendan the Navigator. Lacking a desert in which to make a pilgrimage of com-munion with Jesus, and the patriarchs and prophets of the Bible, these sixth-century monks put to sea in their curraghs, trusting to divine providence to guide them spiritually and temporally into harbor.

This selection is the story of a day trip along the coast of England in bad weather, but the best bit is probably the funniest and most irreverent description of a yacht ever penned.

THE NORTH SEA

It was on or about a Tuesday (I speak without boasting) that my com-panion and I crept in by darkness to the unpleasant harbour of Lowestoft. And I say "unpleasant" because, however charming for the large Colonial yacht, it is the very devil for the little English craft that tries to lie there. Great boats are moored in the Southern Basin, each with two head ropes to a buoy, so that the front of them makes a kind of entanglement such as is used to defend the front of a position in warfare. Through this entanglement you are told to creep as best you can, and if you cannot (who could?) a man comes off in a boat and moors you, not head and stern, but, as it were, criss-cross, or slant-ways, so that you are really foul of the next berth alongside, and that in our case was a little steamer.

Then when you protest that there may be a collision at midnight, the man in the boat says merrily, "Oh, the wind will keep you off," as though winds never changed or dropped.

I should like to see moorings done that way, at Cowes, say, or in Southampton Water. I should like to see a lot of craft laid head and tail to the wind with a yard between each, and, when Lord Isaacs protested, I should like to hear the harbour man say in a distant voice, "*Sic volo, sic jubeo*" (a classical quotation misquoted, as in the South-country way), "the wind never changes here."

Such as it was, there it was, and trusting in the wind and God's providence we lay criss-cross in Lowestoft South Basin. The Great Bear shuffled round the pole and streaks of wispy clouds lay out in heaven.

The next morning there was a jolly great breeze from the East, and my companion said, "Let us put out to sea." But before I go further, let me explain to you and to the whole world what vast courage and meaning underlay these simple words. In what were we to put to sea?

This little boat was but twenty-five feet over all. She had lived since 1864 in inland waters, mousing about rivers, and lying comfortably in mudbanks. She had a sprit seventeen foot outboard, and I appeal to the Trinity Brothers to explain what that means; a sprit dangerous and horrible where there are waves; a sprit that will catch every sea and wet the foot of your jib in the best of weathers; a sprit that weighs down already overweighted bows and buries them with every plunge. "Quid dicam?" A Sprit of Erebus. And why had the boat such a sprit? Because her mast was so far aft, her forefoot so deep and narrow, her helm so insufficient, that but for this gigantic sprit she would never come round, and even as it was she hung in stays and had to have her weather jib-sheet hauled in for about five minutes before she would come round. So much for the sprit.

This is not all, nor nearly all. She had about six inches of free-board. She did not rise at the bows: not she! Her mast was dependent upon a forestay (spliced) and was not stepped, but worked in a tabernacle. She was a hundred and two years old. Her counter was all but awash. Her helm—I will describe her helm. It waggled back and forth without effect unless you jerked it suddenly over. Then it "bit," as it were, into the rudder post, and she just felt it—but only just—the ronyon!

She did not reef as you and I do by sane reefing points, but in a gimcrack fashion with a long lace, so that it took half an hour to take in sail. She had not a jib and foresail, but just one big headsail as high as the peak, and if one wanted to shorten sail after the enormous labour of reefing the main-sail (which no man could do alone) one had to change jibs forward and put up a storm sail—under which (by the way) she was harder to put round than ever.

Did she leak? No, I think not. It is a pious opinion. I think she was tight under the composition, but above that and between wind and water she positively showed daylight. She was a basket. Glory be to God that such a boat should swim at all!

But she drew little water? The devil she did! There was a legend in the yard where she was built that she drew five feet four, but on a close examination of her (on the third time she was wrecked), I calculated with my companion that she drew little if anything under six feet. All this I say knowing well that I shall soon put her up for sale; but that is neither here nor there. I shall not divulge her name.

So we put to sea, intending to run to Harwich. There was a strong flood down the coast, and the wind was to the north of north-east. But the wind was with the tide—to that you owe the lives of the two men and the lec-tion of this delightful story; for had the tide been against the wind and the water steep and mutinous, you would never have seen either of us again: in-deed we should have trembled out of sight for ever.

The wind was with the tide, and in a following lump of a sea, without combers and with a rising glass, we valorously set out, and, missing the South Pier by four inches, we occupied the deep.

For one short half-hour things went more or less well. I noted a white horse or two to windward, but my companion said it was only the sea break-ing over the outer sands. She plunged a lot, but I flattered myself she was carrying Caesar, and thought it no great harm. We had started without food, meaning to cook a breakfast when we were well outside: but men's plans are on the knees of the gods. The god called Æolus, that blows from the north-east of the world (you may see him on old maps—it is a pity they don't put him on the modern), said to his friends: "I see a little boat. It is long since I sank one"; and altogether they gave chase, like Imperialists, to destroy what was infinitely weak.

I looked to windward and saw the sea tumbling, and a great number of white waves. My heart was still so high that I gave them the names of the waves in the eighteenth *Iliad:* The long-haired wave, the graceful wave, the

wave that breaks on an island a long way off, the sandy wave, the wave before us, the wave that brings good tidings. But they were in no mood for
poetry. They began to be great, angry, roaring waves, like the chiefs of
charging clans, and though I tried to keep up my courage with an excellent
song by Mr. Newbolt, "Slung between the round shot in Nombre Dios
Bay," I soon found it useless, and pinned my soul to the tiller. Every sea following caught my helm and battered it. I hung on like a stout gentleman,
and prayed to the seven gods of the land. My companion said things were
no worse than when we started. God forgive him the courageous lie. The
wind and the sea rose.

It was about opposite Southwold that the danger became intolerable,
and that I thought it could only end one way. Which way? The way out,
my honest Jingoes, which you are more afraid of than of anything else in the
world. We ran before it; we were already over-canvased, and she buried her
nose every time, so that I feared I should next be cold in the water, seeing
England from the top of a wave. Every time she rose the jib let out a hun-
dredweight of sea-water; the sprit buckled and cracked, and I looked at the
splice in the forestay to see if it yet held. I looked a thousand times, and a
thousand times the honest splice that I had poked together in a pleasant
shelter under Bungay Woods (in the old times of peace, before ever the sons
of the Achaians came to the land) stood the strain. The sea roared over the
fore-peak, and gurgled out of the scuppers, and still we held on. Till (Æolus
blowing much more loudly, and, what you may think a lie, singing through
the rigging, though we were before the wind) opposite Aldeburgh I thought
she could not bear it any more.

I turned to my companion and said: "Let us drive her for the shore and
have done with it; she cannot live in this. We will jump when she touches."
But he, having a chest of oak, and being bound three times with brass, said:
"Drive her through it. It is not often we have such a fair-wind." With these
words he went below; I hung on for Orfordness. The people on the strand
at Aldeburgh saw us. An old man desired to put out in a boat to our aid.
He danced with fear. The scene still stands in their hollow minds.

As Orfordness came near, the seas that had hitherto followed like giants
in battle now took to a mad scrimmage. They leapt pyramidically, they
heaved up horribly under her; she hardly obeyed her helm, and even in that
gale her canvas flapped in the troughs. Then in despair I prayed to the boat

itself (since nothing else could hear me), "Oh, Boat," for so I was taught the vocative, "bear me safe round this corner, and I will scatter wine over your decks." She heard me and rounded the point, and so terrified was I that (believe me if you will) I had not even the soul to remember how ridiculous and laughable it was that sailors should call this Cape of Storms "the Onion."

Once round it, for some reason I will not explain, but that I believe connected with my prayer, the sea grew tolerable. It still came on to the land (we could sail with the wind starboard), and the wind blew harder yet; but we ran before it more easily, because the water was less steep. We were racing down the long drear shingle bank of Oxford, past what they call "the life-boat house" on the chart (there is no life-boat there, nor ever was), past the look-out of the coastguard, till we saw white water breaking on the bar of the Alde.

Then I said to my companion, "There are, I know, two mouths to this harbour, a northern and a southern; which shall we take?" But he said, "Take the nearest."

I then, reciting my firm beliefs and remembering my religion, ran for the white water. Before I knew well that she was round, the sea was yellow like a pond, the waves no longer heaved, but raced and broke as they do upon a beach. One greener, kindly and roaring, a messenger of the gale grown friendly after its play with us, took us up on its crest and ran us into the deep and calm beyond the bar, but as we crossed, the gravel ground beneath our keel. So the boat made harbour. Then, without hesitation, she cast herself upon the mud, and I, sitting at the tiller, my companion ashore, and pushing at her inordinate sprit, but both revelling in safety, we gave thanks and praise. That night we scattered her decks with wine as I had promised, and lay easy in deep water within.

But which of you who talk so loudly about the island race and the command of the sea have had such a day? I say to you all it does not make one boastful, but fills one with humility and right vision. Go out some day and run before it in a gale. You will talk less and think more; I dislike the memory of your faces. I have written for your correction. Read less, good people, and sail more; and, above all, leave us in peace.

FROM *THE THOUSAND DOLLAR YACHT*
1967

Anthony Bailey

After a childhood spent breathing salt air and sailing a dinghy around Portchester, England, Anthony Bailey found himself living in New York City, married with a child, and lamenting his boatlessness. He went to boat shows, read magazines, amassed a large collection of plans, brochures, and for-sale ads, and dreamed of getting back on the water. But at the same time, he wondered a bit about his own compulsion:

There is a special gaze, a sort of hypnotized stare, that men develop as they look at the sail plan or line drawing of a possible boat. It isn't really an examination or analysis, but more a giving-up of the beholder to the object beheld—a semimystical act, producing little that is concrete and especially annoying to people like wives, who speak to you and receive no answer. Sometimes I had moments of guilt. Was this all a waste of time?

How serious could a man become about boats and still function and suc-
ceed in everyday society? . . . In any event, I now have pleasant memories
of those city dream ships, of Vivette, *a lovely, long East Anglian yawl,*
and Lemster, *a stubby steel sloop. I have a sense of having had real ad-*
ventures in them, finding Vivette *a misery to get out of Harwich harbor*
one foggy morning and Lemster *rather noisy in the short steep seas of the*
Ijsselmeer.

He clearly had it bad, but a move to the port town of Stonington, Connecticut, made
having a boat a real possibility. Bailey rummaged in bilges and poked suspicious gar-
boards for a while, and then happened upon a magazine article extolling the virtues
of the St. Pierre dory. The French islands St. Pierre and Miquelon lie off the coast of
Newfoundland. From them fishermen take their big dories as much as 20 miles to sea.
In an advertisement in the next month's magazine, a builder in New Jersey offered
to build a 28-foot bare hull, mahogany planking on oak frames, for $550. Bailey
bit, and with the addition of a cuddy cabin and centerboard case, ended up paying
$850 for the boat. With the help of some friends who were very adept scavengers, he
managed to rig and finish the boat for less than $1,000. This was 1962, to be sure,
but as Bailey wrote in the introduction to a later edition, inflation is more a ques-
tion of numbers, and the book has been in print ever since. Partly as a sort of inspi-
rational, how-to guide certainly, but also because Bailey simply writes so divertingly.

NAMING

We had already begun to search for a name. It seemed vastly important that we find the right name, though I now see we overestimated that
importance. Whatever name one chooses, it may soon be invested with
properties one didn't mean it to have; it may lack qualities one had hoped
for. Yet one is impressed by names like *Bloodhound* and *Northern Light,* which
seem to evoke the long, lean ocean-racing yawls they are attached to. There
is a martial ring of discipline and strength to *Resolution* and *Despatch,* and an
inescapable romance in *Malay, Bandit,* and *Finisterre.* Carleton Mitchell
claimed the latter as particularly suitable because it had a vowel on the end,
useful for hailing purposes, but there was no doubt the word came to his
mind in the first place because it suggested the Cape jutting out to sea, the
Land's End first to be seen by seafarers at the end of a long ocean voyage.
It seems a big step from that sort of name—romantic, allusive—to a type

equally favored by seamen, which at first sight appears to be chosen with a decided want of imagination, but which in fact bears witness to close and immediate affection: *Elizabeth Alice, Ebenezer Howard, Brown Smith & Jones.* The poetry is practical. I suppose one should therefore tolerate the modern fashion of abbreviation, often to be noticed on the flat transoms of over-powered motorboats—such names, for example, as *Howmar* (owned by Howard and Marlene Smith) and *Alsubagi* (created from the first syllables of the names of the Smiths' four dogs). I suppose they are preferable to *Nautigal,* and *Winsum.*

I have had my own failures. I called my first boat—a ten and a half foot Cadet sailing dingy—*Rhapsody,* which didn't begin to be right for such a snub-nosed, V-bottom, little pram (though it did do justice to her fifteen-year-old skipper's feelings about building, owning, and sailing her). I insisted that my father call our slow and most unlively family dayboat *Caprice.* By the time I reached the ancient Comet on Long Island Sound, the pendulum had swung. Our summer cottage came with a black kitten called Cat. Our laconic Comet was known as *Boat.* I have less irksome memories about the names of the Portchester Duck class dinghies, which were twelvefoot clinker scows with a single dipping lug mainsail, all built by gruff Commander Hammond in his boatshop a few doors away from us. They were excellent boats for the harbor and its muddy creeks, though they tended to bury their noses a trifle dangerously when running before a heavy breeze. Their names had no effect on me as a child, but now seem redolent of the creek, the castle, and the long summer days. They were of course all ducks: *Merganser, Shoveller, Teal, Goosander.* The last one built by the Commander was *Surf Scoter,* which he raced himself, and it was a disappointment to him when she didn't prove fast. The Commander once told me that I wasn't sufficiently public-spirited. He did so much to encourage children to sail that he couldn't understand why I didn't take other boys with me, but preferred to sail alone. But I think I was restored to his favor by a solo voyage I made in *Shoveller,* down the creek, out through Portsmouth harbor, along Southsea beach, and across the five mile width of Spithead to the Isle of Wight. I hauled the Duck up on Seaview beach, had a few ice creams for lunch, and then sailed back again, cheating the fierce ebb in the harbor entrance by getting into the eddies right next to the stone fortifications. For a single-handed voyager in a

Duck the Isle of Wight had been a far country.

Portsmouth harbor now presents itself in memory as one of those miniature profile drawings that used to accompany charts: the stone forts, the
lofty rigging of Nelson's flagship *Victory* in her drydock, the birdlike necks
of the dockyard cranes, and the occasional battleship enjoying a respite on
her way to the shipbreakers. The Napoleonic hulk of the *Foudroyant* was
tethered between two mooring buoys, while across the width of the harbor
moved the Portsmouth-Gosport ferry, a sort of floating platform bearing a
load of standing people, among which reared an even higher standing brass
funnel. There were paddlewheel naval tugs and the *Shanklin,* an elderly
paddlewheel Isle of Wight passenger steamer—the newer *Ryde* and *Sandown*
were twin-screw driven. My father was born at Ryde, grew up on a farm
over the downs behind Shanklin, and in prewar summers took us to spend
our holidays with my grandmother, who lived at Sandown. We went by
paddle steamer. Bells rang, pistons thumped. There was a smell of tea from
the third-class saloon, a smell of oil from the engine room, and the clang of
shoes on the chequered steel plating underfoot. Polished brass plaques gave
the date of the ship's construction by Mr. Denny on the Clyde. On the deck,
the wooden seats had ropes looped along them, indicating their possible
use as life rafts if the steamer sank. A few years ago it was still possible to
see, at the Tate Gallery in London, similar seats in the large rooms where the
spectacular Turners hang, showing fire at sea and great storms; slatted seats
that were robustly curvaceous, combining the properties of heating ducts
and places to sit, and looking like roll-top desks turned inside-out. Indeed,
at the Tate one could rest on them opposite an appropriate Turner and,
hearing the Tate boilers below, imagine oneself on the deck of the old
Shanklin, thrashing her way across Spithead toward Ryde Pier.

Although it was never too rough on the trips we made, it was sometimes
too early, in regard for the tide, and taking a short cut across Spit Sand the
steamer would ground momentarily and have to wait for the assistance of
the flood. Then the regular passengers would smirk at one another and
throw accusing glances at the bridge. The captain—I used to wonder if it
mattered to him—had the gold letters SOUTHERN RAILWAY on his cap.

For a child, as perhaps for adults too, the Isle of Wight was the seaside
rather than the sea: it was beaches, piers, sand castles, small towns with
curving streets, and shops with sweets, postcards, and spades and buckets

in them. And now, if forced to choose between the sea and seaside I would say I liked the seaside more. I have no ambition to cross oceans in a small boat, either to make long passages to windward against North Atlantic gales or to scoot day after day downwind, rolling horribly, before the beneficent trades. For me the sea is seasickness, and weariness, and the readiness to admit "This is it—I'm through." The sea is continual wetness and apprehension and often an absolute terror, and the fact that one is experiencing it not to make a living but for "pleasure" adds an element of madness to it. To my mind, there is more to be said for sailing in shallow water, making use of the eddies along beaches and watching the current swirl through the sand; or to pole through marsh channels with eel grass stroking the topsides and the smell of mud fairly high. I like wharves and jetties and, living in America, I miss piers—those quaint iron structures, the last push of the Victorian railway-building age, poking out from the land, with bars, amusements, cafes, windbreaks for anglers and sunbathers, and a theater on the seaward end where comedians treated holiday audiences to the corniest gags of the previous fifty years. You could stand on a pier in a storm and look down through the cracks in the decking to watch the sea rising and falling like a concertina, and thank goodness you were not out in it. In America, on the other hand, I like the relative lack of promenades and beach huts. I like the possibility one has of walking, say, from Watch Hill along a curved sand beach, with dunes on one side and the sea on the other for half the width of Rhode Island. As Matthew Arnold made clear in his poem "Dover Beach," the shore is as good as the sea for somber philosophy—perhaps a little better, for the sea gives one a large foretaste of eternity, and one can readily turn back to the land for the mortal present.

Is this a long way from the names of boats? I believe a name, like a title, should be a touchstone indicating some of the qualities one hopes the named object will possess, and at the same time perhaps recreating or at least recalling a moment past. I like the names Shoveller, Vol-au-Vent, and Tristram Shandy, the hero of which is nine months and several hundred pages being born. It seemed to me a good name for a comic sort of boat on which one would make picaresque voyages, at any rate for France. Since the dory was an impromptu sort of craft, I felt it needed not too dignified a name. Margot said one day, "How about Bellerophon, or rather Billy Ruffian?"

She explained that *H.M.S. Bellerophon* was the British warship on which

Napoleon formally surrendered in 1815 after Waterloo. The British tars aboard her called her the *Billy Ruffian*. Bellerophon himself I looked up in Robert Graves's *Greek Myths*. He had managed to survive the day-to-day troubles of a Greek boyhood in Corinth—two murders (one his brother) and the misfortune of not knowing whether Poseidon or Glaucus was his father—only to have Anteia, wife of the King of Tiryus, fall in love with him. When Bellerophon honorably refused her, she accused him of having tried to seduce her. Her husband Proteus, however, didn't dare risk the vengeance of the Furies by liquidating Bellerophon on the spot, but sent him on to Anteia's father with a sealed note saying "Pray remove the bearer from this world; he has tried to violate my wife, your daughter." But Anteia's father was also a king and similarly reluctant to kill a household guest. He therefore asked Bellerophon to do a chore: namely, get rid of the chimaera, which was a fire-breathing she-monster with a lion's head, goat's body, and serpent's tail. The king didn't doubt that the chimaera would take care of the young upstart from Corinth. However, Bellerophon tamed Pegasus, the flying horse, and strafed the chimaera with bow and arrow, finally thrusting a lead-tipped spear into her mouth. The monster's fiery breath melted the lead, which (writes Graves) "trickled down her throat, searing her vitals."

Anteia's father was, of course, ungrateful, and sent off Bellerophon to battle the Solymians and Amazons. From the back of his winged steed, our young hero successfully bombed them with boulders. In the next reel, the king attempted to ambush Bellerophon, but Poseidon came to his rescue and flooded the plain; as Bellerophon advanced on the king's palace, the waves advanced with him. Nothing appeared to stop him. As a last resort the women of the country were called for and lifting up their skirts, they rushed forward, offering themselves to him one and all. At this point, Bellerophon—still a modest fellow—lost his nerve and ran.

But the king had now seen the light. He had been given the truth about his daughter's conduct. He made Bellerophon his heir and gave him another daughter for his own, taking a moment to praise his female subjects for their resourcefulness. Bellerophon thereupon lost his simple ways and (in Graves's words) "presumptuously undertook a flight to Olympus, as though he were an immortal; but Zeus sent a gadfly, which stung Pegasus under the tail, making him rear and fling Bellerophon ingloriously to earth. Pegasus completed the flight to Olympus, where Zeus now uses him as a pack beast for thunderbolts; and Bellerophon, who had fallen into a thorn bush, wandered about the earth, lame, blind, lonely and accursed, always avoiding the paths of men, until death overtook him."

The name *Billy Ruffian* might enable us to avoid some of the misfortunes that came to poor Bellerophon. It lacked hubris and had a jaunty, ragamuffin ring. It would do well.

FIRST CRUISE

We made our first cruise on September 1. Here is the log, as I wrote it immediately afterward, lacking polish but preserving, perhaps, the freshness of our adventure.

After Margot and Liz returned from Church and Sunday school, decided today might as well be the day. Gathered gear and junk, all ready by noon, except for Liz, who had disappeared in the direction of the Holy Ghost parade, celebrating the feeding of the starving masses of Portugal by Queen Isabella. Found her at the Portuguese Holy Ghost Club, downing free Portuguese soup. Finally reached the dory, stowed gear, fed other members of the crew.

Made sail at 1:30 p.m. Clear blue sky, not too warm, light breeze. Sailed behind Sandy Point and anchored opposite Elihu Island, south of the channel. Went ashore by dinghy, and Liz, Anny and I walked on the beach prospecting while Margot went clamming on the flat that spreads out to the east of Sandy. Haul, a dozen cherrystones. Margot said she hadn't quite got the clamming technique of the Chipperfield boys, who were searching for clams with the toes and doing a sort of twist. We went aboard again, retrieved the anchor, drifted aground, pushed off with Yaacov's boathook, and sailed over to the entrance of Wequetequock Cove where we anchored again. I fed Gerber's Tropical Fruit to Anny while Liz and Margot fished, using some of the clams for bait. They caught nothing. Liz kept bringing up her line to see what was on it and kept losing her bait. Lots of water skiers around. Other boats nearby with men rodfishing catching fish. At five-thirty we weighed anchor and sailed over to Barn Island game preserve area, ghosting into a little anchorage behind a tree-covered point. The bottom, a clear six feet down, was firm mud—a few shells and underwater plants were visible. The harbor was formed of low, marsh-grass covered banks.

It was a lovely evening. Liz and I went for a sail in the dinghy for a way up a ditch that drained the marsh, and then made a second trip, with Margot and Anny, who refused to go to sleep, up a wider creek that wound into the woods. We ran fast up this miniature river, our wake lapping the banks. We saw herons, cormorants, duck, and gulls. The sun began to go down over Stonington. We rowed back down our creek until we reached the little harbor which gave us room again to sail.

On the *Billy Ruffian,* Margot cooked her first shipboard meal, while I rigged an awning over the boom. Anny still refused to go off watch, and had a second dinner, this time of minestrone and Dinty Moore stew. (She refused the fried clams, which turned out to be a wise move.) By ten-fifteen, Liz and Anny were at last sacked out on the cabin floor in sleeping bags. Margot and I sat in the after-cockpit. A huge yellow moon rose over Osbrook Point, and across the water from Stonington came the sound of revelry at the Holy Ghost. The tide fell, and the dory pointed her nose inland. In the marshes a few birds piped, and overhead we heard the loud buzz of mosquitoes.

Margot and I slept in the main cockpit under the awning, the centerboard case between us like Sir Gawain's sword. We had air mattresses and found it hard to discover the exact point of comfort where the mattress was not too hard nor too soft. Margot had the sleeping bag. I had two blankets, an old genoa jib, and a sail bag, into which I stuck my feet. It was a cold night, and the awning proved to be permeable.

Liz woke at seven.

Anny woke at seven plus ten seconds.

I got up, creaking like a tin man.

Fine clear morning, flat calm. Margot got up, refused to talk, took four baby aspirins and gave four to me.

It was Labor Day. Margot dressed L and A, while I sorted blankets, sleeping bags, folded awning and pumped ship. M, heroine, cooked on the gimballed Sterno stove pan-fried cornbread, which was delicious with boiled eggs and coffee. Anny crawled into a locker under the bridge deck and had her bottle there.

We were underway at 9 a.m. Light breeze from the south-west. We tacked out of our bay and then swung round Ostbrook Point to the Pawcatuck River. We spent the morning on the river, sailing up it with the wind against the tide, and then down with the tide against the wind. We admired the houses at Avondale and the boats on the moorings off Paines Yard, and Frank Hall's, and we answered questions from passing yachts: "Say, is that a converted Coast Guard rescue boat?" The question was—we thought—better put in Fishers the week before by an Alden Challenger which pursued us across the sound and caught us by East Harbor, coming up to leeward, and deliberately slowing with a great release of genoa sheet— "What is she? She's dandy!" I doffed my beret and yelled out, "A French dory." "Lovely boat!" came the reply, then they cranked on the winches and were away.

Around lunchtime we got to Napatree and anchored in the bay behind the fort. Liz made sand puddings with children from other boats, Anny splashed in the shallows, Margot sketched, and I slept for an hour. When I woke, I felt thick and groggy from the sun, but a hundred feet away across the dunes was the sea and I stumbled over and plunged into a foaming breaker. Soon I had a clear cool head. We raced home against Charlie and Anne Storrow's Woodpussy, but they made it through the cut and we, bouncing hard, had to jibe around and go the long way back. It was a slow trip, tide-cheating. Liz and Anny were flat out in the cabin. We turned down the offer of a tow from the senior Dodsons in a Boston Whaler. A Marshall cat-boat passed us at tremendous speed and we hoped she had an engine on, but there was no sound or sign of it. We made our mooring on the second attempt and I rowed ashore with the gear and then the crew. Liz, contrary, didn't want to leave the ship. We were all sun reddened and strangely enough without colds or coughs. I took ashore with me at the end of this maiden cruise the knowledge that I needed a lighter more easily handled anchor, and also that I needed a compass that didn't, at certain times of day, acquire a bubble. Home, Margot turned to me: "It was just awful, but I suppose I liked it."

FROM **THE BOAT WHO WOULDN'T FLOAT**
1969

Farley Mowat

In the early 1960s Farley Mowat found himself on the east coast of Newfoundland looking to buy a boat. The "Why Newfoundland?" bit was straightforward. As Mowat wrote:

One night a few weeks after I bought the departed chandler's stock Jack McClelland and I were moored to a bar in Toronto. It was a dismal day in a dismal city so we stayed moored to the bar for several hours. I kept no notes of what was said nor do I recall with any clarity how it all came to pass. I know only that before the night ended we were committed to buying ourselves an ocean-going vessel in which to roam the salt seas over.

We decided we should do things the old-fashioned way (we both have something of the Drake and Nelson complex) and this meant buying an *old-fashioned boat; the kind of boat that was once sailed by iron men.*

The only place we knew where such a boat might be procured was in the remote and foggy island of Newfoundland.

The "Why a boat?" bit was, as these things often are, more complicated. Not to spoil the story should one buy the book, but it involved a World War II Motor Torpedo Boat, the purchase of thirty hives of bees by Mowat's father during Mowat's childhood, and the aforementioned auction of a ship chandler's goods (I bought this anchor but I'd get arrested if I started chucking it out the window of my car when I needed to slow down, so what else can I do?).

Of course, any normal person would run out and buy a boat to go with their new anchor. But perhaps only someone with Farley Mowat's ear for the poetry of the absurd could have ended up at sea in a boat of the type known as a "Southern Shore bummer."

The book is one of those rare tales that gets drier and more understated as the absurdities mount. Mowat, trained as a biologist, has written something like forty books. They deal mostly with the outdoors, Canada's native peoples, and the environment, and share an extraordinarily finely tuned appreciation of the picaresque—of the margins of society where civilization is more a foil than a blanket. It is hard to go wrong when picking one up.

FARLEY MOWAT BUYS A BOAT

Time was drawing on and we were no forwarder. Harold's red beard jutted at an increasingly belligerent angle; his frosty eyes took on a gimlet stare and his temper grew worse and worse. He was not used to being thwarted and he did not like it. He arranged to have a news item printed in the papers describing the arrival of a rich mainlander who was looking for a local schooner.

Two days later he informed me that he had found the perfect vessel. She was, he said, a small two-masted schooner of the type known generally as a jack-boat and, more specifically, as a Southern Shore bummer. I can't say that the name enthralled me, but by this time I, too, was growing desperate so I agreed to go and look at her.

She lay hauled out at Muddy Hole, a small fishing village on the east coast of the Avalon Peninsula—a coast that is rather inexplicably called the

Southern Shore, perhaps because it lies south of St. John's and St. John's is, in its own eyes at least, the centre of the universe.

Tourist maps showed Muddy Hole as being connected to St. John's by road. This was a typical Newfoundland "jolly." Muddy Hole was not connected to St. John's at all except by a tenuous trail which, it is believed, was made some centuries ago by a very old caribou who was not only blind but also afflicted with the staggers.

In any event it took us six hours to follow where he had led. It was a typical spring day on the east coast of the island. A full gale was blowing from seaward, hurling slanting rain heavily against the car. The Grand Banks fog, which is forever lurking just off the coast, had driven in over the high headlands obscuring everything from view. Guided by some aboriginal instinct inherited from his seagoing ancestors, Harold somehow kept the course and just before ten o'clock, in impenetrable darkness, we arrived at Muddy Hole.

I had to take his word for it. The twin cones of the headlights revealed nothing but rain and fog. Harold rushed me from the car and a moment later was pounding on an unseen door. It opened to allow us to enter a tiny, brilliantly lit, steaming hot kitchen where I was introduced to the brothers Mike and Paddy Hallohan. Dressed in thick homespun sweaters, heavy rubber boots and black serge trousers they looked like a couple of characters out of a smuggling yarn by Robert Louis Stevenson. Harold introduced me explaining that I was the "mainland feller" who had come to see their boat.

The brothers wasted no time. Rigging me up in oilskins and a sou'wester they herded me out into the storm.

The rain beat down so heavily that it almost masked the thunder of breakers which seemed to be directly below me and at no great distance away.

"Tis a grand night for a wreck!" Paddy bellowed cheerfully.

It was also a grand night to fall over a cliff and break one's neck; a matter of more immediate concern to me as I followed close on Paddy's heels down a steep path that was so slippery your average goat would have thought twice about attempting it. Paddy's storm lantern, fuelled for economy reasons with crude cod-liver oil, gave only a symbolic flicker of light through a dense cloud of rancid smoke. Nevertheless the smoke was useful. It enabled me to keep track of my guide simply by following my nose.

Twenty minutes later I bumped heavily into Paddy and was bumped into as heavily by Mike who had been following close behind. Paddy thrust the lamp forward and I caught a maniacal glimpse of his gnome-like face, streaming with rain and nearly split in two by a gigantic grin.

"Thar she be, Skipper! T'foinest little bummer on t'Southern Shore o' Newfoundland!"

I could see nothing. I put my hand out and touched the flank of something curved and wet. Paddy shoved the lantern forward to reveal reflections from the most repellent shade of green paint I have ever seen. The color reminded me of the naked belly of a long-dead German corpse with whom I once shared a foxhole in Sicily. I snatched my hand away.

Mike roared in my ear. "Now dat you'se seen her, me dear man, us'll nip on back t'house and have a drop o' tay."

Whereupon Mike and Paddy nipped, leaving me stumbling anxiously in their wake.

Safely in the kitchen once more I found Harold had never left that warm sanctuary. He later explained that he had felt it would have been an intrusion for him to be present at my first moment of communion with my new love. Harold is such a thoughtful man.

By this time I was soaked, depressed, and very cold; but the Hallohan brothers and their ancient mother, who now appeared from a back room, went to work on me. The began by feeding me a vast plate of salt beef and turnips boiled with salt cod which in turn engendered within me a monumental thirst. At this juncture the brothers brought out a crock of Screech.

Screech is a drink peculiar to Newfoundland. In times gone by it was made by pouring boiling water into empty rum barrels to dissolve whatever rummish remains might have lingered there. Molasses and yeast were added to the black, resultant fluid and this mixture was allowed to ferment for a decent length of time before it was distilled. Sometimes it was aged for a few days in a jar containing a plug of nigger-twist chewing tobacco.

However the old ways have given way to the new, and Screech is now a different beast. It is the worst conceivable quality of Caribbean rum, bottled by the Newfoundland government under the Screech label, and sold to poor devils who have no great desire to continue living. It is not as powerful as it used to be but this defect can be, and often is, remedied by the addition of quantities of lemon extract. Screech is usually served mixed with boiling water. In its consequent near gaseous state the transfer of the alcohol to the blood stream is instantaneous. Very little is wasted in the digestive tract.

This was my first experience with Screech and nobody had warned me. Harold sat back with an evil glitter in his eye and watched with delight as I tried to quench my thirst. At least I think he did. My memories of the balance of that evening are unclear.

At a much later date I was to be accused by Jack of having bought our boat while drunk, or of having bought her sight unseen, or both. The last part of the accusation is certainly not true. As I sat in the overwhelming heat of the kitchen with steam rising to maximum pressure inside my own boilers, the brothers Hallohan drew on the wizardry of their Irish ancestors and conjured up for me a picture of their little schooner using such vivid imagery that I saw her as clearly as if she had been in the kitchen with us. When I eventually threw my arms around Paddy's neck and thrust a bundle of bills into his sharkskin textured hand, I knew with sublime certainty that I had found the perfect vessel.

As we drove back to St. John's the next morning, Harold rhapsodised about the simple-hearted, honest, God-fearing Irish fishermen of the Southern Shore.

"They'd give you their shirt as soon as look at you," he said. "Generous? Migod, there's nobody in the whole world like them! You're some lucky they took to you."

In a way I suppose Harold was right. Because if the Hallohans had not taken to me I might have remained in Ontario where I could conceivably have become a solid citizen. I bear the Hallohans no ill will, but I hope I never again get "took to" the way I was taken on that memorable night at Muddy Hole.

Two days later I returned to Muddy Hole to do a survey on my vessel and to get my first sober (in the sense of calm, appraising) look at her. Seen from a distance she was indeed a pretty little thing, despite her nauseous color. A true schooner hull in miniature, she measured thirty-one feet on deck with a nine-foot beam and a four-foot draft. But she was rough! On close inspection she looked as though she had been flung together by a band of our Palaeolithic ancestors—able shipbuilders perhaps, but equipped only with stone adzes.

SMALL BOATS ON GREEN WATERS

Her appointments and accommodations left a great deal to be desired. She was flush-decked, with three narrow fishing wells in each of which one man could stand and jig for cod, and with two intervening fish holds in each of which the ghosts of a million long-dead cod tenaciously lingered. Right up in her eyes was a cuddy two feet high, three feet wide, and three feet long, into which one very small man could squeeze if he did not mind assuming the foetal position. There was also the engine room; a dark hole in which lurked the enormous phallus of a single-cylinder, make-and-break (but mostly broke) gasoline engine.

Her rigging also left something to be desired. Her two masts had apparently been manufactured out of a couple of walking sticks. They were stayed with lengths of telephone wire and cod line. Her sails were patched like Joseph's coat and seemed to be of similar antiquity. Her bowsprit was hardly more than a mop handle tied in place with netting twine. It did not appear to me that the Hallohans had sailed her very much. I was later to hear that they had never sailed her and shared the general conviction that any attempt to do so would probably prove fatal.

She was not a clean little vessel. In truth, she stank. Her bilges had not been cleaned since the day she was built and they were encrusted with a gelatinous layer of fish slime, fish blood, and fish gurry to a depth of several inches. This was not because of bad housekeeping. It was done "a-purpose" as the Muddy Holers told me *after* I had spent a solid week trying to clean her out.

"Yee see, skipper," one of them explained, "dese bummers now, dey be built o' green wood, and when dey dries, dey spreads. Devil a seam can yee keep tight wit corkin (caulking). But dey seals dersel's, yee might say, wit' gurry and blood, and dat's what keeps dey tight."

I have never since had reason to doubt his words.

Since the sum the Hallohans had demanded for their vessel was, oddly enough, exactly the sum I had to spend, and since this nameless boat (the Hallohans had never christened her, referring to her only as She, or sometimes as That Bitch) was not yet ready to go, I had to make a serious decision.

The question really was whether to walk away from her forever, telling Jack McClelland a suitable lie about having been waylaid by highwaymen in St. John's, or whether to try and brazen it out and somehow make a vessel out of a sow's ear. Because I am essentially a coward, and anyway Jack is onto my lies, I chose the latter course.

Upon asking the Hallohans where I could find a boat builder who could make some necessary changes for me I was directed to Enarchos Coffin—the very man who had built the boat four years earlier. Enos, as he was called, was a lean, lank, dehydrated stick of a man. In his younger days he had been a master shipwright in Fortune Bay building vessels for the Grand Banks fishery, but when the Banking fleet faded into glory he was reduced to building small boats for local fishermen. The boats he built were beautifully designed; but a combination of poverty amongst his customers, a shortage of decent wood, failing vision, and old age, somewhat affected the quality of his workmanship. The Hallohan boat was the last one he had built and was to be the last one he would ever build.

When I went to visit him, armed with an appropriate bottle, he was living in a large, ramshackle house in company with his seven unmarried daughters. Enos proved amiable and garrulous. The Southern Shore dialect is almost unintelligible to the ear of an outsider and when it is delivered in a machine gun clip it becomes totally incomprehensible. For the first hour or two of our acquaintance I understood not a single word that he addressed to me. However after the first burst of speed had run its course, he slowed down a little and I was able to understand quite a lot.

He was delighted to hear I had bought the boat; but when he heard what I had paid for her, he was only able to cure his attack of apoplexy by drinking half the bottle of rum, neat.

"Lard livin' Jasus!" he screeched when he got his breath back. "An' I built her for they pirates fer two hunnert dollars!"

At which point I snatched the bottle from him and drank the other half of it, neat.

When we had recovered our breath, I asked him if he would undertake repairs, modifications and a general refit. He willingly agreed. We arranged that he would fit a false keel and outside ballast; a cabin trunk over the fish wells; bunks, tables, lockers and other internal essentials; re-spar, re-rig her properly, and do a hundred other smaller but necessary jobs. Enos thought the work would take him about two months to complete.

I returned to St. John's and thence to Ontario in moderately good spirits. I did not worry about the boat being ready on time, since we did not plan on sailing her until midsummer. Occasionally I wrote to Enos (he himself could neither read nor write) and one or other of his strapping daughters would reply with a scrawled postcard of which this one is typical.

Dear Mister Mote

Dad say yor boat come fine lots fish this month Gert got her baby

Nellie Coffin

During the waiting months Jack and I dreamed many a dream and made many a plan. We agreed that I should precede him to Newfoundland near the end of June taking with me a jeep-load of gear and equipment, and that I would have the few finishing touches to the boat completed so that she would be ready to sail when Jack arrived in mid-July. After that, well, we would see. Bermuda, the Azores, Rio de Janeiro—the world lay waiting!

FROM AN OLD GAFFER'S TALE

1984

Martin Eve

Martin Eve spent most of his life building Seafarer Books, a small, independent British nautical publisher. But An Old Gaffer's Tale, *about his time with an old wooden smack, was the only book he ever published of his own. In this excerpt, Eve takes a couple of young women on a two-week charter cruise. There were two things that drew me to it from all the book's other good bits. The first was probably the driest and most understated two sentences in a literature famous for its dry and understated humor:*

From Dunkirk we moved on to Nieuport, where we sailed up the narrow gut and careened on the mud. It was a messy place for scraping,

but the girls waded in gamely although this activity was not I think in my brochure.

The second was that this is a happily-ever-after story, and it is hard to go too far wrong with one of those.

CHARTERING

The discerning reader will have noticed that this story is like all the accounts they have ever read about owners of old boats in one respect at least; I was hard up. Buying a nine-tonner like *Privateer* had stretched my finances to the limit, and it was not through perversity that I made do with an engine that didn't work half the time, with sails that were apt to tear, and with old gear that needed replacing. I managed for many years to run *Privateer* on the proverbial shoestring, but there would come a time, I knew, when I should have to lay out some money. Where was this going to come from?

I remembered how I used to sail charter yachts, in the days before *Privateer*, and how I would pay thirty or forty pounds a week for this, out of season too. Of course, I could not trust anyone with *Privateer*, that was out of the question; not for me the arrangement Dick had made with his Eventide, handing her over to Blackwater Charters for a whole season and sailing her only when she wasn't booked. But, I thought, if I chartered her complete with skipper, I should be able to ask that much more. I began to count the chickens and raised the idea with Frank Mulville, the sort of man to know about these things.

Frank was horrified; he had not chartered himself, but was full of terrible stories of would-be charterers who had sailed to seek their fortunes in the West Indies and had suffered every degradation before giving up in despair. Franked advised me in the strongest possible terms not to consider chartering, and warned me solemnly that I should regret it if I didn't heed his advice.

Of course we don't ask our friends for advice in order to take it, so I went ahead and put a notice in *The Times,* offering a week or two's holiday at what seemed like a competitive rate, and implying a slightly flattering picture of *Privateer*. I had ready a duplicated sheet, again containing no untruths, or hardly any, and setting out the details.

There were quite a few replies to the original advertisement, but less to the duplicated follow-up. I had paid this much attention to Frank's warning, that I resolved to be careful about whom I took. So as a result of telephone conversations I eliminated anyone that I didn't take to immediately. This left me with one or two weekenders, but for the August holiday the booking was for two girls, Pat and her friend Christine, to be joined in the second week by another girl, Jill.

For some reason *Privateer* was not on her mooring then but had been left up in the Twizzle at Walton; I collected Pat and Christine at the London terminus and drove them up to Walton. *Privateer* had, I suppose, been left at Walton in a hurry, and without time to clear up properly. She must have been in a bit of a shambles, and I saw the disgust on the girls' faces as they emptied the teapot, full of mouldy tea-leaves, over the side. We met at Walton a young American boy (the cousin of a friend) who was coming with us, and he didn't help by first getting stuck in the Walton Carnival and keeping us all waiting for hours, and then asking if anyone had any grass with them.

In fine and almost windless weather we had made our way gently to Mersea, and then on across the estuary, where we drifted on the ebb towards Herne Bay pier. We all had a swim alongside, and when the tide turned we anchored; there was not a breath of wind. The American lad, Mel, either because of the shortage of grass, or because he didn't take to this slow and stately way of life, for whatever reason, asked to be put ashore. Pat rowed him to the end of the mile-long pier, he scrambled up a gangway and we never saw him again. After we had done this, I noticed that there was a bit missing in the middle of the pier and worried that we might have marooned Mel, but there was no sign of him, and in fact we heard later that he had managed to get across the gap and onto the mainland. However, this was not the end of his troubles; an alert policeman had seen him scrambling ashore and had asked him to identify himself. Mel had no passport with him and spent some time in the local police station before his English cousins could be reached on the phone to vouch for him.

We meanwhile remained becalmed at anchor for the night, but were woken early by sounds of frapping. A wind had got up, and so we wasted no time but raised the anchor and made our way swiftly through the channel between Hook Sands and the Kentish shore, past Margate and round the corner of the North Foreland. Here there was a fine beam wind, later backing slightly to make a quartering breeze of force 5 or 6. By lunchtime we were passing the Goodwin Lightship and making direct for Calais. With a rolling sea and a wind on the quarter it is impossible to hold a course exactly, but Pat made a very good job of steering in what is the only situation where *Privateer* is heavy on the helm. By one of those happy coincidences the large pillar buoy that lies off Calais turned up dead ahead of us, and I acquired a reputation for accurate navigation that Pat has never abandoned despite all evidence to the contrary. Exactly three hours after passing the Goodwin Light we were sailing between the twin piers of Calais harbour, the fastest channel crossing I have made in *Privateer* so far.

We moved into the inner harbour, where we were joined by Jill, while the wind outside blew up and then away altogether. We made a slow passage on to Dunkirk, where we entered harbour so slowly that we could row the tender off and take a photo of *Privateer* against the stones of the breakwater. As can be seen, Privateer was wearing her brand new Number 3 jib, a tiny storm sail which was the only one we had now, not counting the so-called Genoa, or acting spinnaker. From Dunkirk we moved on to Nieuport, where we sailed up the narrow gut and careened on the mud. It was a messy place for scraping, but the girls waded in gamely although this activity was not I think in my brochure. We soon had the barnacles biting the dirt.

We came off the mud and lay alongside a Belgian boat, whose owner was also chartering. He was persuaded, with much show of reluctance, to get out his guitar and sing to us, and I have never heard a man with so much self confidence as a musician based on so little technique. I think he had only one chord, but he sang and played with such conviction that no-one seemed to notice. We moved on to Ostend, where I managed to get *Privateer* through the entrance to the boat harbor and alongside the pontoons without using the engine. Perhaps the girls thought this was a display of seamanship, but the real reason was that it was a safer method than with our uncertain engine. From Ostend we took the train up to Bruges, one of the most beautiful cities in Europe and one that is strangely underrated. It has the necessary history for a perfect result, having been prosperous in the late middle ages, when all the houses were built, and then gone into decline, so that they were never replaced. In its heyday it was the great port to which all the English wool was sent—difficult to imagine now that it is so far from the sea.

Our leisurely progress was beginning to run us out of time; we had to turn for home. We left Ostend, with some wondering stares from some of the all-male crew of the yachts there, drifted back past Nieuport, then ran into thick fog, keeping well inshore and hoping to miss the traffic that way. Dunkirk lights showed up through gaps in the fog, and we finally worked into the harbour as the fog cleared and dawn broke. Here we were met by a large number of visitors, including Will, who had been staying with a French family. After a day of junketing it was time to go home. On the return journey we broke no cross channel records; it took us seven hours to get from Dunkirk to the South Goodwin, and another seven to get round the corner to Whitstable, where we anchored off the Street.

At that time my sister lived in Whitstable, and it was her constant anxiety that one day she would awake to see her brother aground on the Street, that great spit that sticks out at right angles to Whitstable. The thought of the shame this would cause her was too awful to contemplate, and I always supposed this was why she moved inland. Of course I never did get aground on the Street, though I did once, with my sister aboard, take the ground at high water up the Swell.

Making a very early start from Whitstable, we made our way slowly across the estuary and round to Barrow, where the wind headed us. The ebb took us as far as the south side of the Whitaker sand and no further; no way could we bear round the corner against wind and tide. I took *Privateer* as close in to the sand as I dared and anchored. We sat and watched the flood tide gradually covering the sands. With the wind about 4-5 from the North-east our anchorage was becoming more and more uncomfortable. We now looked across the choppy sea rolling over the sands to the Crouch channel, only about half a mile away from us, with the channel buoys showing clearly, and many craft sailing up and down. It was tempting to say the least, and I worked out the depths over the sand more than once. After four hours of flood, I waited no longer, we hoisted sail, up anchor and with the wind on the beam foamed across the sands. I switched off the echo sounder, there wasn't a thing I could do whatever story it told. After a few exhilarating minutes we were off the edge of the sand and into the deep water of the Crouch, where we turned hard left and found ourselves in the middle of Burnham regatta, with class after class of yachts racing up behind us, alongside us and in front of us. We surfed down the steep waves, doing about eight or nine knots over the river bed. In no time we were up to Burnham and swinging to an anchor in the quiet lee of the town. That was the end of the charter cruise, as Pat and Christine had to leave immediately and we put them ashore on the hard as soon as we had cleared Customs.

It was time to draw up a balance on the success of chartering. Looked at financially it was a dead failure; all the charterers were going to come sailing again, but next time as guests, not as paying customers. This meant that however many charters I got, if things went this way it could not be profitable. Frank had been right about that. On the other hand, looked at from other points of view, it had not turned out badly. Pat signed on as regular crew; and in due course we got married and lived happily ever after.

FROM *LAST OF THE SAILORMEN*
2001

Bob Roberts

The Thames sailing barges emerged as a type in the 16th and 17th centuries. They started as lighters, designed to unload the cargo ships—which needed too much water to approach the wharves to unload—that had started to come to England at the time, carrying all the riches of empire. With time they evolved into handy coastal traders, carrying everything from corn to sand to hay through the estuaries of south-east England. If one looks at a building in London from before about 1910, odds are good most of the materials, clay, sand, timber, were brought up the Thames in a barge.

They were sloop rigged, with a spritsail main, and even the largest of them, as much as 300 tons, could be handled by two men and a boy. In the early 1900s, as modern London was being built, there were something like 2,000 of them trading. By the end of World War II they had dwindled to a handful. But the last one, the last vessel working under sail in Britain, was the Cambria. *She was 170 tons, sailed with two men, and Roberts, the last sailorman, kept her trading until 1971.*

Born in 1907, Roberts first went to sea in the barquentine Waterwitch *at 15. He later crossed the Atlantic in a 27-foot smack, and had two ships sunk under him while serving in the merchant marine during World War II. He traded and fished the coasts of East Anglia and the North Sea, as well as places as far flung as the West Indies, Ascension Island, West Africa, and Brazil. Along the way he did a bit of many things: journalism, singing and playing his squeezebox, boxing ("Don't look so pleased when you win, son, just pick up the money.") Early in life, he began writing of his time on the sea, and eventually published four books—guaranteed good reads for anyone with any interest in those who worked the sea.*

In this piece, Roberts writes of some tricky sailing to make harbor in another barge, the Greenhithe, *during some dodgy weather, and then having to do some even trickier sailing in front of half a town forced to wait and watch one Sunday morning because the bridge over the river had swung to let him pass. Like all of Roberts' yarns, it is well spun, but what struck me was the thought of all those people watching. No doubt few could appreciate the first-class seamanship they were seeing. Some were probably fuming at the delay, while others watched with interest a sight that had grown rare.*

The account of the townsfolk stays with me, because I remember driving one evening out of my hometown and having to stop while a switching engine pulled a crucible car full of molten steel across a rail bridge over the road. It was just dark, and the steel spat a shower of glowing chunks of slag out of the top of the car. By the time the crucible had passed and the glowing slag had cooled, a bunch of cars were waiting. One guy honked his horn, but most just sat and watched. And then we all went on our way. A couple of weeks later I heard that the steel works, one of the last in an area where there had been many, had closed that day. But it wasn't until a couple of months later, passing under the bridge again at dusk, that I reflected that there would be no more fireworks displays on that stretch of road, and that I had without knowing it watched the passing of the industry that built my town.

So it must have been for the people of Lowestoft that day. For as long as the town had been a town, a thousand years or so at least, the harbor would have been full of working sail. Then came World War II and there were fewer and fewer. One day they saw what was by then a novelty, a sailing barge working its way into harbor. And then, maybe only years later, they were somehow reminded of that Sunday morning, the sailing barge, and a gale blowing out on the estuary, and thought "You know, I never did see another one of those."

PIERHEADS IN BAD WEATHER

In the hurly burly life of coasting under canvas it was hardly noticeable for a time that our companions in sail were gradually getting fewer and fewer. But a few years after the war had ended there came another rapid decline in the red sailed fleets that used to set out from London for the East Coast ports and we could do a round trip from London to Yarmouth, the Humber and back to London without seeing a single barge under sail.

Sometimes when lying in the docks in London in company with other barges I would ask for news of vessels which seemed to have slipped out of existence.

"Where's old so-and-so? Haven't seen her about lately."

"Oh, she's gone to have her engine put in"—or—"she's being turned into a houseboat"—or—"she's being broken up."

It seemed incredible to think that just before the war broke out I had been among fifty-one barges getting under way together from Sea Reach, outward bound after a spell of easterly weather. The river mouth was a mass of bellying canvas, the barges almost aboard of one another and not room for a steamboat to get past them. There was some smart seamanship to be seen on days like that and a sailorman who did not know his job could bring accident and disaster to himself and several others by a false manoeuvre or bad judgement.

But all that was done. We became lonelier and lonelier. People began to marvel at us being able to get from place to place in reasonable time without the assistance of an engine and that in itself was an indication that a sailing barge was well on the way to becoming a curio in the new era of machine-driven ships.

Month by month, year by year, little odd incidents began to impress upon me that the days of sail were nearly over at last. I remember once when we were heaving the *Greenhithe* into the dock at King's Lynn, holding up a motor ship for a few minutes while we did so, to the great annoyance of her skipper and pilot. Some lads on the deck of a training ship nearby were watching, some with pity and some with derision, and I heard one of them remark that he believed we had come from London without an engine.

"Then how did she get here?" asked his companion. "Strewth! I wouldn't go to sea in that."

These were British boys being trained as seamen. As we sprung the barge ahead round the dockhead knuckle with a line on the leeboard crab winch I realised, judging by their attitude of wonder and ridicule, that to these bright lads of the new generation such sailormen as we might just as well belong to the Stone Age.

There were still a fair number of river barges, mostly in the cement and ballast work, but, like us big 'uns, their days were numbered as new motor craft came to be built. In the small barges the crews could not earn a decent living. In the face of competition from fast power craft, the coasting barges had to be thankful for any cargo they could get—and then deliver it as quickly as possible so as not to show up too badly against the motors. In fact there was more pressing and cracking on and sleepless nights in this last struggle for survival than there had been in the flourishing days of coasting sail.

Young Ken left after twelve months to join his father aboard a new floating oil refinery. There was good pay for him there and the prospect of steady advancement. He liked the barges and was none too eager to go, but he realised, being a young man, that he had better start carving out his career in a job that was going to lead to something.

For his last freight we loaded raw sugar in Ipswich Dock, and when the news got round among the barging fraternity that the mate of the *Greenhithe* was leaving, young Hazelton (who had been mate with me for three months while waiting to take the *Saltcote Belle*) jumped aboard and asked for his old job back. He had had enough of the *Saltcote Belle* when she fell short of work and seemed very pleased to get back to the *Greenhithe*.

He was a very different type from Ken Fry, but a fine seaman all the same. He had been aboard barges from schoolboy days and I can only say that he deserved the somewhat hackneyed phrase of being "quietly efficient."

With Hazelton as mate and his young friend Jim Godfrey, also of Ipswich, as third hand, I had as good a crew as any barge skipper could wish for.

Hazelton was sensible, workmanlike and experienced while Godfrey (unlike many third hands in barges) was clean, obedient and a good cook.

We were a happy ship. They relied on me, and I knew that I could rely on them.

It was while they were my crew that we once made a spectacular entry into Lowestoft harbor in a gale of wind on a Sunday and made a lot of people late for church. We had flour in for the wharf in the Inner Harbor and had made a fast night passage from London in rough weather. Between the North-east Gunfleet and Southwold so many seas had peeled the full length of her deck that she was a clean as a new pin. The ship was, but the crew were not. We had not had time for such luxuries as washing and shaving and in any case were were too anxious to get into harbor to worry about what we looked like. It took two of us to steer and the gallant Jim, wet and weary, emerged periodically with mugs of steaming tea or cocoa and sandwiches which can only be described as hefty, each one being a meal in itself. In between times he saw to the navigation lights at night, kept an eye on the lashings and wedges, tended the leeboard winches when required and carried out the many duties which the mate did not have time to do when helping me at the wheel.

Approaching the South Barnard buoy, which was rearing up and down like a kid's Jack-in-the-box, the wind backed to the south-east and it was obvious that the gale was likely to become worse. But I had a plan in mind and I knew of a low way across the Barnard shoals into Pakefield Road, which runs close under the cliffs to the south of Lowestoft. Once in this inshore channel, we could run close to Lowestoft pierheads and see if conditions were fit to take the harbour. If not we should have to run on through Yarmouth Roads and probably round the cockle to find shelter off the sandy beaches along by Winterton and Happisburgh.

The Barnard shoal looked white and wicked. The seas were steep and curly, too much like the breakers on a sandy beach to feel comfortable, even though I was confident that there was enough water for us. Young Jim, being a better third hand than most, was trusted with the lead because I wanted the mate to help me at the wheel. He was a good helmsman and when I needed to step clear of the wheelhouse to judge my bearings he struggled manfully and kept her from gybing or broaching-to.

Jim called three fathoms, then three again, then two and a half, not quite two and a half (I stopped breathing for a bit when he said this), then two and a half again (Thank God) three, three and a half. All was well. We were in Pakefield Road.

We eased our mainsheet a little and sped along by the beaches toward the stone walls of Lowestoft harbor. The seas were thundering on the pierheads, sending up clouds of spray and presenting to us weary mariners a fearsome aspect. But we were looking at the worst side, the windward side, of the harbor entrance and with a free wind such as we had I knew that she ought to go in. She was nicely loaded, being not too deep and a bit by the stern, and was travelling at such a rate that she would batter her way through the broken water in the opening.

Hazelton looked at me inquiringly. He was a bit anxious—and he had reason to be by the look of the spray flying over the south pier. I told him that we would take the harbor.

"Down jib and up bobstay as soon as she's inside, and get your anchor off the bow."

I had the pair of them pull in the mainsheet as far as they could, up to the backsides in water at times, and then heave the weather vang in on the crab winch. With everything trimmed ready for either a luff or a bear up, I ran her off shore a little and then headed in for the entrance.

It was not so bad as it had looked. She careered through the confused and broken water in the entrance like a bronco and as we gained the welcome shelter of the harbor walls I saw two men on one of the inner piers vigourously beckoning to us to keep coming.

"They're ready for you with the bridge," they yelled.

This was indeed a great slice of luck. Instead of performing intricate manoeuvres within the confines of the outer harbor in order to get the sail off her and probably let go the anchor, we could now go surging up through the cutting right into our berth. The older men on the swing bridge, which carries the roadway through the town, had in days gone by been accustomed to making a quick swing if they saw a sailing smack taking the harbour in rough weather and unable to check her way. There used to be a big fleet of splendid ketches belonging to Lowestoft and my forbears had owned and sailed in them. I had sailed to South American in one of them and although she was only fifty-seven feet long, I had kept my feet dryer than I did in the old *Greenhithe*.

Heeling over with the weight of wind in her topsail, the barge glided swiftly up the narrow cutting, through the bridgehole and and into the Inner Harbor. We were so busy with our own affairs that it was only then that I noticed we were being watched by a great crowd of people. Apparently we had virtually split the population of Lowestoft into two sections, marooned on each side of the opened bridge.

It transpired that when the harbor master saw that we were safely within the outer walls he had stopped all traffic and got the bridge open in good time. There everyone was compelled to stop and watch our little struggle, whether they were interested or not, and I have to confess to a little touch of conceit as we went sailing up between them and through the center of the town.

Things had to happen quickly while this was being done. I rapped out orders to the mate and third hand and then jumped to it like a couple of heroes. It is on occasions like this when an inefficient crew can bungle the whole affair and cause the ship, themselves and the master's reputation a deal of damage.

Down jib, up bobstay, anchor off the bow, brail up your mainsail, down foresail, down topsail, clew in your topsail sheet, lower the boat in the water, swing your davits in, fenders ready to go alongside. I will hand it to Hazelton that I have never seen a mate fly round a barge's deck as fast as he did during the few minutes he had to do all these things. But, with Jim's help, he accomplished it.

I learned afterwards that when the crew were recognised ashore that evening there was more than one pot of ale stood up for them—"for the lads in that barge what took the harbor this morning".

They deserved it too, for they had been a credit to the old *Greenhithe* that day.

FROM *SHORT VOYAGES: FORAYS ALONG THE LITTORAL*
1985

Stephen Jones

Illustration by Brian Anderson

When I started putting this book together, I sent a prospective list of authors to several fellow boat nuts whom I figured would be able to suggest some writers I didn't know. Stephen Jones topped the list of several of them, and it only took a chapter or two for me to agree. It isn't easy, though, to say exactly why.

This fall, I couldn't resist reading, among too many other things, a couple of this year's "big books." I enjoyed several of them—bright, erudite, well written. But when Short Voyages *turned up in the mail and I opened it to read, I was struck from the first by a feeling of density, of the words somehow being bound together across the pages in a way that is very rare, and far too often lacking in the books one finds on special display in the front of the big bookstores.*

It is to some extent a cliché, but the difference seems to be in the lives of the authors. On the one hand, school, university, often a stint in one of the well-known creative writing programs. So many of the "big" books are like a board of clear spruce—light, clean, easy to work—but you can split it with your hands.

Jones' books feel more like white oak—dense, tough, with rays that run from the pith out through the annular rings of heart and sapwood, binding them together. Not to say that Jones is just some salty old sea dog. He teaches literature at the University of Connecticut, among many other things, and it is obvious from the word go that he can "erudite" with the best of them. It is the many other things, the rays, that make the books: the harbor towns built along the fresh and salt waters of the tiny stretch of Connecticut coastline where Jones has lived his whole life; the people who wander in and out of the stories and the years; the Groton Shellfish Commission; the boatyards he frequented as a child, extending through the years to the boatyard where he now works with his son; the lobster boat he went to sea in as a child with his grandfather and the other boats he has owned in which his children have gone to sea with him.

Good stuff.

STAND UP FOR SHORT VOYAGES

Short voyages may not only extend one's space, but add to one's time. There was a man in one of our harbors who was told by his doctor he had six months to live.

He went home and said to himself, "Then I must hurry and get that old boat in the yard next to the house rebuilt."

It had been sitting in his yard for twenty years since his own father had died.

But he went to work immediately and kept working on it every day, trying to remember how it had looked when his father first had it built in 1927 in Crocker's yard down in New London. She was a twenty-foot launch that looked like a catboat without a mast. Her cockpit was mahogany, vertically sheathed and curved at the stern end. Up forward was a two-bunk cabin with an icebox and round portholes on each side. The Palmer engine was in the cockpit in a raised box and went *dunk-dunk-dunk*. She was steered at the starboard after end of the cabin just outside the doors that went below, and she had a bronze clutch lever in the cockpit floor and a bronze throttle quadrant on the cabin face by the wheel that connected by an ancient bell crank system.

The six months passed and he hadn't finished the restoration, but he hadn't died either, so he kept at the boat. Three years later he had her completely restored, better than new, and the next summer he took her out every evening. We'd watch him chug around the harbour, *dunk, dunk, dunk,* steering her, sitting on a stool in his stocking cap and waving to the people on shore. When everyone cheered, he doffed his stocking cap.

That fall he sat in her cockpit on the stool in his stocking cap and sweater and baggy flannel pants while they took her up in the hoist and set him and his boat ashore. I rowed over, and when he climbed down from his boat I told him how much we'd miss his sundowners.

"Hey, I'm going moose hunting this fall," he said, "not that I expect to shoot anything, but in moose hunting you get way up there."

"Way up there," I said, "where the doctor can't get you."

"You got it."

He didn't die until later that winter.

That, apparently, is the ultimate short voyage of them all. According to the literature, death seems a bit like a Prince Henry trip, an installment, that is, both a little excursion in itself and part of the Big Voyage of Discovery. For this kind of voyage, Dante, of course, has the reputation of being the great cartographer. However, he has only a thwartwise notion of navigation, and of his four crossings, he's passed out in the bilge on one and two are mere fordings. True, the Egyptians and the Norse saw the transport over into the other world as requiring a boat, but judging by the provisions discovered in tomb excavations, these journeys are expected to be long ones.

Still, for final voyages, be they short or long, I prefer my old moose-hunting friend on his restored launch. This was the voyage he always took. It was around the harbor, counterclockwise: the home dock; the creek with the swans; the right-field fence of the softball field; the old white, wooden CPO club; the Coast Guard pier with the bell buoys up out of the water lying on top, their roots exposed; the long, low rock with all the cormorants; the sou'west surge at the mouth of the inlet; the crumbling concrete pier on Pine Island; the east breachway where the lobstermen go out; the pine trees on Bushy Point where the deer hide their young; the lagoon at the far end of which hangs the osprey; the mouth of the river where the scallop channel begins and where once he saw nine blue herons watching him, their eyes, as the sun set, glittering in the tall, blond grass.

Some Related Websites

Duckworks Magazine—Online magazine on small-boat building and cruising, giant archive, plans index, new articles daily:
www.duckworksmagazine.com

The Ash Breeze—Newsletter of The Traditional Small Boat Association. Excellent quarterly magazine online in PDF format:
www.tsca.net/tscaash.html

The Compass Rose Review—Peter Spectre's website devoted to all things Maine and maritime:
www.compassrosereview.blogspot.com

Svenson's Free Boat Plans—Dozens of free boat plans, from the simplest kid's rowboat to houseboats and cabin sailboats:
www.svensons.com/boat

PD Racer home page—Simple, small one-design sailboat, with free plans and lots of photos and step-by-step directions on how to build:
www.pdracer.com

Craig O'Donnell's "The Cheap Pages"—Dozens of articles on canoe and small-boat cruising, sailing, and building, many e-book links:
www2.friend.ly.net/~dadadata/index.html

Simplicity Boats—a half-dozen small skiffs that can be built in a long weekend, some simple toys, free plans, photos:
www.simplicityboats.com

Gavin Atkin's Free Boat Design—Boat design software, lots of free plans, lots of links:
http://home.clara.net/gmatkin/design.htm

The Mother of All Maritime Links:
www.boat-links.com/boatlink.html

Uncle John's General Store—Simple pirogue, skiff, and jonboat kits:
www.unclejohns.com

Jim Michalak's Boat Designs—Many informative articles on boatbuilding and boat design.
http://homepages.apci.net/~michalak